FOREWORD

Congratulations on making a very important investme̶ ̶̶ ̶̶̶ ̶̶̶y ̶̶ppy you have chosen us to help you on your journey- the transition from military service to your next life chapter as a civilian. Just so you know who we are, we are an organization called Veterans Informing Veterans, LLC. We are a small group of Disabled Veterans, with close advisement from Veterans Service Officers, who have one goal- to help you! We all have been where you are-looking into a black hole of information for answers to transition questions. All of us here at VIV have had to navigate the transition process without any assistance. There was no guide book, there was no plan. Instead, there was a lot of discovery learning and countless conversations which usually ended with one of us saying something like 'that would have been helpful to know'. Not anymore! We've put together what we believe is the most comprehensive Veterans self-help book series on the market. Please register on our website at www.veteransinformingveterans.com for updates made after your book purchase, and like and follow us on Facebook at www.facebook.com/veteransinformingveterans/ and Instagram @veteransinformingveterans. Don't forget to tell us how you heard about us so we can compensate our affliliates.

Truth in advertising up front. We don't have secret information you can't get on your own. In fact, everything you will read, except for personal anecdotes and some best practices, can be found online on the VA and other websites- we'll even give you the links! What this book series does for you is give you something most of us find extremely precious- time. We have spent over 5,000 hours compiling the information in this book series. You don't have to invest that time. With this series you get answers to your questions without going to the end of the internet to find them.

So, welcome to Book I! We wrote this book to give you a blueprint to help you with the military-to-civilian transition process. There are a lot of moving parts during your transition-typically, we think of this timeframe from one year before transition, whether for retirement or end of your service obligation, until about three months before your transition. We call this book, the 'doing your homework' book, hence the workbook section at the end. With this book you will prepare your transition timeline; learn how to research and document your medical disabilities for your VA claim; learn about service-specific and VA medical screenings; and finally, you will find a comprehensive list of all VA recognized disabilities, diseases and ailments. Ready?

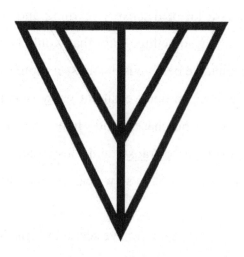

THIS PAGE LEFT INTENTIONALLY BLANK

In Section 1 of this book we provide you with a proven timeline blueprint to help you organize your required transition events, which include: requesting medical records, Transition Assistance initiation, continuing medical documentation, and more. We will walk you through a step-by-step construction of your timeline which is based upon your transition date. Once your timeline is constructed you will know exactly when critical tasks need to be accomplished.

In Section 2 we will discuss how to ensure proper documentation of your ailments, diseases, and disabilities in your medical records. We will show you examples of ailment queries used by actual Veterans Service Officers, which will help you paint your medical issues picture.

In Section 3 we identify the differences between service physicals and the VA disability physical, which is part of your VA claim. These are both critical, and we will explain why.

In Section 4 we provide you a comprehensive list of all VA-recognized ailments, disabilities and diseases for you to conduct your own health assessment of potential VA claims. Section 4 also provides all ailments ratings. The VA applies the same disabilities and ratings standards to each branch of service, so this information applies regardless of your service.

In Section 5 we provide you with a take-away workbook for you to complete while working through your interactive exercises and models. This workbook can be removed for easy reference.

Once you have completed your review of this book, to include the interactive exercises, you will be well-organized to complete your transition and VA disability claim. In Book II – *VA Claims, Compensation, and Appeals*, you will be walked through the claim process and beyond. To get there, however, you must complete your homework in this book.

THIS PAGE LEFT INTENTIONALLY BLANK

SECTION 1

TRANSITION TIMELINE BLUEPRINT

In this section we will help you avoid the same obstacles we went through when we navigated this process. After significant research, which included many hours reviewing Veterans Affairs policies, procedures and regulations, hours of interviews with subject matter experts from Veterans Service Organizations (VSO), and recommendations from many transitioning service members, we are providing you this plan to succeed during your transition. You will likely find most of the information you will receive from your transition briefings would have been helpful to you months before you receive it. Our goal is to bridge that gap. Ok, let's get into your timeline.

Planning is the key to success. To properly plan, you must understand how much time this process takes. In a perfect world, you would want to begin your transition process about two years out. We know- who lives in a perfect world, right? The timeline we've laid out for you is based upon a one-year transition model. That is, you should begin your transition process about one year before your actual transition. Later in this section we will show you our proven timeline, and then we will help you develop your transition timeline. Depending on where you are in your transition process, you may find yourself either behind, ahead, or on-target with these gate times. If you are behind, don't worry, there are opportunities to make up ground and get your affairs in order, and get your VA claim submitted on time. Some things to think about as you start your planning:

What is your transition date? This is the date on your retirement or end of service obligation orders which defines your last official date of military service. If you are taking terminal or transition leave, this is the date your leave ends. If you are not taking transition or terminal leave, this will be the last day you will wear your uniform, regardless of whether you are leaving service for retirement or end of your service obligation. This date is important because it is the starting point for your planning. All other dates for your planning will be determined from your transition date. Don't forget that no plan survives the first contact. You don't know what life will throw at you while you are working though your transition plan. The earlier you can get things done, the better off you will be in the end.

1

Your VA packet submission process. There are two different ways to go about this. You can elect go right into the VA process by establishing a VA claim, and then ensuring everything is documented in your medical records prior to final transition. This program, which is called *Benefits Delivery at Discharge,* or *BDD,* allows Service members to file claims for disability compensation from 180 to 90 days prior to separation or final transition from active duty. Claims processing and adjudication timelines tend to be much shorter for claims submitted prior to discharge. The other way is to hold off on the VA packet submission process to ensure everything is documented in your medical records first. It is very important to stress that, in hindsight, neither method is right or wrong, merely personal preference. But, if you have the time to do so, it may be cleaner to have everything documented in your medical records first, and then establish your VA claim in accordance with the VA or VSO representative availability. Ideally, you would have been documenting your medical issues throughout your career. Regardless of which method you chose, either documenting your ailments first, or after the VA physical process, it still needs to be done. Many of us were behind the timeline, because we didn't know what the timeline was. Now that we know what works, we're sharing it with you.

The VA will not begin to compensate you until you are out of the service; that is, after your actual retirement or end of service obligation date. Again, the VA will not compensate you until you are out of the service. We've purposely written this twice because it is very important to remember. The VA could possibly decide your claim prior to your official transition date, but do not expect any compensation prior to your transition. As long as you have your VA disability claim packet submitted the day before you either retire or end your service obligation, then you are "on-time"; but in order to process your pre-discharge claim the VA requires you have your claim submitted between 180 and 90 days prior to your transition date. This is why the timeline has a little wiggle-room built into it; but it's best to follow the timeline as closely as possible, so you can focus on the transition assistance portion to set you up for success outside the VA arena.

This is an example of one of the author's timeline followed through his process. What we can tell you, with the benefit of hindsight, is that he was late on almost every one of these tasks when compared to our approved timeline. Had he been given the information we are sharing with you, he would not have been doing VA-related requirements until nearly his last day in uniform.

His checklist (with a separation date of June 30th, 2017):

- Requested Medical Records — January 27th, 2017
- Lab Work for Retirement Physical — January 30th, 2017
- Began Retirement Physical — February 13th, 2017
- Follow-on Appointments — February 14th –March 21st, 2017
- Transition Assistance Program — March 6th – 10th, 2017
- Completed Retirement Physical — March 21st, 2017
- Scheduled appointment with VSO — April 10th, 2017
- Compiled claim with VSO — April 20th, 2017
- Initial VA screening — May 11th, 2017
- Picked up clearing papers — May 12th, 2017
- Clearing — May 13th – 23rd, 2017
- Follow-on VA appointments — May 15th – 22nd, 2017
- Load household goods — May 18th – 19th, 2017
- Transition Date (Final out) — May 23rd, 2017
- Retirement Date — June 30th, 2017
- VA Claim development complete — July 1st, 2017
- VA Disability Decision — September 20th, 2017

He also realized there was a lot more which needed to be done, and certainly done in a more organized manner. So, we went back to his timeline and developed a 365-day model for transition. If you follow this model we are confident you will have plenty of time to get the disability claim in order, which will allow more time to focus on other aspects of transition to civilian life.

On the next page is our example transition timeline with some key dates. Don't get too wrapped up in the details of the chart. After the example we will get into the specifics of developing your timeline, which will address all data points in the chart. To show you what this looks like filled out, we are providing you with an actual transition model- the transition date was June 30th, 2017. With that date, the following dates in bold would have been used for the timeline. Compare the key dates above with the transition model on the next page. As you can see, the author was late on nearly all of these. This is why we had to create a functional timeline to share with you.

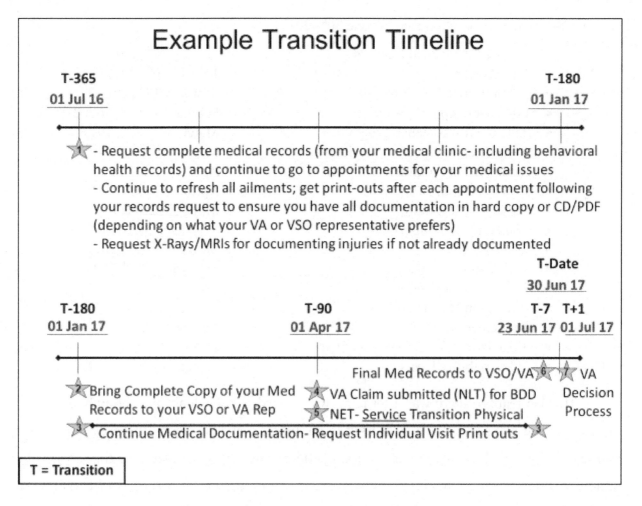

Example Transition Timeline

T-365
01 Jul 16

T-180
01 Jan 17

- Request complete medical records (from your medical clinic- including behavioral health records) and continue to go to appointments for your medical issues
- Continue to refresh all ailments; get print-outs after each appointment following your records request to ensure you have all documentation in hard copy or CD/PDF (depending on what your VA or VSO representative prefers)
- Request X-Rays/MRIs for documenting injuries if not already documented

T-Date
30 Jun 17

T-180
01 Jan 17

T-90
01 Apr 17

T-7   T+1
23 Jun 17 01 Jul 17

Final Med Records to VSO/VA   VA Decision Process

Bring Complete Copy of your Med Records to your VSO or VA Rep

VA Claim submitted (NLT) for BDD

NET- Service Transition Physical

Continue Medical Documentation- Request Individual Visit Print outs

T = Transition

OK, now that we have shown you what the recommended timeline looks like, let's look at your Transition timeline. You can complete your working draft of your timeline on the next page, and then transfer your final timeline to the VIV Workbook section on page 243, for your easy reference and take-away. This is an interactive model- you can fill in your specific dates for the critical gate tasks identified on this chart. The following are the step-by-step instructions for filling out this chart correctly. Once complete, you will have your transition timeline.

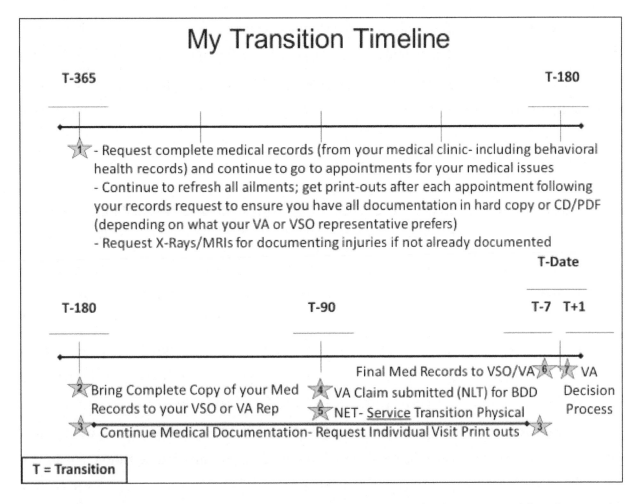

My Transition Timeline

T-365   **T-180**

★1 - Request complete medical records (from your medical clinic- including behavioral health records) and continue to go to appointments for your medical issues
- Continue to refresh all ailments; get print-outs after each appointment following your records request to ensure you have all documentation in hard copy or CD/PDF (depending on what your VA or VSO representative prefers)
- Request X-Rays/MRIs for documenting injuries if not already documented

T-Date

T-180   **T-90**   **T-7   T+1**

Final Med Records to VSO/VA ★6 ★7 VA
★2 Bring Complete Copy of your Med   ★4 VA Claim submitted (NLT) for BDD   Decision
Records to your VSO or VA Rep   ★5 NET- Service Transition Physical   Process
★3 Continue Medical Documentation- Request Individual Visit Print outs ★3

T = Transition

First, fill in the T-Date in the bottom right of the chart- this is your transition date- again, the last day you will be in uniform. This date will be given to you on your transition orders. If you are not taking leave and retiring or ending your service obligation, it is the last day you will be in service. If you are retiring or ending your service obligation and taking transition or terminal leave, it will be the day prior to that leave period starting. Fill in your T-Date now.

Next, fill in the T+1 date in the bottom right of this chart- this is your first day as a civilian. If you are not taking transition or terminal leave, it will be the day after your T-Date. If you are taking transition or terminal leave, it will be the day after your leave period ends. Star 7- the T+1 date is the date in which the VA will "officially" review your claims and can begin compensation anytime after their decision has been made. Fill in your T+1 date now.

Next, fill in the T-7 date in the bottom right of this chart- this is seven (7) days before you stop working. If you are not taking transition or terminal leave, it will be seven (7) days before you become a civilian. If you are taking transition or terminal leave, it will be seven (7) days before your leave period begins. Star 6- the T-7 date should be the date you would bring any final medical or other supporting documents, to include your completed DD Form 214 to your VSO or VA representative to upload into the VA system. Fill in your T-7 date now.

Finally, walk back 90 days, 180 days and 365 days, and fill those days in the corresponding timeline. If you are not taking transition or terminal leave, it will be 90 days, 180 days and 365 days before you become a civilian. If you are taking transition or terminal leave, it will be 90 days, 180 days and 365 days before your leave period begins. Star 1- between T-365 and T-180 days you would continue to document your medical issues with your Primary Care Manager (PCM) or specialty provider. You would also request your medical and behavioral health records, if applicable, and ensure you have your records in the format your local VSO or VA representative requires- some want single-sided hard copy; others want digital copies- you will find this out when you meet with your VSO or VA representative. Star 2- at T-180 you should be prepared to turn in your medical records, behavioral health records, and other supporting documentation required by your VSO or VA representative. Star 3- when you turn in your medical records to the VSO or VA representative handling your VA claim, you will want to continue to document your medical issues- just ensure you get copies of each medical visit so you can give one last batch of records to your representative for uploading prior to your separation- typically at the T-7 date. Star 4- as we discussed earlier, for Benefits Delivery at Discharge (BDD) you will want to have your VA claim submitted prior to your T-90 date. Star 5- each military installation and service has different rules for completing separation physicals- find out the standard on your installation and follow that guidance. Fill in your T-90, T-180, and T-365 dates now.

Note, the Star tasks are not all-encompassing- that is, there may be a couple other tasks you will need to accomplish during these times- things that may be either service-specific, or installation specific. If that's the case, document them on your chart as you progress through this process to keep track of your requirements. Specifically, VA medical appointments are not depicted here, as those will vary greatly.

If you have more than 365 days, we recommend you continue to document your medical issues in your medical records. If you are less than 365 days out, which is what happened to us, then condense your timeline and get your medical records to your VSO or VA representative as close to 180 days from transition as possible. If you are short on time, begin your VA claims process with your VSO or VA representative and continue to document your medical conditions with your Primary Care Manager simultaneously, rather than sequentially.

Ensure you find out what your installation-specific requirements are as soon as possible. As we address in detail in Book II, you will want to find out exactly how your VSO or VA representative wants your documentation and when. This is critical information to help you refine your timeline.

THIS PAGE LEFT INTENTIONALLY BLANK

SECTION 2

DOCUMENTING DISABILITIES IN YOUR MEDICAL RECORDS

As we stated earier, there are two main ways you can document your medical issues in your records: sequentially and simultaneously. A sequential method would be to ensure you had all your medical issues properly documented prior to beginning the VA disability claim process. The simultaneous method would be to continue to document your medical disabilities while completing your VA disability claim. We work with people who have done both. The method that you choose is exactly that- your choice. It truthfully doesn't matter which you choose, but we will offer some thoughts that may help you shape your decision.

VA or VSO Requirements. How much time does your VSO require? If your VSO representative will not accept your packet until six (6) months before you transition, then that may impact your methodology going forward. If your VSO representative will begin your packet prior to six months, then you have options. If you have enough time, ~12 months before you transition, then we recommend you do the sequential method of documentation. That is, get all your ailments properly documented prior to the 6-month mark, then hand-over your complete medical records to your VA or VSO representative and begin your pre-discharge disability claim process. If you are short on time, like less than six months before you transition, then we recommend you do the simultaneous method of documentation. That is, continue to document your ailments in your medical records while you begin your pre-discharge disability claim process at the same time. Regardless of documentation method, there is one thing both plans have in common- the need to document your medical ailments. What we are going to talk about next is how to properly document your ailments, diseases, and disabilities in your medical records to support your pre-discharge claim.

In the Section 4 of this book, we outline all the VA-recognized ailments, diseases, and disabilities, and walk you through step-by-step to identify all issues you will be putting on your VA claim. Even though your service physical and VA disability claim physical are separate, the VA will have access to your medical records once the VA or VSO representative provides them as part of the pre-discharge claim or VA uploads. The VA will typically use your service records to justify service-related issues as part of your claim.

Checklist. The VA and each VSO representative will have different requirements, such as records preferences- hard copy vs. digital copy; other required documents- such as a working copy of your DD Form 214, dependency documents, etc. Get with your VA or VSO representative early to get their checklist so you can ensure you have all required documentation. You can do this now.

Identifying your medical concerns. Make a list with all your ailments and review your records. Some choose to create a spreadsheet with all their issues; others just write it down on a piece of paper. Regardless of how you keep track of your issues, you then must cross-reference all those issues with your medical records. Again, figure out what works for you. Even if you have no record of a condition, the pre-discharge exam alone can still diagnose and document a condition or issue, which can warrant service connection. Ensure your VA or VSO representative knows of any conditions found in this manner. VSO tip!~ obtaining your behavioral health records and any sleep studies is a must. You will also want to separate both of these types of records as it makes it easier for the VA decision-maker to find, which is always a good practice- a happy rater, rates well in a good mood!

Organizing your medical concerns. How do I maximize my claim? It's simple- you must find a way to identify all the things which are causing you issues. Big things, little things, doesn't matter- you have been broken as a result of your service to this great country. So, we are going give you a way to identify all the things which are not quite right. We are going to do this in a logical, organized manner to ensure we don't forget anything. We are not trying to give you secret information here- all this information can be found on the internet, which is how we were able to compile this information. The difference is, you won't have to spend thousands of hours gathering the information- we have already done it for you. What we will do now is a small exercise to determine what you think your disabilities are. We would like you to go to the workbook on page 245 and write down in Column A all your medical issues you believe you will claim during your VA process. Please do that now, we'll be right here when you're done.

Welcome back! The biggest benefit we can provide you is to help you organize your medical situation, which will help you maximize your VA disability claim. After you complete your medical review using the information in this book you can write down your updated list of those medical issues you will claim during your VA process in Column B. What you'll notice is that your revised claim under Column B on page 245 is most likely longer, more comprehensive, and far more organized. It is this comprehensive list that you'll take forward to the VA or your VSO representative for your VA claim. We'll get into putting together your VA claim in Book II of this series. Remember, the stronger the list, the greater the chances of getting the benefits you deserve for your service! Now, let's prove the value of this book- read the rest of this section, and let's work together and fill out Column B.

The Silhouette. On page 244 in your workbook you'll find a silhouette with a bunch of blanks. This is a simple silhouette, but it will yield tremendous results when you are finished filling in those blanks. This silhouette represents you. What we're going to do is start at your head and work our way down to your feet. At every piece of the silhouette we want you to envision things that aren't quite the way they used to be, and then write down the problem next to the corresponding body part. For example, if you suffer from migraine headaches, write down migraine headaches in the box labled "Head, Brain, Psych Issues" of your silhouette. On the next seven pages we break down these body groupings with a few thoughts which may help jog some ideas as to your possible issues. Again, the purpose of this is to prove to you that this system will help you organize your thoughts and allow you to create a more wholistic picture as you get ready to complete your VA claim using Book II. Things to consider when completing your silhouette- you may feel great today, but you didn't yesterday, or you may not tomorrow. It is important when you fill out your silhouette to think of days in which something may not have felt as good as it does today. A classic example are headaches- you may not have one today, but you may have them several times a week or month. Don't forget those things which may cause you pain or suffering, even if you don't feel them right this minute. Once your silhouette is completely filled out, transfer your issues to Column B on page 245.

The Head to Toe Process. One common strategy used by many VSO representatives is the head-to-toe method of investigating what issues to potentially claim on your VA disability claim. If you meet the 90-180 days remaining on active duty rule, as previously outlined, any issues claimed on your Pre-Discharge claim will typically be examined by the VA. As such, an easy way to ensure we are not missing out on any issue is to follow a simple format. Note, this is not an all-inclusive list, and more importantly you do not want to claim any conditions which are non-existent. Your conditions must be diagnosed in your records, or at a minimum, during the VA examination. We strongly recommend having your condition(s) diagnosed by your military treatment providers if possible. The following head-to-toe list is a typical one- there are certainly many different formats, but this one works just fine. There are also plenty of different chronic conditions not on this list which may be deemed a disability. When in doubt, check with the VA or especially your VSO representative, as certain conditions are not considered chronic disabilities- like high cholesterol. Important- for Pre-Discharge claims, you do not need to list the actual disability name for most things. You want to list them generically, such as 'bilateral foot conditions.' The reason for this is simple- legally, if you list Bilateral Pes Planus (Flat feet) the VA technically should only examine and decide on that condition. The proper way to claim the feet in this case would be 'Bilateral foot conditions to include Pes Planus'- which leaves some room for medical examiners to annotate additional issues discovered with your feet. The VSO representatives who assisted us with preparing our claims missed nothing. They essentially asked us the inquiries by body system listed below, while reviewing our military Service Treatment Records (STRs). When our inqueries were complete, we all had a complete list of disabilities which were then forwarded to the VA for examination scheduling. Now let's fill out the silhouette and Column B in your list of ailments. What we want you to do is to follow the head-to-toe query we've outlined for you below. As you read the head-to-toe, make any additions to your silhouette and chart in column B. What you should find is your likely random list of ailments in Column A will now be more methodically developed and complete in Column B.

Head, Brain and Pysch Issues. Some common issues in this box include chronic or recurring headaches- cluster, migraine, tension- ensure you have frequency, duration, intensity and treatment all documented in your medical records; Traumatic Brain Injuries (TBI)- either with or without loss of consciousness; Post-concussive syndrome; Post Traumatic Stress Disorder (PTSD); and other psychological disorders you have been diagnosed with, such as depression, anxiety, or bi-polar disorder. Consider sleep impairments, such as insomnia, here. Any skull damage, like fractures or scarring you may have incurred. Ensure you are considering both training and live or combat environments. Regardless of whether you have been seen by a PCM or medical professional, write it down. Additional note, behavioral health records are typically kept separate from your normal medical records- you will have to request them separately and they will be included in your VA claim packet submitted through the VA or your VSO representative.

Eyes, Ears, Nose, Mouth Issues. Some common issues in this group include double vision; issues with your eyes; hearing loss; tinnitus (ringing in the ears); issues with your ears; diagnosed vestibular conditions such as Meniere's; vertigo or balance issues; deviated nasal septum which causes issues; sinus or allergy issues, like sinusitis or rhinitis, which affect breathing and senses of smell or taste; issues with your nose; temporomandibular joint (TMJ) disorders, or lock-jaw; issues with teeth or jaw due to injury; broken bones; and surgeries. If you have suffered a tongue injury resulting in the loss of taste, claim it. It's important to note that normal age-related decreases in vision is not considered a disability, but if you have a disease process or injury, claim those. Regular dental cavities and conditions such as gingivitis are also not compensable disabilities. Bruxism, or teeth grinding is also not a disability, but it does get granted on some VA decisions, typically when the Veteran has TMD. It also may be a sign of another condition, such as PTSD- if you grind your teeth, you need to find out why. Again, ensure you are considering both training and live or combat environments. Regardless of whether you have been seen by a PCM or medical professional, write it down.

Neck, Throat, and Respiratory Issues. Some common issues in this group include Degenerative Disk Disease (DDD), arthritis, and Degenerative Joint Disease (DJD). When considering injuries suffered to the cervical spine- very common with foot marches, parachute operations, getting in and out of small vehicles and vessels- make note if these injuries also result in upper extremity radiculopathy (numbness)- a neck condition may result in numbness of the hands or fingers; broken bones; surgeries. You should also consider injuries to the throat such as hoarseness, loss of voice, etc. Additional considerations for the throat include hyperthyroidism, hypothyroidism, cancers and nodules. Finally, breathing conditions such as asthma, reactive airway disease, and sleep apnea with any breathing devise such as an APAP, Bi-PAP, CPAP, or oral appliance. Again, ensure you are considering both training and live or combat environments. Regardless of whether you have been seen by a PCM or medical professional, write it down.

Upper Torso, Chest, Cardiovascular and Blood issues. Some common issues in this group include any heart conditions, like hypertension or high blood pressure, and blood conditions like leukemia, lymphoma, and sickle cell anemia. Ensure you note if any medical procedures have been done for one of these conditions; and chronic residuals associated with a broken rib, or rib injuries. Also consider Gastro-esophageal reflux disease (GERD / acid reflux) and make sure to indicate if you have had surgery or an EGD (camera down your esophagus), any hernias or ulcers; and kidney stones or kidney conditions such as kidney disease. Finally, annotate breast cancer, and if you've had surgery, breast lumps for females- such as fibroids- or gynocomastia for guys who may have suffered from this. Again, consider both training and live or combat environments. Regardless of whether you have been seen by a PCM or medical professional, write it down.

Left Arm, Shoulder, Elbow, Wrist, Hand and Finger issues. This is where you would put down all the injuries you've suffered to your left arm; tenderness to your left elbow/wrist could be medial epidcondylitis; numbness or other neurological issues such as carpal or cubital tunnel syndrome and indicate any surgeries as necessary; arthritis in any arm joint; stress fractures to fingers; and cold weather injuries. Also, identify if your issue occurs in both your left and right side, which is refered to as 'bilateral', or if the issue you have is with your dominant hand- for example, dislocated left shoulder/elbow/wrist- dominant hand; broken bones; amputations; and surgeries. Again, considering both training and live or combat environments. Regardless of whether you have been seen by a PCM or medical professional, write it down.

Right Arm, Shoulder, Elbow, Wrist, Hand and Finger issues. This is where you would put down all the injuries you've suffered to your right arm; tenderness to your right elbow/wrist could be medial epidcondylitis; numbness or other neurological issues such as carpal or cubital tunnel syndromes; arthritis in any arm joint; stress fractures to fingers; and cold weather injuries. If these injuries happen on both arms, like carpal tunnel syndrome, then you have bilateral carpal tunnel syndrome- annotate that on your claim. Also, identify your dominant hand if you have an issue with it- for example, broken right wrist- dominant hand; broken bones; amputations; and surgeries. If the issue happens in both arms, like medial epycondylitis in both elbows, then it's bilateral medial epycondylitis. Again, consider training and live or combat environments. Regardless of whether you have been seen by a PCM or medical professional, write it down.

14

Left Leg, Hip, Knee, Ankle, Foot and Toes issues. This is where you would put down all the injuries you've suffered to your left leg; injuries to your knee, hip and ankle; arthritis in any leg joint; stress fractures your leg bones and toes; if you have pain in your feet when you first wake up and that pain disappears within a few minutes of walking you may have plantar fasciitis; cold weather injuries; broken bones; amputations; and surgeries; radiating pain or numbness; and sciatica. Ensure you consider both training and live or combat environments. Regardless of whether you have been seen by a PCM or medical professional, write it down.

Right Leg, Hip, Knee, Ankle, Foot and Toes issues. This is where you would put down all the injuries you've suffered to your right leg; injuries to your knee, hip and ankle; arthritis in any leg joint; stress fractures your leg bones and toes; if you have pain in your feet when you first wake up and that pain disappears within a few minutes of walking you may have plantar fasciitis; cold weather injuries; broken bones; amputations; and surgeries; radiating pain or numbness; and sciatica. Again, ensure you are considering both training and live or combat environments. Regardless of whether you have been seen by a PCM or medical professional, write it down. If the issue happens in both feet, like plantar fasciitis, then it's bilateral plantar fasciitis. Make sure you annotate it that way on your claim.

Urology and Gynecology Issues. If you have noticed you have increased frequency in the number of times you go to the bathroom every day/night then you need to annotate it here; increased urge to go to the bathroom; inability to completely empty your bladder, resulting in accidents- annotate all of these. For females, if you have documented gynecological issues, you would annotate them here as well. Any damage to either male or female reproductive organs would be annotated here. For females, annotate if you have had a partial or total hysetectomy, uterine fibroids, chronic HPV, and of course any cancers. For males, annotate erectile dysfunction- which will almost always be rated as 0%, but that is because the VA will add a Special Monthly Compensation (SMC) award, $108.57/month for 2019; testicular cancer, hydrococeles, spermatoceles, etc; Prostate cancer and enlarged prostate are also annotated here. Regardless of whether you have been seen by a PCM or medical professional, write it down.

Thoraco-Lumbar Spine Issues. Many people have mid-to-lower back issues, thoracolumbar issues, and don't realize it. Unfortunately, you can't just list 'lumbar spine' here, but you can of course list Degenerative Disk Disease if applicable. Make sure to list Sciatica, which is lower extremity radiculopathy (numbness, tingling, pain) on the same line with your back. Also annotate any coccyx (tailbone) issues you may have. If you have pain in your lower back, you should consult your PCM and request an x-ray, or preferably an MRI of your lower back. If you know of issues you have with your lower back, like bulging or herniated discs, degenerative disc disease, or arthritis, annotate it. Write down your spine issues now.

Digestive Issues, Lower Torso, and Infectious Disease Issues. Common lower GI tract issues here include Irritable Bowel Syndrome, Diverticulitis / Colitis, Recurring Hemorrhoids; include any surgeries such as anal fissure repair, etc. It is also very helpful for the VA if you indicate on your claim if you have had a colonoscopy and ensure there is a copy in your records. Annotate anything else here so you don't forget to claim it. Again, ensure you are considering both training and live or combat environments. If you served in Southwest Asia theater of operations on or after August 2nd, 1990, or served in Afghanistan or Djibouti after September 11th, 2001, you should consider registering with the VA burn-pit registry to help document your exposures to airborne hazards like burn pit smoke, air pollution, and oil-well fires. You can also document other exposures you have as a result of your service in these locations. If you have not already done so, we recommend you register with the Airborne Hazards and Open Burn Pit Registry at: https://veteran.mobilehealth.va.gov/AHBurnPitRegistry/#page/home. Regardless of whether you have been seen by a PCM or medical professional, write it down.

Skin and Miscellaneous Conditions for Consideration. Annotate any recurring chronic skin conditions. You will want to list the area where the skin condition is present, such as Psedufolliculitis barbae (PFB), which is typically on the face and back of the neck; Eczema, dermatitis, etc. If any skin condition affects multiple areas such as bilateral arms and legs, chest, back etc, it is fine to list "Multiple areas", since the VA examiner must check the current area of coverage as part of the evaluation. Scars are not typically a chronic condition unless they are deemed as tender/painful, cause swelling, or bleeding, or are visible on the face, including the nose. It is important to note normal hair loss is not typically considered a disability with the VA-however, Alopecia due to a medical condition, such as Lupus or chemical burns, are a disability and should be reported. Finally, diagnosed specialty conditions should be claimed, such as Fibromyalgia, Chronic Fatigue syndrome, Rheumatoid arthritis, etc. It is important to note these conditions must be medically diagnosed by an M.D. or medical specialist, such as a Rheumatologist.

Last thing you can do in compiling your list of issues is to research the repository of ailments and diseases in Section 4 of this book. We're not suggesting you should go 'looking for an ailment to add', but rather review the comprehensive list of ailments to ensure you didn't forget anything. One of our authors almost forgot to write down cold weather exposure injuries to the hands and feet. He is very glad he didn't. There is a non-exhaustive glossary of medical terms beginning on page 233 of this book. As you research ailments, refer to the glossary for added clarity. Note, this glossary is not designed to explain and diagnose every ailment and disease- rather, it serves to define words which are used throughout this book to break the medical terms down, so we commoners can understand.

Now that you've seen a few things to consider in each group, does this change your silhouette? Hopefully you saw something which made you think of another issue you have but it slipped your mind.

If you've done this properly, your list should be longer, more inclusive, and more organized than your first attempt in Column A. After your VA claim is complete, you will be able to compare the percentage you would have received in Column A with the one you did receive in Column B- the difference between the two is what makes this book series so worth it! Even if your increase is only 10% between Column A and Column B, this book will have paid for itself several hundreds of times over, every year, for the rest of your life. Worst case scenario, even if you went from a combined disability rating of 0% to 10%, that means you have $140.05 per month in tax exemptions- or $1680.60 per year that you wouldn't have had without this book. The savings are far more dramatic the higher the VA disability rating you get. We are looking forward to hearing your success story when this is all said and done.

Now that you've identified all the issues you have, go back to your medical records and confirm they have been documented. That is, anything you claim is wrong with you should hopefully be in your medical records after you brought this issue to the attention of a health care provider. If there are things in your claim not annotated in your medical records, either on or off a federal installation, you should strongly consider making an appointment with your PCM and getting it documented. If you are claiming left shoulder pain but have no medical records showing you have a left shoulder issue, you may be fighting a tough battle with the VA. If you attempt to claim Tinnitus, or ringing in your ears, and don't have it mentioned in your medical records, you may be fighting a tough battle with the VA.

Refresh your issues. Once you've made a comprehensive list of all issues and reviewed to ensure those issues are in your records, then take a close look at the frequency of complaints you have for an issue. We are not suggesting you go to your PCM and complain about every issue every time you go to an appointment. Rather, if you have issues you need to ensure you are continually addressing them with your PCM. Our guys have several hundred parachute jumps- a couple of us with some serious back issues- so, every time we went to see our PCM, we made sure to mention our backs bothering us. If you had a shoulder issue 15 years ago, and have said nothing since, then someone reviewing your records may find it hard to believe that you have a serious issue with your shoulder. On the other hand, if you have seen your PCM on and off for the same issue over the years, then this issue is well documented and less likely to be challenged. You need to do this for every issue you have. Review your records- if it looks like it's been awhile since you've addressed an ailment, we strongly recommend you make an appointment and readdress it, or at a minimum address it during your separation or retirement physical and during your VA disability physical. We will eventually be adding examples of ailment tracking mechanisms to our website under the webinars and blogs section.

Once you have completed Section 2 you should have a rock-solid understanding of your medical situation, clearly identified what you believe to be the medical issues you plan to claim during your VA disability claim, have a strong plan to identify any medical issues which need to either be initially added to your records, or reviewed as a recurring issue with your PCM. Now we will talk in detail about the two different types of physicals- service and VA.

SECTION 3

SERVICE PHYSICALS VS. VA PHYSICALS

Typically, your service physical and your VA disability claim physical are two completely different physicals. The information on each, however, is connected so it's important to make sure you have proper documentation for both. In this section we are going to talk about the differences between your service transition physical and the VA disability claim physical. It's important to remember that your service transition physical is not required by the VA. A new change, however, is most DOD facilities (Military bases) have a shared agreement between the Physical exam section and the VA. This substitutes a separation examination such as ETS, Retirement, and Chapter physicals with a Standard Health Assessment (SHA). If you are clear with the DOD exam section that you will be filing a VA disability claim, the VA examination will include this SHA, which will include standard exam procedures such as blood pressure, chest X-ray, and others such as ordering a final hearing test or anything that needs to be rectified as found on the exam. Please make sure though that you are within the 90-180 day time-frame for your Pre-Discharge claim to participate in this program. Some installations are requiring the SHA instead of having a service physical. In order to clear most installations medical records section, you will need a memorandum from the VA office on your installation indicating that you will have the SHA as part of your claim.

Service physical. Your service physical is the last physical you will take for your branch of service before you transition. This physical is typically completed during outprocessing and is part of your transition checklist. Installation requirements for when these service physicals vary, so find out when you will need to complete yours as part of your transition. These physicals are completed on these Department of Defense Forms (DD Forms):

- DD Form 2697 (Report of Medical Assessment), dated Feb 95
- DD Form 2807-1 (Report of Medical History), dated Aug 11
- DD Form 2808 (Report of Medical Examination), dated Oct 05

Key take-away. This physical is the last physical you will take in service. So, any issue you address on this physical will be something viewed as service connected, unless you identify a pre-existing condition. It is very important you take your time and explain any issues in detail on these forms. This physical will be part of your enduring records for the rest of your life. The VA may reference them as proof of an existing issue while in service, so please make sure you do this right!

Of the three Forms, you will fill out the headers of each, and provide your specific individual health assessment on the DD Form 2697 and DD Form 2807-1. The DD Form 2808 will be completed by your medical examiner. On the next few pages we highlighted the critical boxes for the first two forms to ensure you are focused on what needs to be filled out. There, you should highlight everything you have medically wrong with you- essentially, your taking your claims from Column B, annotating them in the respective bubbles, and describing them in boxes we've identified. When you do this, you have at least ensured all your claims have been annotated a minimum of one time. The VA will have this document during consideration.

DD Form 2697. Fill out Section I. Answer Boxes 10-18 and explain. Sign and Date.

REPORT OF MEDICAL ASSESSMENT	REPORT CONTROL SYMBOL

PRIVACY ACT STATEMENT

AUTHORITY: PL 103-160, EO 9397.
PRINCIPAL PURPOSE: To be used by the Medical Services to provide a comprehensive medical assessment for active and reserve component service members separating or retiring from active duty.
ROUTINE USES: A copy of this form will be released to the Department of Veterans Affairs.
DISCLOSURE: Voluntary; however, failure to disclose the requested personal information may result in delay in processing any disability claim.

SECTION I - TO BE COMPLETED BY SERVICE MEMBER. Any service member who requests a physical examination may have one.

1. NAME (Last, First, Middle)		2. SOCIAL SECURITY NUMBER	3. RANK

4. COMPONENT	5. UNIT OF ASSIGNMENT

6a. HOME STREET ADDRESS (Or RFD, including apartment number)	b. CITY	c. STATE	d. ZIP CODE	7. HOME TELEPHONE NUMBER (Include area code)

8. DATE OF LAST PHYSICAL EXAMINATION BY THE MILITARY (YYMMDD)	9. DATE ENTERED ON CURRENT ACTIVE DUTY (YYMMDD)

10. COMPARED TO MY LAST MEDICAL ASSESSMENT/PHYSICAL EXAMINATION, MY OVERALL HEALTH IS (X one. If "Worse," explain.)

- [ ] THE SAME
- [ ] BETTER
- [ ] WORSE

11. SINCE YOUR LAST MEDICAL ASSESSMENT/PHYSICAL EXAMINATION, HAVE YOU HAD ANY ILLNESSES OR INJURIES THAT CAUSED YOU TO MISS DUTY FOR LONGER THAN 3 DAYS? (X one. If "Yes," explain.)

- [ ] NO
- [ ] YES

12. SINCE YOUR LAST MEDICAL ASSESSMENT/PHYSICAL EXAMINATION, HAVE YOU BEEN SEEN BY OR BEEN TREATED BY A HEALTH CARE PROVIDER, ADMITTED TO A HOSPITAL, OR HAD SURGERY? (X one. If "Yes," explain.)

- [ ] NO
- [ ] YES

13. HAVE YOU SUFFERED FROM ANY INJURY OR ILLNESS WHILE ON ACTIVE DUTY FOR WHICH YOU DID NOT SEEK MEDICAL CARE? (X one. If "Yes," explain.)

- [ ] NO
- [ ] YES

14. ARE YOU NOW TAKING ANY MEDICATIONS? (X one. If "Yes," list medications.)

- [ ] NO
- [ ] YES

15. DO YOU HAVE ANY CONDITIONS WHICH CURRENTLY LIMIT YOUR ABILITY TO WORK IN YOUR PRIMARY MILITARY SPECIALTY OR REQUIRE GEOGRAPHIC OR ASSIGNMENT LIMITATIONS? (X one. If "Yes," explain.)

- [ ] NO
- [ ] YES

16. DO YOU HAVE ANY DENTAL PROBLEMS? (X one. If "Yes," explain.)

- [ ] NO
- [ ] YES

17. DO YOU HAVE ANY OTHER QUESTIONS OR CONCERN ABOUT YOUR HEALTH? (X one. If "Yes," explain.)

- [ ] NO
- [ ] YES

18. AT THE PRESENT TIME, DO YOU INTEND TO SEEK DEPARTMENT OF VETERANS AFFAIRS (VA) DISABILITY? (X one. If "Yes," list conditions for which you will ask for VA Disability.)

- [ ] NO
- [ ] YES
- [ ] UNCERTAIN

19. CERTIFICATION. I certify that the information provided above is true and complete to the best of my knowledge.

a. SIGNATURE OF SERVICE MEMBER	b. DATE SIGNED

DD FORM 2697, FEB 95 (EG)   Designed using Perform Pro, WHS/DIOR, Feb 95

Your evaluating physician will complete Section II.

SECTION II - TO BE COMPLETED BY INDIVIDUALLY PRIVILEGED HEALTH CARE PROVIDER

This Report of Medical Assessment is to be used by the Medical Services to provide a comprehensive medical assessment for active and reserve component service members separating or retiring from active duty. The assessment will cover, as a minimum, the period since the service member's last medical assessment/physical examination, or the period of this call or order to active duty. Any service member who requests a physical examination may have one. Any service member who has indicated "yes" to Item 18 will have an appropriate physical examination, if the last examination is more than 12 months old and/or there are new signs and/or symptoms. If the service member answers "Worse" to Item 10 or "Yes" to Items 11, 12, or 14 through 18, documentation of the injury, illness, or problem should be included in the service member's medical or dental record.

20. HEALTH CARE PROVIDER COMMENTS *(All patient complaints must be addressed)*

21. WAS PATIENT REFERRED FOR FURTHER EVALUATION? *(X one. If "Yes," specify where.)*

	NO
	YES

22. PURPOSE OF ASSESSMENT *(X one. If "Other," explain.)*

	SEPARATION *(Includes discharge from military service and release from active duty, including release of National Guard and Reserve personnel voluntarily or involuntarily called or ordered to active duty.)*
	RETIREMENT
	OTHER

23. MEDICAL FACILITY	24. DATE OF ASSESSMENT *(YYMMDD)*

25. HEALTH CARE PROVIDER

a. NAME *(Last, First, Middle Initial)*	b. GRADE/RANK	c. SIGNATURE

DD FORM 2697, FEB 95 (BACK)

DD Form 2807-1. Fill out header. Highlight issues in Boxes 10a-28; then explain in Box 29.

REPORT OF MEDICAL HISTORY

(This information is for official and medically confidential use only and will not be released to unauthorized persons.)

OMB No. 0704-0413
OMB approval expires
Aug 31, 2014

The public reporting burden for this collection of information is estimated to average 10 minutes per response, including the time for reviewing instructions, searching existing data sources, gathering and maintaining the data needed, and completing and reviewing the collection of information. Send comments regarding this burden estimate or any other aspect of this collection of information, including suggestions for reducing the burden, to the Department of Defense, Washington Headquarters Services, Executive Services Directorate, Information Management Division, 1155 Defense Pentagon, Washington, DC 20301-1155 (0704-0413). Respondents should be aware that notwithstanding any other provision of law, no person shall be subject to any penalty for failing to comply with a collection of information if it does not display a currently valid OMB control number.

PLEASE DO NOT RETURN YOUR FORM TO THE ABOVE ORGANIZATION. RETURN COMPLETED FORM AS INDICATED ON PAGE 2.

PRIVACY ACT STATEMENT

AUTHORITY: 10 U.S.C. 136, DoD Instruction 6130.03, and E.O. 9397, as amended (SSN).
PRINCIPAL PURPOSE(S): The primary collection of this information is from individuals seeking to join the Armed Forces. The information collected on this form is used to assist DoD physicians in making determinations as to acceptability of applicants for military service and verifies disqualifying medical condition(s) noted on the prescreening form (DD 2807-2). An additional collection of information using this form occurs when a Medical Evaluation Board is convened to determine the medical fitness of a current member and if separation is warranted. Completed forms are covered by recruiting, medical evaluation board, and official military personnel file SORNs maintained by each of the Services.
ROUTINE USE(S): The Blanket Routine Uses found at http://privacy.defense.gov/blanket_uses.shtml apply to this collection.
DISCLOSURE: Voluntary. However, failure by an applicant to provide the information may result in delay or possible rejection of the individual's application to enter the Armed Forces. An applicant's SSN is used during the recruitment process to keep all records together and when requesting civilian medical records. For an Armed Forces member, failure to provide the information may result in the individual being placed in a non-deployable status. The SSN of an Armed Forces member is to ensure the collected information is filed in the proper individual's record.

WARNING: The information you have given constitutes an official statement. Federal law provides severe penalties (up to 5 years confinement or a $10,000 fine or both), to anyone making a false statement. If you are selected for enlistment, commission, or entrance into a commissioning program based on a false statement, you can be tried by military courts-martial or meet an administrative board for discharge and could receive a less than honorable discharge that would affect your future.

1. LAST NAME, FIRST NAME, MIDDLE NAME (SUFFIX)	2. SOCIAL SECURITY NUMBER	3. TODAY'S DATE (YYYYMMDD)

4.a. HOME ADDRESS (Street, Apartment No., City, State, and ZIP Code)	5. EXAMINING LOCATION AND ADDRESS (Include ZIP Code)
b. HOME TELEPHONE (Include Area Code)	

X ALL APPLICABLE BOXES:

7.a. POSITION (Title, Grade, Component)

6.a. SERVICE	b. COMPONENT	c. PURPOSE OF EXAMINATION	
Army / Coast Guard	Regular	Enlistment	Medical Board / Other (Specify)
Navy	Reserve	Commission	Retirement
Marine Corps	National Guard	Retention	U.S. Service Academy
Air Force		Separation	ROTC Scholarship Program

b. USUAL OCCUPATION

8. CURRENT MEDICATIONS (Prescription and Over-the-counter)	9. ALLERGIES (Including insect bites/stings, foods, medicine or other substance)

Mark each item "YES" or "NO". Every item marked "YES" must be fully explained in Item 29 on Page 2.

HAVE YOU EVER HAD OR DO YOU NOW HAVE:	YES	NO	12. (Continued)	YES	NO
10.a. Tuberculosis	○	○	f. Foot trouble (e.g., pain, corns, bunions, etc.)	○	○
b. Lived with someone who had tuberculosis	○	○	g. Impaired use of arms, legs, hands, or feet	○	○
c. Coughed up blood	○	○	h. Swollen or painful joint(s)	○	○
d. Asthma or any breathing problems related to exercise, weather, pollens, etc.	○	○	i. Knee trouble (e.g., locking, giving out, pain or ligament injury, etc.)	○	○
e. Shortness of breath	○	○	j. Any knee or foot surgery including arthroscopy or the use of a scope to any bone or joint	○	○
f. Bronchitis	○	○	k. Any need to use corrective devices such as prosthetic devices, knee brace(s), back support(s), lifts or orthotics, etc.	○	○
g. Wheezing or problems with wheezing	○	○	l. Bone, joint, or other deformity	○	○
h. Been prescribed or used an inhaler	○	○	m. Plate(s), screw(s), rod(s) or pin(s) in any bone	○	○
i. A chronic cough or cough at night	○	○	n. Broken bone(s) (cracked or fractured)	○	○
j. Sinusitis	○	○	13.a. Frequent indigestion or heartburn	○	○
k. Hay fever	○	○	b. Stomach, liver, intestinal trouble, or ulcer	○	○
l. Chronic or frequent colds	○	○	c. Gall bladder trouble or gallstones	○	○
11.a. Severe tooth or gum trouble	○	○	d. Jaundice or hepatitis (liver disease)	○	○
b. Thyroid trouble or goiter	○	○	e. Rupture/hernia	○	○
c. Eye disorder or trouble	○	○	f. Rectal disease, hemorrhoids or blood from the rectum	○	○
d. Ear, nose, or throat trouble	○	○	g. Skin diseases (e.g. acne, eczema, psoriasis, etc.)	○	○
e. Loss of vision in either eye	○	○	h. Frequent or painful urination	○	○
f. Worn contact lenses or glasses	○	○	i. High or low blood sugar	○	○
g. A hearing loss or wear a hearing aid	○	○	j. Kidney stone or blood in urine	○	○
h. Surgery to correct vision (RK, PRK, LASIK, etc.)	○	○	k. Sugar or protein in urine	○	○
12.a. Painful shoulder, elbow or wrist (e.g. pain, dislocation, etc.)	○	○	l. Sexually transmitted disease (syphilis, gonorrhea, chlamydia, genital warts, herpes, etc.)	○	○
b. Arthritis, rheumatism, or bursitis	○	○	14.a. Adverse reaction to serum, food, insect stings or medicine	○	○
c. Recurrent back pain or any back problem	○	○	b. Recent unexplained gain or loss of weight	○	○
d. Numbness or tingling	○	○	c. Currently in good health (If no, explain in Item 29 on Page 2.)	○	○
e. Loss of finger or toe	○	○	d. Tumor, growth, cyst, or cancer	○	○

DD FORM 2807-1, AUG 2011 DoD exception to SF 93 approved by ICMR, August 3, 2000. PREVIOUS EDITION IS OBSOLETE. Page 1 of 3 Pages Adobe Professional 8.0

23

Any item checked as 'yes' will be explained in detail in Box 29. Continuation sheets are good!

LAST NAME, FIRST NAME, MIDDLE NAME (SUFFIX)	SOCIAL SECURITY NUMBER

Mark each item "YES" or "NO". Every item marked "YES" must be fully explained in Item 29 below.

HAVE YOU EVER HAD OR DO YOU NOW HAVE:	YES	NO		YES	NO
15.a. Dizziness or fainting spells	○	○	19. Have you been refused employment or been unable to hold a job or stay in school because of:		
b. Frequent or severe headache	○	○	a. Sensitivity to chemicals, dust, sunlight, etc.	○	○
c. A head injury, memory loss or amnesia	○	○	b. Inability to perform certain motions	○	○
d. Paralysis	○	○	c. Inability to stand, sit, kneel, lie down, etc.	○	○
e. Seizures, convulsions, epilepsy or fits	○	○	d. Other medical reasons (If yes, give reasons.)	○	○
f. Car, train, sea, or air sickness	○	○	20. Have you ever been treated in an Emergency Room? (If yes, for what?)	○	○
g. A period of unconsciousness or concussion	○	○			
h. Meningitis, encephalitis, or other neurological problems	○	○	21. Have you ever been a patient in any type of hospital? (If yes, specify when, where, why, and name of doctor and complete address of hospital.)	○	○
16.a. Rheumatic fever	○	○			
b. Prolonged bleeding (as after an injury or tooth extraction, etc.)	○	○			
c. Pain or pressure in the chest	○	○	22. Have you ever had, or have you been advised to have any operations or surgery? (If yes, describe and give age at which occurred.)	○	○
d. Palpitation, pounding heart or abnormal heartbeat	○	○			
e. Heart trouble or murmur	○	○			
f. High or low blood pressure	○	○	23. Have you ever had any illness or injury other than those already noted? (If yes, specify when, where, and give details.)	○	○
17.a. Nervous trouble of any sort (anxiety or panic attacks)	○	○			
b. Habitual stammering or stuttering	○	○	24. Have you consulted or been treated by clinics, physicians, healers, or other practitioners within the past 5 years for other than minor illnesses? (If yes, give complete address of doctor, hospital, clinic, and details.)	○	○
c. Loss of memory or amnesia, or neurological symptoms	○	○			
d. Frequent trouble sleeping	○	○			
e. Received counseling of any type	○	○			
f. Depression or excessive worry	○	○	25. Have you ever been rejected for military service for any reason? (If yes, give date and reason for rejection.)	○	○
g. Been evaluated or treated for a mental condition	○	○			
h. Attempted suicide	○	○	26. Have you ever been discharged from military service for any reason? (If yes, give date, reason, and type of discharge; whether honorable, other than honorable, for unfitness or unsuitability.)	○	○
i. Used illegal drugs or abused prescription drugs	○	○			
18. FEMALES ONLY. Have you ever had or do you now have:					
a. Treatment for a gynecological (female) disorder	○	○	27. Have you ever received, is there pending, or have you ever applied for pension or compensation for any disability or injury? (If yes, specify what kind, granted by whom, and what amount, when, why.)	○	○
b. A change of menstrual pattern	○	○			
c. Any abnormal PAP smears	○	○			
d. First day of last menstrual period (YYYYMMDD)					
e. Date of last PAP smear (YYYYMMDD)			28. Have you ever been denied life insurance?	○	○

29. EXPLANATION OF "YES" ANSWER(S) (Describe answer(s), give date(s) of problem, name of doctor(s) and/or hospital(s), treatment given and current medical status.)

NOTE: HAND TO THE DOCTOR OR NURSE, OR IF MAILED MARK ENVELOPE "TO BE OPENED BY MEDICAL PERSONNEL ONLY."

DD FORM 2807-1, AUG 2011   Page 2 of 3 Pages

Your medical examiner will fill out Box 30a.

LAST NAME, FIRST NAME, MIDDLE NAME (SUFFIX)	SOCIAL SECURITY NUMBER

30. EXAMINER'S SUMMARY AND ELABORATION OF ALL PERTINENT DATA *(Physician/practitioner shall comment on all positive answers in questions 10 - 29. Physician/practitioner may develop by interview any additional medical history deemed important, and record any significant findings here.)*

a. COMMENTS

b. TYPED OR PRINTED NAME OF EXAMINER *(Last, First, Middle Initial)*	c. SIGNATURE	d. DATE SIGNED *(YYYYMMDD)*

DD FORM 2807-1, AUG 2011

VA CLAIM PHYSICALS

The VA disability claim physical is a completely different animal. Your service medical treatment facility has nothing to do with this physical, as it did with your transition physical. The VA physicals are performed by contracted medical examinars or a VA medical center. These examiners are responsible for the receipt of your comprehensive ailments list from the VA or your VSO representative, the scheduling of your examinations, and compilation and delivery of reports to the VA to review when determining the results of your pre-discharge claim.

In Book II in this series we will walk you through the process of submitting your claim through the VA or your VSO representative. When the VA or your VSO representative submits your comprehensive ailments list for your pre-discharge claim, it goes to a medical facility for scheduling, which will then contact you to inform you of your appointment(s) to provide medical evaluation for each of your claims. Some things to think about when you conduct your medical examination(s):

Range of Motion. Pain means little to your claim by itself, except when the medical examiner diagnoses a condition which causes the pain. Any musculoskeletal issues you may have will be evaluated for pain and range of motion limitations. The examining physician will use a goniometer to determine your ranges of motion. Expect the examining physician to check each range of motion three times for an accurate reading. This is required for the worksheets; it is not a physician trying to catch you faking an injury. Ranges of motion are assigned a percentage, which are depicted under then musculoskeletal system in Section 4 of this book.

Know your pain limits. Again, not everything you have an issue with hurts you every day. During your examination you need to move as much as you are comfortable with. Remember, range of motion and pain. If you are told to bend over and touch your toes, and you are able to do so, then don't expect a report of significant lumbar spine issues. Don't lie about your range of motion or threshold of pain, but don't try to tough through it either. As soon as you feel pain, stop. We would also recommend having a good understanding of where your ranges of motion are on your 'bad days'- so you have an understanding of what usually limits your motion.

Check your ego at the door. If something hurts, say so. If your range of motion is compromised, stop. This is not the time to reflect on what it took to get all of your badges and tabs- being a hard-ass isn't going to get you anything starting the day you retire. Too many guys we know tried to tough through the pain- they got a lot of 0% ratings. Again, we are not suggesting you try to win the next academy award- be truthful. However, if you feel pain, stop! That is your range of motion. You are not going to get better in time. If you are feeling pain in one of your ranges of motion, you will continue to feel that pain. You need to be compensated at that range of motion.

Now that you have a good understanding of how to organize your ailments, how to ensure they are documented, and how to prepare for service-related and VA disabilities physicals, the rest of this book is dedicated to outlining the VA-recognized ailments, diseases, and disabilities with their respective compensation. Study this book carefully to ensure you have identified all issues you may have. When researching disabilities in 38 Code of Federal Regulations (C.F.R) it is important to note that changes occur often! Rating criteria are updated periodically by the VA mainly based on Court of Appeal decisions which affect all Veterans. The VA has two newer websites to accompany the eCFR websites where they plan to post updates, which are https://www.knowva.ebenefits.va.gov and https://www.vapulse.net/. These sites mainly discuss VHA healthcare success stories, but this can be an invaluable tool to keep up with health care changes and trends in treatment, eligibility and such. These websites are inter-locked with Ebenefits, but you do not have to have an account. Keep in mind these are new sites, and for now are a work in progress. You can check with these websites, but also ensure you register and continue to check back regularly on our website, at www.veteransinformingveterans.com, as we will have an update section for each book. As we hear of any additions to or changes in the ailments, diseases or disabilities, we will add them to the site for you.

Once you have identified all of your ailments, diseases and disabilities, you will be ready for the next piece of the claims process, which we will walk you through in detail in Book II. If you have already left the service, you can find out how to add another disability to your VA claim, or have the VA reconsider a claim if you did not get a favorable rating, by following the plan outlined in detail in Book II.

THIS PAGE LEFT INTENTIONALLY BLANK

SECTION 4

VA RECOGNIZED AILMENTS, DISEASES, AND DISABILITIES

Ok, now that we know how we should ensure our disabilities are documented, let's make sure we have all our disabilities accounted for. This section can be daunting, but it's broken down into multiple chapters. Each of these chapters correspond with a specific bodily group or system. Disclaimer- this section has many medical professional terms- we have compiled a glossary of terms in Chapter 18 of this section, but there will be terms you may need to look up. This information is taken from the VA's Code of Federal Regulations (CFR)-38.

If you aren't sure which system a specific ailment, disease or disability falls under, we have also provided you with an alphabetical listing of ailments. You can simply find your diagnosed ailment and where to get more specific information about it. You can find this list in Chapter 18, beginning on page 213.

With this section you can research any VA-recognized ailment or disability to preview the rating range. To do so, it is necessary to understand which chapter your ailment or disability resides. For example, if you suffer from Chronic Urticaria (a fancy term for the hives), that condition is housed under Skin Conditions, in Chapter 13 of this section- see Table of Contents on the next page. Go to Chapter 13 and in the Table of Contents and you see it begins on page 159. If you go to page 159 you will see the quick glance at the beginning of Chapter 13, which shows all disabilities for skin conditions. Look down the left side of the chart until you find Chronic Urticaria. You'll see the VA code for Chronic Urticaria is 7825, with specific details on page 167. You would then go to that page, find VA Code 7825, and you will see Chronic Urticaria has a minimum rating of 10% and a maximum rating of 60%, depending on the described severity. Repeat this process for all disabilities to see what the rating range will be for any ailment you have.

It is important to remember that this book is not designed to diagnose you with any issues- that's your primary care manager's responsibility- but it is designed to help you ensure you have all issues addressed. The information here allows you to see what the rating ranges are for each of your diagnosed disabilities.

THIS PAGE LEFT INTENTIONALLY BLANK

Section 4- Table of Contents

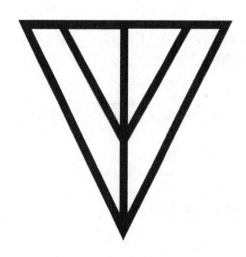

THIS PAGE LEFT INTENTIONALLY BLANK

CHAPTER 1

MUSCULOSKELETAL SYSTEM

Quick Reference:

	THE SPINE (Continued)	
5237	Lumbosacral or cervical strain	54
5238	Spinal stenosis	54
5239	Spondylolisthesis or segmental instability	54
5240	Ankylosing spondylitis	54
5241	Spinal fusion	54
5242	Degenerative arthritis of the spine (see also diagnostic code 5003)	54
5243	Intervertebral disc syndrome (IVDS)	54
	Intervertebral Disc Syndrome Based on Incapacitating Episodes Formula	55
	Range of Motion Diagrams of the Cervical and Thoracolumbar Spine	55-56
	THE HIP AND THIGH	
5250	Hip, ankylosis of	57
5251	Thigh, limitation of extension of	57
5252	Thigh, limitation of flexion of	57
5253	Thigh, impairment of	57
5254	Hip, flail joint	57
5255	Femur, impairment of	57
	Range of Motion Diagrams of Hip	57
	THE KNEE AND LEG	
5256	Knee, ankylosis of	58
5257	Knee, other impairment of	58
5258	Cartilage, semilunar, dislocated, with frequent episodes of "locking," pain, and effusion into the joint	58
5259	Cartilage, semilunar, removal of, symptomatic	58
5260	Leg, limitation of flexion of	58
5261	Leg, limitation of extension of	58
5262	Tibia and fibula, impairment of	58
5263	Genu recurvatum (acquired, traumatic, with weakness and insecurity in weight-bearing objectively demonstrated)	58
	Range of Motion Diagrams of the Knee	58
	THE ANKLE	
5270	Ankle, ankylosis of	59
5271	Ankle, limited motion of	59
5272	Subastragalar or tarsal joint, ankylosis of	59
5273	Os calcis or astragalus, malunion of	59
5274	Astragalectomy	59
	SHORTENING OF THE LOWER EXTREMITIES	
5275	Bones, of the lower extremity, shortening of	60
	THE FOOT	
5276	Flatfoot, acquired	60
5277	Weak Foot, bilateral	60
5278	Claw foot (pes cavus), acquired	61
5279	Metatarsalgia, anterior (Morton's disease), unilateral, or bilateral	61
5280	Hallux valgus, unilateral	61

THE FOOT (Continued)		
5281	Hallux rigidus, unilateral, severe	61
5282	Hammer toe	61
5283	Tarsal, or metatarsal bones, malunion of, or nonunion of	61
5284	Foot injuries, other	61
	Foot Diagram	62
THE SKULL		
5296	Skull, loss of part of, both inner and outer tables	63
THE RIBS		
5297	Ribs, removal of	63
THE COCCYX		
5298	Coccyx, removal of	63

ACUTE, SUBACUTE, OR CHRONIC DISEASES

Rating

- 5000 Osteomyelitis, acute, subacute, or chronic:
  - Of the pelvis, vertebrae, or extending into major joints, or with multiple localization or with long history of intractability and debility, anemia, amyloid liver changes, or other continuous constitutional symptoms 100%
  - Frequent episodes, with constitutional symptoms 60%
  - With definite involucrum or sequestrum, with or without discharging sinus 30%
  - With discharging sinus or other evidence of active infection within the past 5 years 20%
  - Inactive, following repeated episodes, without evidence of active infection in past 5 years 10%

  - Note (1): A rating of 10 percent, as an exception to the amputation rule, is to be assigned in any case of active osteomyelitis where the amputation rating for the affected part is no percent. This 10 percent rating and the other partial ratings of 30 percent or less are to be combined with ratings for ankylosis, limited motion, nonunion or malunion, shortening, etc., subject, of course, to the amputation rule. The 60 percent rating, as it is based on constitutional symptoms, is not subject to the amputation rule. A rating for osteomyelitis will not be applied following cure by removal or radical resection of the affected bone.

  - Note (2): The 20 percent rating on the basis of activity within the past 5 years is not assignable following the initial infection of active osteomyelitis with no subsequent reactivation. The prerequisite for this historical rating is an established recurrent osteomyelitis. To qualify for the 10 percent rating, 2 or more episodes following the initial infection are required. This 20 percent rating or the 10 percent rating, when applicable, will be assigned once only to cover disability at all sites of previously active infection with a future ending date in the case of the 20 percent rating.

- 5001   Bones and joints, tuberculosis of, active or inactive:
  - Active.. 100%
  - Inactive: VA will rate based upon residuals

- 5002   Arthritis rheumatoid (atrophic) *as an active process*:
  - With constitutional manifestations associated with
  active joint involvement, totally incapacitating 100%
  - Less than criteria for 100% but with weight loss and anemia
  productive of severe impairment of health or severely
  incapacitating exacerbations occurring 4 or more times a year
  or a lesser number over prolonged periods 60%
  - Symptom combinations productive of definite impairment of
  health objectively supported by examination findings or
  incapacitating exacerbations occurring 3 or more times a year 40%
  - One or two exacerbations a year in a well-established diagnosis.................... 20%
  - For chronic residuals: For residuals such as limitation of motion or ankylosis,
  favorable or unfavorable, rate under the appropriate diagnostic codes for the
  specific joints involved. Where, however, the limitation of motion of the specific
  joint or joints involved is noncompensable under the codes a rating of 10 percent
  is for application for each such major joint or group of minor joints affected by
  limitation of motion, to be combined, not added under diagnostic code 5002.
  Limitation of motion must be objectively confirmed by findings such as swelling,
  muscle spasm, or satisfactory evidence of painful motion.
  - Note: The ratings for the active process will not be combined with the residual
  ratings for limitation of motion or ankylosis. Assign the higher evaluation.

- 5003   Arthritis, degenerative (hypertrophic or osteoarthritis):
  - Degenerative arthritis established by X-ray findings will be rated on the basis of
  limitation of motion under the appropriate diagnostic codes for the specific joint or
  joints involved (DC 5200 etc.). When however, the limitation of motion of the
  specific joint or joints involved is noncompensable under the appropriate
  diagnostic codes, a rating of 10 percent is for application for each such major joint
  or group of minor joints affected by limitation of motion, to be combined, not
  added under diagnostic code 5003. Limitation of motion must be objectively
  confirmed by findings such as swelling, muscle spasm, or satisfactory evidence of
  painful motion. In the absence of limitation of motion, rate as below:
  - With X-ray evidence of involvement of 2 or more major joints
  or 2 or more minor joint groups, with occasional incapacitating
  exacerbations 20%
  - With X-ray evidence of involvement of 2 or more major joints
  or 2 or more minor joint groups.. 10%
  - Note (1): The 20% and 10% ratings based on X-ray findings, above, will not
  be combined with ratings based on limitation of motion.

- Note (2): The 20% and 10% ratings based on X-ray findings, above, will not be used in rating conditions listed under diagnostic code 5013 to 5024, inclusive.

FOR DIAGNOSTIC CODES 5004 THROUGH 5009, RATE THE DISABILITY AS RHEUMATOID ARTHRITIS

Rating

- 5004   Arthritis, gonorrheal.
- 5005   Arthritis, pneumococcic.
- 5006   Arthritis, typhoid.
- 5007   Arthritis, syphilitic.
- 5008   Arthritis, streptococcic.
- 5009   Arthritis, other types (specify):

- 5010   Arthritis, due to trauma, substantiated by X-ray findings:
  - Rate as arthritis, degenerative.

- 5011   Bones, caisson disease of:
  - Rate as arthritis, cord involvement, or deafness, depending on the severity of disabling manifestations.

- 5012   Bones, new growths of, malignant.. 100%

  - Note: The 100 percent rating will be continued for 1 year following the cessation of surgical, X-ray, antineoplastic chemotherapy or other therapeutic procedure. At this point, if there has been no local recurrence or metastases, the rating will be made on residuals.

The diseases under diagnostic codes 5013 through 5024 will be rated on limitation of motion of affected parts, as arthritis, degenerative, except gout which will be rated under diagnostic code 5002.

- 5013   Osteoporosis, with joint manifestations.
- 5014   Osteomalacia.
- 5015   Bones, new growths of, benign.
- 5016   Osteitis deformans.
- 5017   Gout.
- 5018   Hydrarthrosis, intermittent.
- 5019   Bursitis.
- 5020   Synovitis.
- 5021   Myositis.
- 5022   Periostitis.
- 5023   Myositis ossificans.
- 5024   Tenosynovitis.

- 5025 Fibromyalgia (fibrositis, primary fibromyalgia syndrome):
  - With widespread musculoskeletal pain and tender points, with or without associated fatigue, sleep disturbance, stiffness, paresthesias, headache, irritable bowel symptoms, depression, anxiety, or Raynaud's-like symptoms:

  - That are constant, or nearly so, and refractory to therapy 40%

  - That are episodic, with exacerbations often precipitated by environmental or emotional stress or by overexertion, but that are present more than one-third of the time 20%

  - That require continuous medication for control 10%

  - Note: Widespread pain means pain in both the left and right sides of the body, that is both above and below the waist, and that affects both the axial skeleton (i.e., cervical spine, anterior chest, thoracic spine, or low back) and the extremities.

PROSTHETIC IMPLANTS

	Rating	
	Major	*Minor*
■ 5051 Shoulder replacement (prosthesis):		
o Prosthetic replacement of the shoulder joint:		
- For 1 year following implantation of prosthesis	100%	100%
- With chronic residuals consisting of severe, painful motion or weakness in the affected extremity	60%	50%
- With intermediate degrees of residual weakness, pain or limitation of motion, rate by analogy to diagnostic codes 5200 and 5203.		
- Minimum rating	30%	20%
■ 5052 Elbow replacement (prosthesis):		
o Prosthetic replacement of the elbow joint:		
- For 1 year following implantation of prosthesis	100%	100%
- With chronic residuals consisting of severe, painful motion or weakness in the affected extremity	50%	40%
- With intermediate degrees of residual weakness, pain or limitation of motion, rate by analogy to diagnostic codes 5205 and 5208.		
- Minimum rating	30%	20%

- **5053** Wrist replacement (prosthesis):
  - Prosthetic replacement of the wrist joint:
    - For 1 year following implantation of prosthesis ....100% 100%
    - With chronic residuals consisting of severe, painful
    motion or weakness in the affected extremity.....................40%................ 30%
    - With intermediate degrees of residual weakness, pain or
    limitation of motion, rate by analogy to diagnostic code 5214.
    - Minimum rating .... 20%................. 20%

    - Note: The 100% rating for 1 year following implantation of prosthesis will commence after initial grant of the 1-month total rating following hospital discharge.

- **5054** Hip replacement (prosthesis):
  - Prosthetic replacement of the head of the femur or of the acetabulum:
    - For 1 year following implantation of prosthesis... 100%
    - Following implantation of prosthesis with painful
    motion or weakness such as to require use of crutches 90%*
    - Markedly severe residual weakness, pain or limitation of motion
    following implantation of prosthesis. 70%
    - Moderately severe residuals of weakness, pain or limitation of motion 50%
    - Minimum rating... 30%

- **5055** Knee replacement (prosthesis):
  - Prosthetic replacement of the knee joint:
    - For 1 year following implantation of prosthesis.................................... 100%
    - With chronic residuals consisting of severe painful motion or
    weakness in the affected extremity... 60%
    - With intermediate degrees of residual weakness, pain or limitation
    of motion rate by analogy to diagnostic codes 5256, 5261, or 5262.
    - Minimum rating.. 30%

- **5056** Ankle replacement (prosthesis):
  - Prosthetic replacement of the ankle joint:
    - For 1 year following implantation of prosthesis... 100%
    - With chronic residuals consisting of severe painful motion or
    weakness 40%
    - With intermediate degrees of residual weakness, pain or limitation
    of motion rate by analogy to diagnostic codes 5270 or 5271.
    - Minimum rating... 20%

    - Note (1): The term "prosthetic replacement" in diagnostic codes 5051 through 5056 means a total replacement of the named joint. However, in DC 5054, "prosthetic replacement" means a total replacement of the head of the femur or the acetabulum.

- Note (2): The 100 percent rating for 1 year following implantation of prosthesis will commence after initial grant of the 1-month total rating following hospital discharge.

- * Special monthly compensation is assignable during the 100% rating period the earliest date permanent use of crutches is established.

COMBINATIONS OF DISABILITIES
Rating

- 5104 Anatomical loss of one hand and loss of use of one foot............................... 100%*
- 5105 Anatomical loss of one foot and loss of use of one hand............................. 100%*
- 5106 Anatomical loss of both hands.. 100%*

- 5107 Anatomical loss of both feet 100%*
- 5108 Anatomical loss of one hand and one foot... 100%*
- 5109 Loss of use of both hands.. 100%*
- 5110 Loss of use of both feet... 100%*
- 5111 Loss of use of one hand and one foot 100%*

*Also entitled to special monthly compensation.

AMPUTATIONS: UPPER EXTREMITY

| | | Rating | |
| | | *Major* | *Minor* |

Arm, amputation of:

- 5120 Disarticulation: ....90%* 90%*
- 5121 Above insertion of deltoid...90%* 80%*
- 5122 Below insertion of deltoid...80%* 70%*

*Also entitled to special monthly compensation.

Forearm, amputation of:

- 5123 Above insertion of pronator teres:...................................80%* 70%*
- 5124 Below insertion of pronator teres:...................................70%* 60%*
- 5125 Hand, loss of use of: ....70%* 60%*

*Also entitled to special monthly compensation.

			Rating	
			Major	*Minor*
▪	5126	Five digits of one hand, amputation:.....................................	70%*	60%*

*Also entitled to special monthly compensation

Four digits of one hand, amputation of:

▪	5127	Thumb, index, long, and ring:..	70%*	60%*
▪	5128	Thumb, index, long, and little:.......................................	70%*	60%*
▪	5129	Thumb, index, ring and little:	70%*	60%*
▪	5130	Thumb, long, ring, and little:..	70%*	60%*
▪	5131	Index, long, ring, and little:	60%	50%

*Also entitled to special monthly compensation

Three digits of one hand, amputation of:

▪	5132	Thumb, index, and long:..	60%	50%
▪	5133	Thumb, index, and ring:..	60%	50%
▪	5134	Thumb, index, and little:	60%	50%
▪	5135	Thumb, long, and ring:...	60%	50%
▪	5136	Thumb, long, and little:	60%	50%
▪	5137	Thumb, ring and little:...	60%	50%
▪	5138	Index, long, and ring:	50%	40%
▪	5139	Index, long and little:	50%	40%
▪	5140	Index, ring, and little:	50%	40%
▪	5141	Long, ring, and little:	40%	30%

Two digits of one hand, amputation of:

▪	5142	Thumb and index:	50%	40%
▪	5143	Thumb and long:	50%	40%
▪	5144	Thumb and ring:	50%	40%
▪	5145	Thumb and little:	50%	40%
▪	5146	Index and long:	40%	30%
▪	5147	Index and ring:	40%	30%
▪	5148	Index and little:	40%	30%
▪	5149	Long and ring:	30%	20%
▪	5150	Long and little:	30%	20%
▪	5151	Ring and little:	30%	20%

- (a) The ratings for multiple finger amputations apply to amputations at the proximal interphalangeal joints or through proximal phalanges.

- (b) Amputation through middle phalanges will be rated as prescribed for unfavorable ankylosis of the fingers.

- (c) Amputations at distal joints, or through distal phalanges, other than negligible losses, will be rated as prescribed for favorable ankylosis of the fingers.

- (d) Amputation or resection of metacarpal bones (more than one-half the bone lost) in multiple fingers injuries will require a rating of 10 percent added to (not combined with) the ratings, multiple finger amputations, subject to the amputation rule applied to the forearm.

- (e) Combinations of finger amputations at various levels, or finger amputations with ankylosis or limitation of motion of the fingers will be rated on the basis of the grade of disability; i.e., amputation, unfavorable ankylosis, most representative of the levels or combinations. With an even number of fingers involved, and adjacent grades of disability, select the higher of the two grades.

- (f) Loss of use of the hand will be held to exist when no effective function remains other than that which would be equally well served by an amputation stump with a suitable prosthetic appliance.

SINGLE FINGER AMPUTATIONS

Rating

- 5152   Thumb, amputation of:
    - With metacarpal resection..40%.............. 30%
    - At metacarpophalangeal joint or through proximal phalanx... 30%.............. 20%
    - At distal joint or through distal phalanx...........................20% 20%

- 5153   Index finger, amputation of:
    - With metacarpal resection (more than one-half the bone lost).....30%.......... 20%
    - Without metacarpal resection, at proximal interphalangeal
        joint or proximal thereto ....20%.......... 20%
    - Through long phalanx or at distal joint ....10%.......... 10%

- 5154   Long finger, amputation of:
    - With metacarpal resection (more than one-half the bone lost).....20%.......... 20%
    - Without metacarpal resection, at proximal interphalangeal
        joint or proximal thereto ....10%.......... 10%

- 5155   Ring finger, amputation of:
    - With metacarpal resection (more than one-half the bone lost).....20%.......... 20%
    - Without metacarpal resection, at proximal interphalangeal
        joint or proximal thereto ....10%.......... 10%

43

- 5156 Little finger, amputation of:
  - With metacarpal resection (more than one-half the bone lost).....20%.......... 20%
  - Without metacarpal resection, at proximal interphalangeal
    joint or proximal thereto...…10%........ 10%

- Note: The single finger amputation ratings are the only applicable ratings for amputations of whole or part of single fingers.

AMPUTATIONS: LOWER EXTREMITY

Thigh, amputation of:

- 5160 Disarticulation, with loss of extrinsic pelvic girdle muscles 90%*
- 5161 Upper third, one-third of the distance from perineum to knee joint
  measured from perineum 80%*
- 5162 Middle or lower thirds 60%*

Leg, amputation of:

- 5163 With defective stump, thigh amputation recommended 60%*
- 5164 Amputation not improvable by prosthesis controlled by
  natural knee action 60%*
- 5165 At a lower level, permitting prosthesis 40%*
- 5166 Forefoot, amputation proximal to metatarsal bones (more than
  one-half of metatarsal loss).. 40%*
- 5167 Foot, loss of use of... 40%*
- 5170 Toes, all, amputation of, without metatarsal loss...................................... 30%
- 5171 Toe, great, amputation of:
  - With removal of metatarsal head... 30%
  - Without metatarsal involvement.. 10%

  *Also entitled to special monthly compensation.

- 5172 Toes, other than great, amputation of, with removal of metatarsal head:
  - One or two 20%
  - Without metatarsal involvement.. 0%

- 5173 Toes, three or four, amputation of, without metatarsal involvement:
  - Including great toe 20%
  - Not including great toe 10%

Rating

Major   *Minor*

- ▪ 5200   Scapulohumeral articulation, ankylosis of:
  - Unfavorable, abduction limited to 25° from side:...............50% 40%
  - Intermediate between favorable and unfavorable:...............40% 30%
  - Favorable, abduction to 60°, can reach mouth and head: ......30%................ 20%

  - Note: The scapula and humerus move as one piece.

- ▪ 5201   Arm, limitation of motion of:
  - To 25° from side:..40% 30%
  - Midway between side and shoulder level:.........................30% 20%
  - At shoulder level:...20% 20%

- ▪ 5202   Humerus, other impairment of:
  - Loss of head of (flail shoulder): ....80% 70%
  - Nonunion of (false flail joint): ....60% 50%
  - Fibrous union of:..50%................ 40%
  - Recurrent dislocation of at scapulohumeral joint:
  - With frequent episodes and guarding of all arm movements:...30%............... 20%
  - With infrequent episodes, and guarding of movement
  only at shoulder level:...20%............... 20%
  - Malunion of:
  - Marked deformity: ....30%............... 20%
  - Moderate deformity: ....20%............... 20%

- ▪ 5203   Clavicle or scapula, impairment of:
  - Dislocation of:..20%............ 20%
  - Nonunion of:
  - With loose movement..20%..........20%
  - Without loose movement...10%..........10%
  - Malunion of: ....10%............ 10%
  Or rate on impairment of function of contiguous joint.

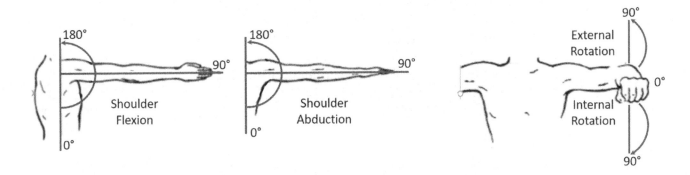

45

- 5205   Elbow, ankylosis of:
  - Unfavorable, at an angle of less than 50° or with complete
  loss of supination or pronation .... 60%.......... 50%
  - Intermediate, at an angle of more than 90°, or between
  70° and 50° .... 50%.......... 40%
  - Favorable, at an angle between 90° and 70° .... 40%.......... 30%

- 5206   Forearm, limitation of flexion of:
  - Flexion limited to 45°.. 50%.......... 40%
  - Flexion limited to 55°.. 40%.......... 30%
  - Flexion limited to 70°.. 30%.......... 20%
  - Flexion limited to 90°.. 20%.......... 20%
  - Flexion limited to 100° .... 10%.......... 10%
  - Flexion limited to 110°.. 0%............ 0%

- 5207   Forearm, limitation of extension of:
  - Extension limited to 110°... 50%.......... 40%
  - Extension limited to 100°... 40%.......... 30%
  - Extension limited to 90°... 30%.......... 20%
  - Extension limited to 75°... 20%.......... 20%
  - Extension limited to 60°... 10%.......... 10%
  - Extension limited to 45°... 10%.......... 10%

- 5208   Forearm, flexion limited to 100° and extension to 45°................. 20%.......... 20%

- 5209   Elbow, other impairment of Flail joint:.................................. 60%......... 50%
  - Joint fracture, with marked cubitus varus or cubitus valgus
  deformity or with ununited fracture of head of radius:.................20%........ 20%

- 5210   Radius and ulna, nonunion of, with flail false joint:.................. 50%........ 40%

- 5211   Ulna, impairment of:
  - Nonunion in upper half, with false movement:
  With loss of bone substance (1 inch (2 5 cms.) or more)
  and marked deformity...40%.....30%
  - Without loss of bone substance or deformity:.........................30%..... 20%
  - Nonunion in lower half...20%.....20%
  - Malunion of, with bad alignment ....10%.....10%

- 5212   Radius, impairment of:
  - Nonunion in upper half, with false movement:
  With loss of bone substance (1 inch (2 5 cms.) or more)
  and marked deformity ....40%.....30%
  - Without loss of bone substance or deformity:............................30%.... 20%
  - Nonunion in lower half..20%.....20%
  - Malunion of, with bad alignment ....10%.....10%

- 5213   Supination and pronation, impairment of:
  - o   Loss of (bone fusion):
    - The hand fixed in supination or hyperpronation ....40%.....30%
    - The hand fixed in full pronation ....30%.....20%
    - The hand fixed near the middle of the arc or
    moderate pronation ....20%.....20%
  - o   Limitation of pronation:
    - Motion lost beyond middle of arc...30%.....20%
    - Motion lost beyond last quarter of arc, the hand does
    not approach full pronation..20%.....20%
  - o   Limitation of supination:
    - To 30° or less ....10%.....10%

  - Note: In all the forearm and wrist injuries, codes 5205 through 5213, multiple impaired finger movements due to tendon tie-up, muscle or nerve injury, are to be separately rated and combined not to exceed rating for loss of use of hand.

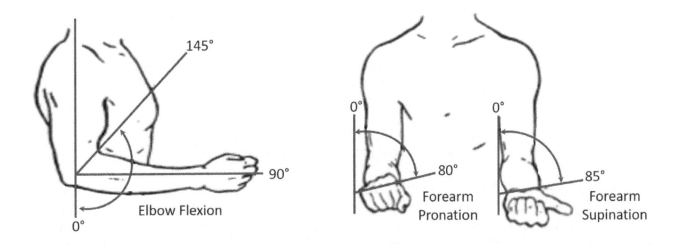

- 5214   Wrist, ankylosis of:
  - Unfavorable, in any degree of palmar flexion, or with
  ulnar or radial deviation ....50%.....40%
  - Any other position, except favorable...40%.....30%
  - Favorable in 20° to 30° dorsiflexion ....30%.....20%

  - Note: Extremely unfavorable ankylosis will be rated as loss of use of hands under diagnostic code 5125.

- 5215   Wrist, limitation of motion of:
  - Dorsiflexion less than 15°..10%.....10%
  - Palmar flexion limited in line with forearm ....10%.....10%

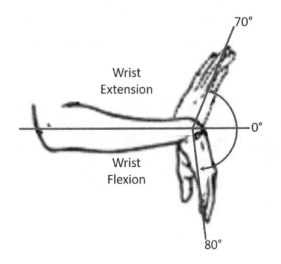

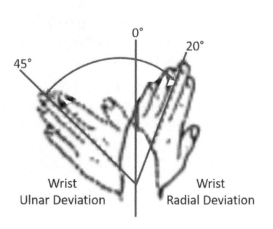

EVALUATION OF ANKYLOSIS OR LIMITATION OF MOTION
OF SINGLE OR MULTIPLE DIGITS OF THE HAND

(1) For the index, long, ring, and little fingers (digits II, III, IV, and V), zero degrees of flexion represents the fingers fully extended, making a straight line with the rest of the hand. The position of function of the hand is with the wrist dorsiflexed 20 to 30 degrees, the metacarpophalangeal and proximal interphalangeal joints flexed to 30 degrees, and the thumb (digit I) abducted and rotated so that the thumb pad faces the finger pads. Only joints in these positions are considered to be in favorable position. For digits II through V, the metacarpophalangeal joint has a range of zero to 90 degrees of flexion, the proximal interphalangeal joint has a range of zero to 100 degrees of flexion, and the distal (terminal) interphalangeal joint has a range of zero to 70 or 80 degrees of flexion.

(2) When two or more digits of the same hand are affected by any combination of amputation, ankylosis, or limitation of motion that is not otherwise specified in the rating schedule, the evaluation level assigned will be that which best represents the overall disability (i.e., amputation, unfavorable or favorable ankylosis, or limitation of motion), assigning the higher level of evaluation when the level of disability is equally balanced between one level and the next higher level.

(3) Evaluation of ankylosis of the index, long, ring, and little fingers:
    (i) If both the metacarpophalangeal and proximal interphalangeal joints of a digit are ankylosed, and either is in extension or full flexion, or there is rotation or angulation of a bone, evaluate as amputation without metacarpal resection, at proximal interphalangeal joint or proximal thereto.

    (ii) If both the metacarpophalangeal and proximal interphalangeal joints of a digit are ankylosed, evaluate as unfavorable ankylosis, even if each joint is individually fixed in a favorable position.

    (iii) If only the metacarpophalangeal or proximal interphalangeal joint is ankylosed, and there is a gap of more than two inches (5.1 cm.) between the fingertip(s) and the proximal transverse crease of the palm, with the finger(s) flexed to the extent possible, evaluate as unfavorable ankylosis.

    (iv) If only the metacarpophalangeal or proximal interphalangeal joint is ankylosed, and there is a gap of two inches (5.1 cm.) or less between the fingertip(s) and the proximal transverse crease of the palm, with the finger(s) flexed to the extent possible, evaluate as favorable ankylosis.

(4) Evaluation of ankylosis of the thumb:
    (i) If both the carpometacarpal and interphalangeal joints are ankylosed, and either is in extension or full flexion, or there is rotation or angulation of a bone, evaluate as amputation at metacarpophalangeal joint or through proximal phalanx.

    (ii) If both the carpometacarpal and interphalangeal joints are ankylosed, evaluate as unfavorable ankylosis, even if each joint is individually fixed in a favorable position.

    (iii) If only the carpometacarpal or interphalangeal joint is ankylosed, and there is a gap of more than two inches (5.1 cm.) between the thumb pad and the fingers, with the thumb attempting to oppose the fingers, evaluate as unfavorable ankylosis.

    (iv) If only the carpometacarpal or interphalangeal joint is ankylosed, and there is a gap of two inches (5.1 cm.) or less between the thumb pad and the fingers, with the thumb attempting to oppose the fingers, evaluate as favorable ankylosis.

(5) If there is limitation of motion of two or more digits, evaluate each digit separately and combine the evaluations.

I. MULTIPLE DIGITS: UNFAVORABLE ANKYLOSIS

Rating

Major   *Minor*

- 5216   Five digits of one hand, unfavorable ankylosis of:……..………..…..60%…..... 50%
  Note: Also consider whether evaluation as amputation is warranted.

- 5217   Four digits of one hand, unfavorable ankylosis of:
  - Thumb and any three fingers ....60%…..50%
  - Index, long, ring and little fingers ....50%…..40%
  - Note: Also consider whether evaluation as amputation is warranted.

- 5218   Three digits of one hand, unfavorable ankylosis of:
  - Thumb and any two fingers ....50%…..40%
  - Index, long, and ring; index, long, and little; or
  index, ring and little fingers ....40%…..30%
  - Long, ring, and little fingers ....30%…..20%
  Note: Also consider whether evaluation as amputation is warranted.

- 5219   Two digits of one hand, unfavorable ankylosis of:
  - Thumb and any finger...40%…..30%
  - Index and long; index and ring; or index and little fingers ....30%…..20%
  - Long and ring; long and little; or ring and little fingers ....20%…..20%
  - Note: Also consider whether evaluation as amputation is warranted.

II. MULTIPLE DIGITS: FAVORABLE ANKYLOSIS

Rating

Major   *Minor*

- 5220   Five digits of one hand, favorable ankylosis of……………………..50%…..... 40%

- 5221   Four digits of one hand, favorable ankylosis of:
  - Thumb and any three fingers ....50%…..40%
  - Index, long, ring, and little ....40%…..30%

- 5222   Three digits of one hand, favorable ankylosis of:
  - Thumb and any two fingers ....40%…..30%
  - Index, long, and ring; index, long, and little fingers; or
  index, ring and little fingers ....30%…..20%
  - Long, ring, and little fingers ....20%…..20%

- 5223   Two digits of one hand, favorable ankylosis of:
  - Thumb and any finger...30%…..20%
  - Index and long; index and ring; or index and little fingers ....20%…..20%
  - Long and ring; long and little; or ring and little fingers ....10%…..10%

III. ANKYLOSIS OF INDIVIDUAL DIGITS

Rating

Major *Minor*

- 5224 Thumb, ankylosis of:
  - Unfavorable ....20%.....20%
  - Favorable ....10%.....10%

  - Note: Also consider whether evaluation as amputation is warranted and whether an additional evaluation is warranted for resulting limitation of motion of other digits or interference with overall function of the hand.

- 5225 Index finger, ankylosis of:
  - Unfavorable or favorable...10%.....10%

  - Note: Also consider whether evaluation as amputation is warranted and whether an additional evaluation is warranted for resulting limitation of motion of other digits or interference with overall function of the hand.

- 5226 Long finger, ankylosis of:
  - Unfavorable or favorable...10%.....10%

  - Note: Also consider whether evaluation as amputation is warranted and whether an additional evaluation is warranted for resulting limitation of motion of other digits or interference with overall function of the hand.

- 5227 Ring or little finger, ankylosis of:
  - Unfavorable or favorable...0%.....0%

  Note: Also consider whether evaluation as amputation is warranted and whether an additional evaluation is warranted for resulting limitation of motion of other digits or interference with overall function of the hand.

IV. LIMITATION OF MOTION OF INDIVIDUAL DIGITS

Rating

Major *Minor*

- 5228 Thumb, limitation of motion:
  - With a gap of more than two inches (5.1 cm.) between the thumb pad and the fingers, with the thumb attempting to oppose the fingers .... 20%.......... 20%

  - With a gap of one to two inches (2.5 to 5.1 cm.) between the thumb pad and the fingers, with the thumb attempting to oppose the fingers................................. .... 10%.......... 10%
  - With a gap of less than one inch (2.5 cm.) between the thumb pad and the fingers, with the thumb attempting to oppose the fingers... 0%............ 0%

- 5229 Index or long finger, limitation of motion:
  - With a gap of one inch (2.5 cm.) or more between the fingertip and the proximal transverse crease of the palm, with the finger flexed to the extent possible, or; with extension limited by more than 30 degrees .... 10%.......... 10%
  - With a gap of less than one inch (2.5 cm.) between the fingertip and the proximal transverse crease of the palm, with the finger flexed to the extent possible, and; extension is limited by no more than 30 degrees .... 0%............ 0%

- 5230 Ring or little finger, limitation of motion:
  - Any limitation of motion……………………………………………..0%........... 0%

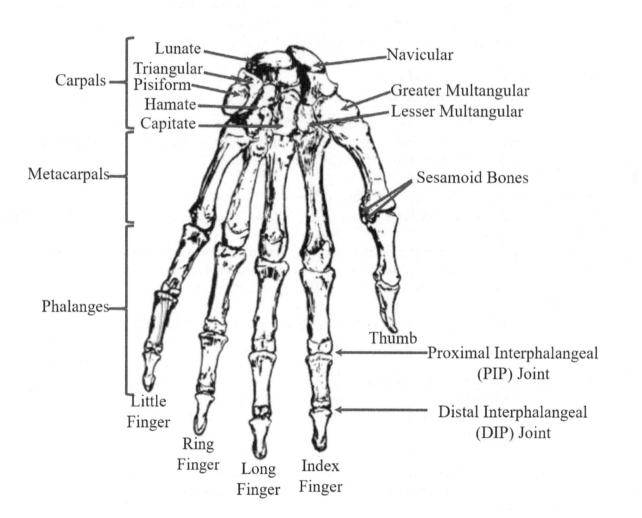

THE SPINE
General Rating Formula For Diseases And Injuries Of The Spine

(For diagnostic codes 5235 to 5243 unless 5243 is evaluated under the Formula for Rating Intervertebral Disc Syndrome Based on Incapacitating Episodes):

With or without symptoms such as pain (whether or not it radiates), stiffness, or aching in the area of the spine affected by residuals of injury or disease:

Rating

- Unfavorable ankylosis of the entire spine 100%
- Unfavorable ankylosis of the entire thoracolumbar spine 50%
- Unfavorable ankylosis of the entire cervical spine; or, forward flexion of the thoracolumbar spine 30 degrees or less; or, favorable ankylosis of the entire thoracolumbar spine 40%
- Forward flexion of the cervical spine 15 degrees or less; or, favorable ankylosis of the entire cervical spine 30%
- Forward flexion of the thoracolumbar spine greater than 30 degrees but not greater than 60 degrees; or, forward flexion of the cervical spine greater than 15 degrees but not greater than 30 degrees; or, the combined range of motion of the thoracolumbar spine not greater than 120 degrees; or, the combined range of motion of the cervical spine not greater than 170 degrees; or, muscle spasm or guarding severe enough to result in an abnormal gait or abnormal spinal contour such as scoliosis, reversed lordosis, or abnormal kyphosis 20%
- Forward flexion of the thoracolumbar spine greater than 60 degrees but not greater than 85 degrees; or, forward flexion of the cervical spine greater than 30 degrees but not greater than 40 degrees; or, combined range of motion of the thoracolumbar spine greater than 120 degrees but not greater than 235 degrees; or, combined range of motion of the cervical spine greater than 170 degrees but not greater than 335 degrees; or, muscle spasm, guarding, or localized tenderness not resulting in abnormal gait or abnormal spinal contour; or, vertebral body fracture with loss of 50 percent or more of the height 10%

- Note (1): Evaluate any associated objective neurologic abnormalities, including, but not limited to, bowel or bladder impairment, separately, under an appropriate diagnostic code.

- Note (2): For VA compensation purposes, normal forward flexion of the cervical spine is zero to 45 degrees, extension is zero to 45 degrees, left and right lateral flexion are zero to 45 degrees, and left and right lateral rotation are zero to 80 degrees. Normal forward flexion of the thoracolumbar spine is zero to 90 degrees, extension is zero to 30 degrees, left and right lateral flexion are zero to 30 degrees, and left and right lateral rotation are zero to 30 degrees. The combined range of motion refers to the sum of the range of forward flexion, extension, left and right lateral flexion, and left and right rotation. The normal combined range of motion of the cervical spine is 340 degrees and of the thoracolumbar spine is 240 degrees. The normal ranges of motion for each component of spinal motion provided in this note are the maximum that can be used for calculation of the combined range of motion.

- Note (3): In exceptional cases, an examiner may state that because of age, body habitus, neurologic disease, or other factors not the result of disease or injury of the spine, the range of motion of the spine in a particular individual should be considered normal for that individual, even though it does not conform to the normal range of motion stated in Note (2). Provided that the examiner supplies an explanation, the examiner's assessment that the range of motion is normal for that individual will be accepted.

- Note (4): Round each range of motion measurement to the nearest five degrees.

- Note (5): For VA compensation purposes, unfavorable ankylosis is a condition in which the entire cervical spine, the entire thoracolumbar spine, or the entire spine is fixed in flexion or extension, and the ankylosis results in one or more of the following: difficulty walking because of a limited line of vision; restricted opening of the mouth and chewing; breathing limited to diaphragmatic respiration; gastrointestinal symptoms due to pressure of the costal margin on the abdomen; dyspnea or dysphagia; atlantoaxial or cervical subluxation or dislocation; or neurologic symptoms due to nerve root stretching. Fixation of a spinal segment in neutral position (zero degrees) always represents favorable ankylosis.

- Note (6): Separately evaluate disability of the thoracolumbar and cervical spine segments, except when there is unfavorable ankylosis of both segments, which will be rated as a single disability.

- 5235   Vertebral fracture or dislocation
- 5236   Sacroiliac injury and weakness
- 5237   Lumbosacral or cervical strain
- 5238   Spinal stenosis
- 5239   Spondylolisthesis or segmental instability
- 5240   Ankylosing spondylitis
- 5241   Spinal fusion
- 5242   Degenerative arthritis of the spine (see also diagnostic code 5003)
- 5243   Intervertebral disc syndrome

- Evaluate intervertebral disc syndrome (preoperatively or postoperatively) either under the General Rating Formula for Diseases and Injuries of the Spine or under the Formula for Rating Intervertebral Disc Syndrome Based on Incapacitating Episodes, whichever method results in the higher evaluation when all disabilities are combined.

FORMULA FOR RATING INTERVERTEBRAL DISC SYNDROME BASED ON INCAPACITATING EPISODES

Rating

o With incapacitating episodes having a total duration of at least 6 weeks during the past 12 months 60%

o With incapacitating episodes having a total duration of at least 4 weeks less than 6 weeks during the past 12 months 40%

o With incapacitating episodes having a total duration of at least 2 weeks but less than 4 weeks during the past 12 months 20%

o With incapacitating episodes having a total duration of at least one week but less than 2 weeks during the past 12 months 10%

- Note (1): For purposes of evaluations under diagnostic code 5243, an incapacitating episode is a period of acute signs and symptoms due to intervertebral disc syndrome that requires bed rest prescribed by a physician and treatment by a physician.

- Note (2): If intervertebral disc syndrome is present in more than one spinal segment, provided that the effects in each spinal segment are clearly distinct, evaluate each segment on the basis of incapacitating episodes or under the General Rating Formula for Diseases and Injuries of the Spine, whichever method results in a higher evaluation for that segment.

RANGE OF MOTION- CERVICAL SPINE

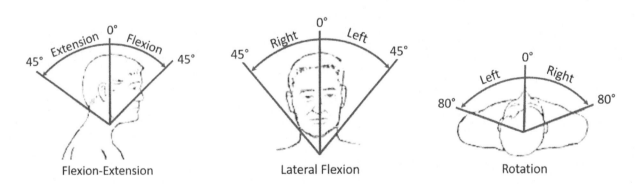

Flexion-Extension   Lateral Flexion   Rotation

RANGE OF MOTION- THORACOLUMBAR SPINE

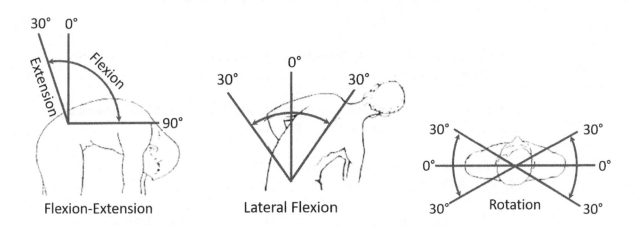

Flexion-Extension   Lateral Flexion   Rotation

Rating

- 5250   Hip, ankylosis of:
  - Unfavorable, extremely unfavorable ankylosis,
  the foot not reaching ground, crutches necessitated 90%*
    - Intermediate 70%
    - Favorable in flexion at an angle between 20° and 40° and
  slight adduction or abduction 60%
  *Also entitled to special monthly compensation.

- 5251   Thigh, limitation of extension of:
    - Extension limited to 5°... 10%

- 5252   Thigh, limitation of flexion of:
    - Flexion limited to 10° 40%
    - Flexion limited to 20° 30%
    - Flexion limited to 30° 20%
    - Flexion limited to 45° 10%

- 5253   Thigh, impairment of:
    - Limitation of abduction of, motion lost beyond 10°.................................... 20%
    - Limitation of adduction of, cannot cross legs... 10%
    - Limitation of rotation of, cannot toe-out more than 15°,
  affected leg.. 10%

- 5254   Hip, flail joint... 80%

- 5255   Femur, impairment of:
  - o   Fracture of shaft or anatomical neck of:
    - With nonunion, with loose motion (spiral or oblique fracture) 80%
    - With nonunion, without loose motion, weight-bearing preserved
  with aid of brace... 60%
  - o   Fracture of surgical neck of, with false joint 60%
  - o   Malunion of:
    - With marked knee or hip disability 30%
    - With moderate knee or hip disability 20%
    - With slight knee or hip disability 10%

Rating

- 5256   Knee, ankylosis of:
  - Extremely unfavorable, in flexion at an angle of 45° or more 60%
  - In flexion between 20° and 45° 50%
  - In flexion between 10° and 20° 40%
  - Favorable angle in full extension, or in slight flexion between 0° and 10° 30%

- 5257   Knee, other impairment of:
  - ○   Recurrent subluxation or lateral instability:
  - Severe 30%
  - Moderate 20%
  - Slight 10%

- 5258   Cartilage, semilunar, dislocated, with frequent episodes of
  "locking," pain, and effusion into the joint 20%

- 5259   Cartilage, semilunar, removal of, symptomatic. 10%

- 5260   Leg, limitation of flexion of:
  - Flexion limited to 15° 30%
  - Flexion limited to 30° 20%
  - Flexion limited to 45° 10%
  - Flexion limited to 60° 0%

- 5261   Leg, limitation of extension of:
  - Extension limited to 45° 50%
  - Extension limited to 30° 40%
  - Extension limited to 20° 30%
  - Extension limited to 15° 20%
  - Extension limited to 10° 10%
  - Extension limited to 5° 0%

- 5262   Tibia and fibula, impairment of:
  - ○   Nonunion of, with loose motion, requiring brace 40%
  - ○   Malunion of:
  - With marked knee or ankle disability 30%
  - With moderate knee or ankle disability 20%
  - With slight knee or ankle disability 10%

- 5263   Genu recurvatum (acquired, traumatic, with weakness and
  insecurity in weight-bearing objectively demonstrated) 10%

Rating

- 5270   Ankle, ankylosis of:
  - In plantar flexion at more than 40º, or in dorsiflexion at more than 10˚ or with abduction, adduction, inversion or eversion deformity..40%
  - In plantar flexion, between 30º and 40º, or in dorsiflexion, between 0º and 10º..30%
  - In plantar flexion, less than 30º 20%

- 5271   Ankle, limited motion of:
  - Marked 20%
  - Moderate 10%

- 5272   Subastragalar or tarsal joint, ankylosis of:
  - In poor weight-bearing position 20%
  - In good weight-bearing position 10%

- 5273   Os calcis or astragalus, malunion of:
  - Marked deformity..20%
  - Moderate deformity..10%

- 5274   Astragalectomy 20%

*Also entitled to special monthly compensation

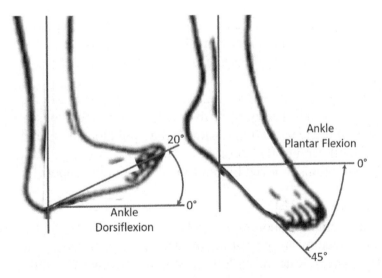

SHORTENING OF THE LOWER EXTREMITY

Rating

- 5275   Bones, of the lower extremity, shortening of:
  - Over 4 inches (1 0.2 cms.) 60%*
  - 3-1/2 to 4 inches (8.9 cms. to 10.2 cms.) 50%*
  - 3 to 3-1/2 inches (7.6 cms.to 8.9 cms.) 40%
  - 2-1/2 to 3 inches (6.4 cms. to 7.6 cms.) 30%
  - 2 to 2-1/2 inches (5.1 cms. to 6.4 cms.) 20%
  - 1-1/4 to 2 inches (3.2 cms. to 5.1 cms.) 10%

- Note: Measure both lower extremities from anterior superior spine of the ilium to the internal malleolus of the tibia. Not to be combined with other ratings for fracture or faulty union in the same extremity.

*Also entitled to special monthly compensation

THE FOOT

Rating

- 5276   Flatfoot, acquired:
  - Pronounced; marked pronation, extreme tenderness of plantar surfaces of the feet, marked inward displacement and severe spasm of the tendo achillis on manipulation, not improved by orthopedic shoes or appliances:
    - Bilateral 50%
    - Unilateral 30%
  - Severe; objective evidence of marked deformity (pronation, abduction, etc.), pain on manipulation and use accentuated, indication of swelling on use, characteristic callosities:
    - Bilateral 30%
    - Unilateral 20%
  - Moderate; weight-bearing line over or medial to great toe, inward bowing of the tendo achillis, pain on manipulation and use of the feet, bilateral or unilateral 10%
  - Mild: symptoms relieved by built-up shoe or arch support 0%

- 5277   Weak Foot, bilateral:
  - A symptomatic condition secondary to many constitutional conditions, characterized by atrophy of the musculature, disturbed circulation, and weakness: Rate the underlying condition, minimum rating 10%

- **5278** Claw foot (pes cavus), acquired:
  - Marked contraction of plantar fascia with dropped forefoot, all toes hammer toes, very painful callosities, marked varus deformity:
    - Bilateral 50%
    - Unilateral 30%
  - All toes tending to dorsiflexion, limitation of dorsiflexion at ankle to right angle, shortened plantar fascia, and marked tenderness under metatarsal heads:
    - Bilateral 30%
    - Unilateral 20%
  - Great toe dorsiflexed, some limitation of dorsiflexion at ankle, definite tenderness under metatarsal heads:
    - Bilateral 10%
    - Unilateral 10%
  - Slight 0%

- **5279** Metatarsalgia, anterior (Morton's disease), unilateral, or bilateral.................... 10%

- **5280** Hallux valgus, unilateral:
  - Operated with resection of metatarsal head.. 10%
  - Severe, if equivalent to amputation of great toe 10%

- **5281** Hallux rigidus, unilateral, severe:
  - Rate as hallux valgus, severe.

  - Note: Not to be combined with claw foot ratings.

- **5282** Hammer toe:
  - All toes, unilateral without claw foot 10%
  - Single toes.. 0%

- **5283** Tarsal, or metatarsal bones, malunion of, or nonunion of:
  - Severe 30%
  - Moderately severe 20%
  - Moderate 10%

  - Note: With actual loss of use of the foot, rate 40 percent.

- **5284** Foot injuries, other:
  - Severe 30%
  - Moderately severe 20%
  - Moderate 10%

  - Note: With actual loss of use of the foot, rate 40 percent.

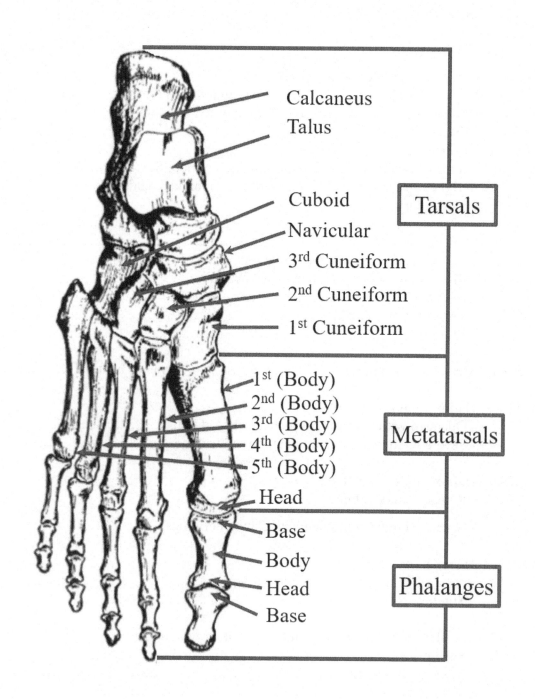

Calcaneus

Talus

Cuboid

Navicular

3rd Cuneiform

2nd Cuneiform

1st Cuneiform

Tarsals

1st (Body)

2nd (Body)

3rd (Body)

4th (Body)

5th (Body)

Head

Base

Body

Head

Base

Metatarsals

Phalanges

THE SKULL

- 5296 Skull, loss of part of, both inner and outer tables:
    o With brain hernia: 80%
    o Without brain hernia:

    - Area larger than size of a 50-cent piece or 1.140 in^2 (7.355 cm^2) 50%
    - Area intermediate 30%
    - Area smaller than size of a 25-cent piece or 0.716 in^2 (4.619 cm^2) 10%

    - Note: Rate separately for intracranial complications.

THE RIBS

- 5297 Ribs, removal of:
    - More than six 50%
    - Five or six 40%
    - Three or four 30%
    - Two 20%
    - One or resection of two or more ribs without regeneration 10%

    - Note (1): The rating for rib resection or removal is not to be applied with ratings for purulent pleurisy, lobectomy, pneumonectomy or injuries of pleural cavity.

    - Note (2): However, rib resection will be considered as rib removal in thoracoplasty performed for collapse therapy or to accomplish obliteration of space and will be combined with the rating for lung collapse, or with the rating for lobectomy, pneumonectomy or the graduated ratings for pulmonary tuberculosis.

THE COCCYX

- 5298 Coccyx, removal of:
    - Partial or complete, with painful residuals 10%
    - Without painful residuals 0%

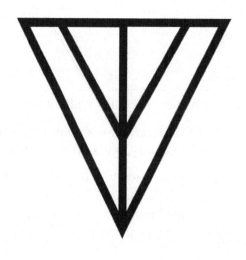

THIS PAGE LEFT INTENTIONALLY BLANK

CHAPTER 2

MUSCLE INJURIES

Quick Reference:

CODE	CATEGORY	PAGE
	THE SHOULDER GIRDLE AND ARM	
5301	Group I. Extrinsic muscles of shoulder girdle: (1) Trapezius; (2) levator scapulae; (3) serratus magnus.	67
5302	Group II. Extrinsic muscles of the shoulder girdle: (1) Pectoralis major II (costosternal); (2) latissimus dorsi and teres major (teres major, although technically an intrinsic muscle, is included with latissimus dorsi); (3) pectoralis minor; (4) rhomboid.	67
5303	Group III. Intrinsic muscles of shoulder girdle: (1) Pectoralis major I (clavicular); (2) deltoid.	67
5304	Group IV. Intrinsic muscles of shoulder girdle: (1) Supraspinatus; (2) infraspinatus and teres minor; (3) subscapularis; (4) coracobrachialis.	67
5305	Group V. Flexor muscles of elbow: (1) Biceps; (2) brachialis; (3) brachioradialis	68
5306	Group VI. Extensor muscles of the elbow: (1) Triceps; (2) anconeus	68
	THE FOREARM AND HAND	
5307	Group VII. Muscles arising from internal condyle of humerus: Flexors of the carpus and long flexors of fingers and thumb; pronator	68
5308	Group VIII. Muscles arising mainly from external condyle of humerus: Extensors of carpus, fingers, and thumb; supinator	68
5309	Group IX. Intrinsic muscles of hand: Thenar eminence; short flexor, opponens, abductor and adductor of thumb; hypothenar eminence; short flexor, opponens and abductor of little finger; 4 lumbricales; 4 dorsal and 3 palmar interossei	69
	THE FOOT AND LEG	
5310	Group X. Intrinsic muscles of the foot: Plantar: (1) Flexor digitorum brevis; (2) abductor hallucis; (3) abductor digiti minimi; (4) quadratus plantae; (5) lumbricales; (6) flexor hallucis brevis; (7) adductor hallucis; (8) flexor digiti minimi brevis; (9) dorsal and plantar interossei. Other important plantar structures: Plantar aponeurosis, long plantar and calcaneonavicular ligament, tendons of posterior tibial, peroneus longus, and long flexors of great and little toes	70
5311	Group XI. Posterior and lateral crural muscles, and muscles of the calf: (1) Triceps surae (gastrocnemius and soleus); (2) tibialis posterior; (3) peroneus longus; (4) peroneus brevis; (5) flexor hallucis longus; (6) flexor digitorum longus; (7) popliteus; (8) plantaris	70
5312	Group XII. Anterior muscles of the leg: (1) Tibialis anterior; (2) extensor digitorum longus; (3) extensor hallucis longus; (4) peroneus tertius	70

	PELVIC GURDLE AND THIGH	
5313	Group XIII. Posterior thigh group, Hamstring complex of 2-joint muscles: (1) Biceps femoris; (2) semimembranosus; (3) semitendinosus	71
5314	Group XIV. Anterior thigh group: (1) Sartorius; (2) rectus femoris; (3) vastus externus; (4) vastus intermedius; (5) vastus internus; (6) tensor vaginae femoris	71
5315	Group XV. Mesial thigh group: (1) Adductor longus; (2) adductor brevis; (3) adductor magnus; (4) gracilis	71
5316	Group XVI. Pelvic girdle group 1: (1) Psoas; (2) iliacus; (3) pectineus	71
5317	Group XVII: Pelvic girdle group 2: (1) Gluteus maximus; (2) gluteus medius; (3) gluteus minimus	72
5318	Group XVIII: Pelvic girdle group 3: (1) Pyriformis; (2) gemellus (superior or inferior); (3) obturator (external or internal); (4) quadratus femoris	72
	THE TORSO AND NECK	
5319	Group XIX: Muscles of the abdominal wall: (1) Rectus abdominis; (2) external oblique; (3) internal oblique; (4) transversalis; (5) quadratus lumborum	72
5320	Group XX: Spinal muscles: Sacrospinalis (erector spinae and its prolongations in thoracic and cervical regions)	73
5321	Group XXI: Muscles of respiration: Thoracic muscle group	73
5322	Group XXII: Muscles of the front of the neck: (Lateral, supra-, and infrahyoid group.) (1) Trapezius I (clavicular insertion); (2) sternocleidomastoid; (3) the "hyoid" muscles; (4) sternothyroid; (5) digastric	73
5323	Group XXIII: Muscles of the side and back of the neck: Suboccipital; lateral vertebral and anterior vertebral muscles	73
	MISCELLANEOUS	
5324	Diaphragm, rupture of, with herniation	74
5325	Muscle injury, facial muscles	74
5326	Muscle hernia, extensive, without other injury to the muscle	74
5327	Muscle, neoplasm of, malignant (excluding soft tissue sarcoma)	74
5328	Muscle, neoplasm of, benign, postoperative	74
5329	Sarcoma, soft tissue (of muscle, fat, or fibrous connective tissue)	74

Note: When evaluating any claim involving muscle injuries resulting in loss of use of any extremity or loss of use of both buttocks (diagnostic code 5317, Muscle Group XVII), determine whether the veteran may be entitled to special monthly compensation.

Rating

Non-
Dominant Domimant

- 5301   Group I. *Function*: Upward rotation of scapula; elevation of arm
  of arm above shoulder level. Extrinsic muscles of shoulder girdle:
  (1) Trapezius; (2) levator scapulae; (3) serratus magnus.
  -Severe ....40%........30%
  -Moderately Severe..30%........20%
  -Moderate ....10%........10%
  -Slight..0%..........0%

- 5302   Group II. *Function*: Depression of arm from vertical overhead
  to hanging at side (1, 2); downward rotation of scapula (3, 4);
  1 and 2 act with Group III in forward and backward swing of arm.
  Extrinsic muscles of shoulder girdle: (1) Pectoralis major II
  (costosternal); ; (2) latissimus dorsi and teres major (teres major,
  although technically an intrinsic muscle, is included with latissimus
  dorsi); (3) pectoralis minor; (4) rhomboid.
  -Severe ....40%........30%
  -Moderately Severe..30%........20%
  -Moderate ....20%........20%
  -Slight..0%..........0%

- 5303   Group III. *Function*: Elevation and abduction of arm to level of
  shoulder; act with 1 and 2 of Group II in forward and backward
  swing of arm. Intrinsic muscles of shoulder girdle: (1) Pectoralis
  major I (clavicular); (2) deltoid.
  -Severe ....40%........30%
  -Moderately Severe..30%........20%
  -Moderate ....20%........20%
  -Slight..0%..........0%

- 5304   Group IV. *Function*: Stabilization of shoulder against injury in
  strong movements, holding head of humerus in socket; abduction;
  outward rotation and inward rotation of arm. Intrinsic muscles of
  shoulder girdle: (1) Supraspinatus; (2) infraspinatus and teres minor;
  (3) subscapularis; (4) coracobrachialis.
  -Severe ....30%........20%
  -Moderately Severe..20%........20%
  -Moderate ....10%........10%
  -Slight..0%..........0%

- 5305 Group V. *Function*: Elbow supination (1) (long head of biceps is
stabilizer of shoulder joint); flexion of elbow (1, 2, 3).
Flexor muscles of elbow: (1) Biceps; (2) brachialis;
(3) brachioradialis.
  -Severe ....40%........30%
  -Moderately Severe..30%.......20%
  -Moderate ....10%.......10%
  -Slight..0%..........0%

- 5306 Group VI. *Function*: Extension of elbow (long head of triceps is
stabilizer of shoulder joint). Extensor muscles of the elbow:
(1) Triceps; (2) anconeus.
  -Severe ....40%.......30%
  -Moderately Severe..30%.......20%
  -Moderate ....10%.......10%
  -Slight..0%..........0%

THE FOREARM AND HAND

- 5307 Group VII. *Function*: Flexion of wrist and fingers. Muscles
arising from internal condyle of humerus: Flexors of the carpus
and long flexors of fingers and thumb; pronator.
  -Severe ....40%.......30%
  -Moderately Severe..30%....20%
  -Moderate ....10%.......10%
  -Slight..0%..........0%

- 5308 Group VIII. *Function*: Extension of wrist, fingers, and thumb;
abduction of thumb. Muscles arising mainly from external condyle
of humerus: Extensors of carpus, fingers, and thumb; supinator.
  -Severe ....30%.......20%
  -Moderately Severe..20%.......20%
  -Moderate ....10%.......10%
  -Slight..0%..........0%

68

- 5309   Group IX. *Function*: The forearm muscles act in strong grasping movements and are supplemented by the intrinsic muscles in delicate manipulative movements. Intrinsic muscles of hand: Thenar eminence; short flexor, opponens, abductor and adductor of thumb; hypothenar eminence; short flexor, opponens and abductor of little finger; 4 lumbricales; 4 dorsal and 3 palmar interossei.

  - Note: The hand is so compact a structure that isolated muscle injuries are rare, being nearly always complicated with injuries of bones, joints, tendons, etc.
  Rate on limitation of motion:.. minimum 10%

- 5310   Group X. *Function*: Movements of forefoot and toes; propulsion thrust in walking. Intrinsic muscles of the foot: Plantar: (1) Flexor digitorum brevis; (2) abductor hallucis; (3) abductor digiti minimi; (4) quadrates plantae; (5) lumbricales; (6) flexor hallucis brevis; (7) adductor hallucis; (8) flexor digiti minimi brevis; (9) dorsal and plantar interossei. Other important plantar structures: Plantar aponeurosis, long plantar and calcaneonavicular ligament, tendons of posterior tibial, peroneus longus, and long flexors of great and little toes.
  - Severe 30%
  - Moderately Severe 20%
  - Moderate 10%
  - Slight 0%

  Dorsal: (1) Extensor hallucis brevis; (2) extensor digitorum brevis. Other important dorsal structures: cruciate, crural, deltoid, and other ligaments; tendons of long extensors of toes and peronei muscles.
  -Severe 20%
  -Moderately Severe 10%
  -Moderate 10%
  -Slight 0%

  - Note: Minimum rating for through-and-through wounds of the foot 10%

- 5311   Group XI. *Function*: Propulsion, plantar flexion of foot (1); stabilization of arch (2, 3); flexion of toes (4, 5); flexion of knee (6). Posterior and lateral crural muscles, and muscles of the calf: (1) Triceps surae (gastrocnemius and soleus); (2) tibialis posterior; (3) peroneus longus; (4) peroneus brevis; (5) flexor hallucis longus; (6) flexor digitorum longus; (7) popliteus; (8) plantaris.
  - Severe 30%
  - Moderately Severe 20%
  - Moderate 10%
  - Slight 0%

- 5312   Group XII. *Function*: Dorsiflexion (1); extension of toes (2); stabilization of arch (3). Anterior muscles of the leg: (1) Tibialis anterior; (2) extensor digitorum longus; (3) extensor hallucis longus; (4) peroneus tertius.
  - Severe 30%
  - Moderately Severe 20%
  - Moderate 10%
  - Slight 0%

Rating

- 5313 Group XIII. *Function*: Extension of hip and flexion of knee; outward and inward rotation of flexed knee; acting with rectus femoris and sartorius (see XIV, 1, 2) synchronizing simultaneous flexion of hip and knee and extension of hip and knee by belt-over-pulley action at knee joint. Posterior thigh group, Hamstring complex of 2-joint muscles: (1) Biceps femoris; (2) semimembranosus; (3) semitendinosus.
  - o Severe 40%
  - o Moderately Severe 30%
  - o Moderate 10%
  - o Slight 0%

- 5314 Group XIV. *Function*: Extension of knee (2, 3, 4, 5); simultaneous flexion of hip and flexion of knee (1); tension of fascia lata and iliotibial (Maissiat's) band, acting with XVII (1) in postural support of body (6); acting with hamstrings in synchronizing hip and knee (1, 2). Anterior thigh group: (1) Sartorius; (2) rectus femoris; (3) vastus externus; (4) vastus intermedius; (5) vastus internus; (6) tensor vaginae femoris.
  - o Severe 40%
  - o Moderately Severe 30%
  - o Moderate 10%
  - o Slight 0%

- 5315 Group XV. *Function*: Adduction of hip (1, 2, 3, 4); flexion of hip (1, 2); flexion of knee (4). Mesial thigh group: (1) Adductor longus; (2) adductor brevis; (3) adductor magnus; (4) gracilis.
  - o Severe 30%
  - o Moderately Severe 20%
  - o Moderate 10%
  - o Slight 0%

- 5316 Group XVI. *Function*: Flexion of hip (1, 2, 3). Pelvic girdle group 1: (1) Psoas; (2) iliacus; (3) pectineus.
  - o Severe 40%
  - o Moderately Severe 30%
  - o Moderate 10%
  - o Slight 0%

- 5317 Group XVII. *Function*: Extension of hip (1); abduction of thigh; elevation
  of opposite side of pelvis (2, 3); tension of fascia lata and iliotibial
  (Maissiat's) band, acting with XIV (6) in postural support of body
  steadying pelvis upon head of femur and condyles of femur on tibia (1).
  Pelvic girdle group 2: (1) Gluteus maximus; (2) gluteus medius;
  (3) gluteus minimus.
  - Severe 50%*
  - Moderately Severe 40%
  - Moderate 20%
  - Slight 0%

  *If bilateral, determine whether the veteran may be entitled to special monthly
  compensation.

- 5318 Group XVIII. *Function*: Outward rotation of thigh and stabilization of hip
  joint. Pelvic girdle group 3: (1) Pyriformis; (2) gemellus (superior or
  inferior); (3) obturator (external or internal); (4) quadratus femoris.
  - Severe 30%
  - Moderately Severe 20%
  - Moderate 10%
  - Slight 0%

THE TORSO AND NECK

- 5319 Group XIX. *Function*: Support and compression of abdominal wall and
  lower thorax; flexion and lateral motions of spine; synergists in strong
  downward movements of arm (1). Muscles of the abdominal wall:
  (1) Rectus abdominis; (2) external oblique; (3) internal oblique;
  (4) transversalis; (5) quadratus lumborum.
  - Severe 50%
  - Moderately Severe 30%
  - Moderate 10%
  - Slight 0%

- 5320   Group XX. *Function*: Postural support of body; extension and lateral movements of spine. Spinal muscles: Sacrospinalis (erector spinae and its prolongations in thoracic and cervical regions).
  - Cervical and thoracic region:
    - Severe 40%
    - Moderately Severe 20%
    - Moderate 10%
    - Slight 0%
  - Lumbar region:
    - Severe 60%
    - Moderately Severe 40%
    - Moderate 20%
    - Slight 0%

- 5321   Group XXI. *Function*: Respiration. Muscles of respiration: Thoracic muscle group.
    - Severe or Moderately Severe 20%
    - Moderate 10%
    - Slight 0%

- 5322   Group XXII. *Function*: Rotary and forward movements of the head; respiration; deglutition. Muscles of the front of the neck: (Lateral, supra-, and infrahyoid group.) (1) Trapezius I (clavicular insertion); (2) sternocleidomastoid; (3) the "hyoid" muscles; (4) sternothyroid; (5) digastric.
    - Severe 30%
    - Moderately Severe 20%
    - Moderate 10%
    - Slight 0%

- 5323   Group XXIII. *Function*: Movements of the head; fixation of shoulder movements. Muscles of the side and back of the neck: Suboccipital; lateral vertebral and anterior vertebral muscles.
    -Severe 30%
    - Moderately Severe 20%
    - Moderate 10%
    - Slight 0%

MISCELLANEOUS

- 5324   Diaphragm, rupture of, with herniation. Rate under diagnostic code 7346.

- 5325   Muscle injury, facial muscles. Evaluate functional impairment as seventh (facial) cranial nerve neuropathy (diagnostic code 8207), disfiguring scar (diagnostic code 7800), etc. Minimum, if interfering to any extent with mastication 10%

- 5326   Muscle hernia, extensive. Without other injury to the muscle. 10%

- 5327   Muscle, neoplasm of, malignant (excluding soft tissue sarcoma). 100%

    - Note: A rating of 100 percent shall continue beyond the cessation of any surgery, radiation treatment, antineoplastic chemotherapy or other therapeutic procedures. Six months after discontinuance of such treatment, the appropriate disability rating shall be determined by mandatory VA examination. If there has been no local recurrence or metastasis, rate on residual impairment of function.

- 5328   Muscle, neoplasm of, benign, postoperative. Rate on impairment of function, i.e., limitation of motion, or scars, diagnostic code 7805, etc.

- 5329   Sarcoma, soft tissue (of muscle, fat, or fibrous connective tissue). 100%

    Note: A rating of 100 percent shall continue beyond the cessation of any surgery, radiation treatment, antineoplastic chemotherapy or other therapeutic procedures. Six months after discontinuance of such treatment, the appropriate disability rating shall be determined by mandatory VA examination. If there has been no local recurrence or metastasis, rate on residual impairment of function.

CHAPTER 3

DISEASES OF THE EYE

Quick Reference:

IMPAIRMENT OF CENTRAL VISUAL ACUITY		
6061	Anatomical loss of both eyes	80
6062	No more than light perception in both eyes	80
6063	Anatomical loss of one eye	80
6064	No more than light perception in one eye	80
IMPAIRMENT OF CENTRAL VISUAL ACUITY (Continued)		
6065	Vision in one eye 5/200 (1.5/60)	80
6066	Visual acuity in one eye 10/200 (3/60) or better	80-81
RATINGS FOR IMPAIRMENT OF VISUAL FIELDS		
6080	Visual field defects	82
6081	Scotoma, unilateral	83
RATINGS FOR IMPAIRMENT OF MUSCLE FUNCTION		
6090	Diplopia (double vision)	83
6091	Symblepharon	83

GENERAL RATING FORMULA FOR DIAGNOSTIC CODES 6000 THROUGH 6009

Rating

-Evaluate on the basis of either visual impairment due to the particular condition or on incapacitating episodes, whichever results in a higher evaluation.
- With documented incapacitating episodes requiring 7 or more treatment visits for an eye condition during the past 12 months 60%
- With documented incapacitating episodes requiring at least 5 but less than 7 treatment visits for an eye condition during the past 12 months 40%
- With documented incapacitating episodes requiring at least 3 but less than 5 treatment visits for an eye condition during the past 12 months 20%
- With documented incapacitating episodes requiring at least 1 but less than 3 treatment visits for an eye condition during the past 12 months 10%

- Note (1): For VA purposes, an incapacitating episode is an eye condition severe enough to require a clinic visit to a provider specifically for treatment purposes.
- Note (2): Examples of treatment may include but are not limited to: Systemic immunosuppressants or biological agents; intravitreal or periocular injections; laser treatments; or other surgical interventions.
- Note (3): For the purposes of evaluating visual impairment due to the particular condition, refer to CRF-38 diagnostic codes 6061-6091.

- 6000 Choroidopathy, including uveitis, iritis, cyclitis, and choroiditis.
- 6001 Keratopathy.
- 6002 Scleritis.
- 6006 Retinopathy or maculopathy not other specified.
- 6007 Intraocular hemorrhage.
- 6008 Detachment of retina.
- 6009 Unhealed eye injury. This code includes orbital trauma, as well as penetrating and non-penetrating eye injury

- 6010   Tuberculosis of eye:
  -Active.. 100%
  -Inactive: VA will evaluate and determine what is appropriate.

- 6011   Retinal scars, atrophy, or irregularities:
  - Localized scars, atrophy, or irregularities of the retina, unilateral
  or bilateral, that are centrally located and that result in an irregular,
  duplicated, enlarged, or diminished image 10%

  - Alternatively, evaluate based on the General Rating Formula for Diseases of the
  Eye, if this would result in a higher evaulation.

- 6012   Angle-closure glaucoma:
  - Evaluate under the General Rating Formula for Diseases of the Eye.

  - Minimum evaluation if continuous medication is required............................ 10%

- 6013   Open-angle glaucoma:
  - Evaluate under the General Rating Formula for Diseases of the Eye.

  - Minimum evaluation if continuous medication is required............................ 10%

- 6014   Malignant neoplasms (eyeball only):
  - Malignant neoplasm of the eye, orbit, and adnexa (excluding skin) that require
  therapy that is comparable to those used for systemic malignancies, i.e., systemic
  chemotherapy, X-ray therapy more extensive than to the area of the
  eye, or surgery more extensive than enucleation 100%

  - Note: Continue the 100-percent rating beyond the cessation of any surgical, X-
  ray, antineoplastic chemotherapy, or other therapeutic procedure. Six months after
  discontinuance of such treatment, the appropriate disability rating will be
  determined by mandatory VA examination. If there has been no local recurrence
  or metastasis, evaluate based on residuals.

  - Malignant neoplasm of the eye, orbit, and adnexa (excluding skin) that do not
  require therapy comparable to that for systemic malignancies:

  - Separately evaluate visual and nonvisual impairment, e.g., disfigurement
  (diagnostic code 7800), and combine the evaluations.

- 6015   Benign neoplasms of the eye, orbit, and adnexa (excluding skin):
  - Separately evaluate visual and nonvisual impairment, e.g., disfigurement
  (diagnostic code 7800) and combine the evaluations.

- 6016   Nystagmus, central.. 10%

- 6017   Trachomatous conjunctivitis:
  -Active: Evaluate under the General Rating Formula for Diseases of the Eye
  Minimum rating 30%
  -Inactive: Evaluate based on residuals, such as visual impairment and
  disfigurement (diagnostic code 7800).

- 6018   Chronic conjunctivitis (nontrachomatous):
  -Active: Evaluate under the General Rating Formula for Diseases of the Eye
  Minimum rating 30%
  -Inactive: Evaluate based on residuals, such as visual impairment and
  disfigurement (diagnostic code 7800).

- 6019   Ptosis, unilateral or bilateral:
  -Evaluate based on visual impairment or, in the absence of visual
  impairment, on disfigurement (diagnostic code 7800).

- 6020   Ectropion:
  -Bilateral 20%
  -Unilateral 10%

- 6021   Entropion:
  -Bilateral 20%
  -Unilateral 10%

- 6022   Lagophthalmos:
  -Bilateral 20%
  -Unilateral 10%

- 6023   Loss of eyebrows, complete, unilateral or bilateral 10%

- 6024   Loss of eyelashes, complete, unilateral or bilateral 10%

- 6025   Disorders of the lacrimal apparatus (epiphora, dacryocystitis, etc.):
  -Bilateral 20%
  -Unilateral 10%

- 6026   Optic neuropathy:
  -Evaluate based on visual impairment.

- 6027   Cataract of any type:
  -Preoperative: Evaluate under General Rating Formula for Diseases of the Eye.
  -Postoperative: If a replacement lens is present (pseudophakia), evaluate based on
  General Rating Formula for Diseases of the Eye. If there is no replacement lens,
  evaluate based on aphakia (diagnostic code 6029).

- 6029 Aphakia or dislocation of crystalline lens:
  - Evaluate based on visual impairment, and elevate the resulting level of visual impairment one step.
  - Minimum (unilateral or bilateral) 30%

- 6030 Paralysis of accommodation (due to neuropathy of the
  Oculomotor Nerve (cranial nerve III)) 20%

- 6032 Loss of eyelids, partial or complete:
  - Separately evaluate both visual impairment due to eyelid loss
  and nonvisual impairment, e.g., disfigurement (diagnostic code 7800),
  and combine the evaluations.

- 6034 Pterygium:
  - Evaluate based on General Rating Formula for Diseases of the Eye,
  disfigurement (diagnostic code 7800), conjunctivitis (diagnostic code 6018), etc.,
  depending on the particular findings, and combine.

- 6035 Keratoconus:

- 6036 Status post corneal transplant:
  - Evaluate under the General Rating Formula for Diseases of the Eye. Minimum,
  if there is pain, photophobia, and glare sensitivity 10%

- 6037 Pinguecula:
  - Evaluate based on disfigurement (diagnostic code 7800).

- 6040 Diabetic Retinopathy:
  - Evaluate based on Disesases of the Eye rating formula.

- 6042 Retinal dystrophy (including retinitis pigmentosa, wet or dry macular
  degeneration, early-onset macular degeneration, rod and/or cone dystrophy):
  - Evaluate based on Disesases of the Eye rating formula.

- 6046 Post-chiasmal disorders:
  - Evaluate based on Disesases of the Eye rating formula.

Rating

- 6061 Anatomical loss of both eyes 100%*

- 6062 No more than light perception in both eyes 100%*

- 6063 Anatomical loss of one eye*:
  -In the other eye 5/200 (1.5/60) 100%
  -In the other eye 10/200 (3/60) 90%
  -In the other eye 15/200 (4.5/60) 80%
  -In the other eye 20/200 (6/60) 70%
  -In the other eye 20/100 (6/30) 60%
  -In the other eye 20/70 (6/21) 60%
  -In the other eye 20/50 (6/15) 50%
  -In the other eye 20/40 (6/12) 40%

- 6064 No more than light perception in one eye*:
  -In the other eye 5/200 (1.5/60) 100%
  -In the other eye 10/200 (3/60) 90%
  -In the other eye 15/200 (4.5/60) 80%
  -In the other eye 20/200 (6/60) 70%
  -In the other eye 20/100 (6/30) 60%
  -In the other eye 20/70 (6/21) 50%
  -In the other eye 20/50 (6/15) 40%
  -In the other eye 20/40 (6/12) 30%

- 6065 Vision in one eye 5/200 (1.5/60):
  -In the other eye 5/200 (1.5/60) 100%*
  -In the other eye 10/200 (3/60) 90%
  -In the other eye 15/200 (4.5/60) 80%
  -In the other eye 20/200 (6/60) 70%
  -In the other eye 20/100 (6/30) 60%
  -In the other eye 20/70 (6/21) 50%
  -In the other eye 20/50 (6/15) 40%
  -In the other eye 20/40 (6/12) 30%

- 6066 Visual acuity in one eye 10/200 (3/60) or better:
  o Vision in one eye 10/200 (3/60):
  -In the other eye 10/200 (3/60) 90%
  -In the other eye 15/200 (4.5/60) 80%
  -In the other eye 20/200 (6/60) 70%
  -In the other eye 20/100 (6/30) 60%
  -In the other eye 20/70 (6/21) 50%
  -In the other eye 20/50 (6/15) 40%
  -In the other eye 20/40 (6/12) 30%

- o Vision in one eye 15/200 (4.5/60):
  - -In the other eye 15/200 (4.5/60) 80%
  - -In the other eye 20/200 (6/60) 70%
  - -In the other eye 20/100 (6/30) 60%
  - -In the other eye 20/70 (6/21) 40%
  - -In the other eye 20/50 (6/15) 30%
  - -In the other eye 20/40 (6/12) 20%
- o Vision in one eye 20/200 (6/60):
  - -In the other eye 20/200 (6/60) 70%
  - -In the other eye 20/100 (6/30) 60%
  - -In the other eye 20/70 (6/21) 40%
  - -In the other eye 20/50 (6/15) 30%
  - -In the other eye 20/40 (6/12) 20%
- o Vision in one eye 20/100 (6/30):
  - -In the other eye 20/100 (6/30) 50%
  - -In the other eye 20/70 (6/21) 30%
  - -In the other eye 20/50 (6/15) 20%
  - -In the other eye 20/40 (6/12) 10%
- o Vision in one eye 20/70 (6/21):
  - -In the other eye 20/70 (6/21) 30%
  - -In the other eye 20/50 (6/15) 20%
  - -In the other eye 20/40 (6/12) 10%
- o Vision in one eye 20/50 (6/15):
  - -In the other eye 20/50 (6/15) 10%
  - -In the other eye 20/40 (6/12) 10%
- o Vision in one eye 20/40 (6/12):
  - -In the other eye 20/40 (6/12) 0%

*Review for entitlement to special monthly compensation.

RATINGS FOR IMPAIRMENT OF VISUAL FIELDS

Rating

- 6080   Visual field defects:
  - Homonymous hemianopsia 30%
  - o Loss of temporal half of visual field:
    - Bilateral 30%
    - Unilateral 10%
    - Or evaluate each affected eye as 20/70 (6/21).
  - o Loss of nasal half of visual field:
    - Bilateral 10%
    - Unilateral 10%
    - Or evaluate each affected eye as 20/50 (6/15).
  - o Loss of inferior half of visual field:
    - Bilateral 30%
    - Unilateral 10%
    - Or evaluate each affected eye as 20/70 (6/21).
  - o Loss of superior half of visual field:
    - Bilateral 10%
    - Unilateral 10%
    - Or evaluate each affected eye as 20/50 (6/15).
  - o Concentric contraction of visual field:
    - With remaining field of 5 degrees:*
    - Bilateral 100%
    - Unilateral 30%
    - Or evaluate each affected eye as 5/200 (1.5/60).
  - o With remaining field of 6 to 15 degrees:
    - Bilateral 70%
    - Unilateral 20%
    - Or evaluate each affected eye as 20/200 (6/60).
  - o With remaining field of 16 to 30 degrees:
    - Bilateral 50%
    - Unilateral 10%
    - Or evaluate each affected eye as 20/100 (6/30).
  - o With remaining field of 31 to 45 degrees:
    - Bilateral 30%
    - Unilateral 10%
    - Or evaluate each affected eye as 20/70 (6/21).
  - o With remaining field of 46 to 60 degrees:
    - Bilateral 10%
    - Unilateral 10%
    - Or evaluate each affected eye as 20/50 (6/15).

*Review for entitlement to special monthly compensation.

▪ 6081 Scotoma, unilateral:
- Minimum, with scotoma affecting at least one-quarter of the visual
Field (quadrantanopsia) or with centrally located scotoma of any size............. 10%
- Alternatively, evaluate based on visual impairment due to scotoma,
if that would result in a higher evaluation.

RATINGS FOR IMPAIRMENT OF MUSCLE FUNCTION

Degree of diplopia	Equivalent visual acuity

▪ 6090 Diplopia (double vision):
- ○ Central 20 degrees.. 5/200 (1.5/60)
- ○ 21 degrees to 30 degrees:
  - -Down 15/200 (4.5/60)
  - -Lateral..20/100 (6/30)
  - -Up 20/70 (6/21)
- ○ 31 degrees to 40 degrees:
  - -Down 20/200 (6/60)
  - -Lateral...20/70 (6/21)
  - -Up 20/40 (6/12)

Note: Diplopia that is occasional or that is correctable with spectacles is evaluated at 0%.

▪ 6091 Symblepharon:
- Evaluate under the General Rating Formula for Disease of the Eye,
lagophthalmos (diagnostic code 6022), disfigurement (diagnostic code 7800), etc.,
depending on the particular findings, and combine.

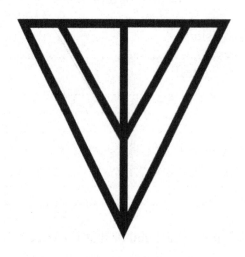

THIS PAGE LEFT INTENTIONALLY BLANK

CHAPTER 4

DISEASES OF THE EAR

Quick Reference:

Rating

- 6200   Chronic suppurative otitis media, mastoiditis, or cholesteatoma (or any combination):
  -During suppuration, or with aural polyps 10%
  -Note: Evaluate hearing impairment, and complications such as labyrinthitis, tinnitus, facial nerve paralysis, or bone loss of skull, separately.

- 6201   Chronic nonsuppurative otitis media with effusion (serous otitis media):
  -Rate hearing impairment

- 6202   Otosclerosis:
  -Rate hearing impairment

- 6204   Peripheral vestibular disorders:
  -Dizziness and occasional staggering 30%
  -Occasional dizziness... 10%

  -Note: Objective findings supporting the diagnosis of vestibular disequilibrium are required before a compensable evaluation can be assigned under this code. Hearing impairment or suppuration shall be separately rated and combined.

- 6205   Meniere's Syndrome (endolymphatic hydrops):
  -Hearing impairment with attacks of vertigo and cerebellar gait
  occurring more than once weekly, with or without tinnitus 100%
  -Hearing impairment with attacks of vertigo and cerebellar gait occurring
  from one to four times a month, with or without tinnitus 60%
  -Hearing impairment with vertigo less than once a month, with or without
  tinnitus.. 30%
  -Note: Evaluate Meniere's syndrome either under these criteria or by separately
  evaluating vertigo (as a peripheral vestibular disorder), hearing impairment, and
  tinnitus, whichever method results in a higher overall evaluation. But do not
  combine an evaluation for hearing impairment, tinnitus, or vertigo with an
  evaluation under diagnostic code 6205.

- 6207   Loss of auricle:
  -Complete loss of both.. 50%
  -Complete loss of one 30%
  -Deformity of one, with loss of one-third or more of the substance.................. 10%

- 6208   Malignant neoplasm of the ear (other than skin only): 100%
  -Note: A rating of 100 percent shall continue beyond the cessation of any surgical,
  radiation treatment, antineoplastic chemotherapy or other therapeutic procedure.
  Six months after discontinuance of such treatment, the appropriate disability
  rating shall be determined by mandatory VA examination. If there has been no
  local recurrence or metastasis, rate on residuals.

- 6209   Benign neoplasms of the ear (other than skin only):
  -Rate hearing impairment of function

- 6210   Chronic otitis externa:
  -Swelling, dry, and scaly or serous discharge, and itching requiring
  frequent and prolonged treatment 10%

- 6211   Tympanic membrane, perforation of 0%

- 6260   Tinnitus, recurrent... 10%

  -Note (1): A separate evaluation for tinnitus may be combined with an evaluation
  under diagnostic codes 6100, 6200, 6204, or other diagnostic code, except when
  tinnitus supports an evaluation under one of those diagnostic codes.
  -Note (2): Assign only a single evaluation for recurrent tinnitus, whether the sound
  is perceived in one ear, both ears, or in the head.
  -Note (3): Do not evaluate objective tinnitus (in which the sound is audible to other
  people and has a definable cause that may or may not be pathologic) under this
  diagnostic code but evaluate it as part of any underlying condition causing it.

CHAPTER 5

OTHER SENSE ORGANS

Quick Reference:

CODE	CATEGORY	PAGE
6275	Sense of smell, complete loss	87
6276	Sense of taste, complete loss	87

Rating

- 6275　Sense of smell, complete loss 10%

- 6276　Sense of taste, complete loss.. 10%

    - Note: Evaluation will be assigned under diagnostic codes 6275 or 6276 only if there is an anatomical or pathological basis for the condition.

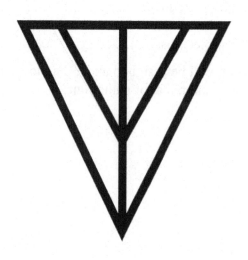

THIS PAGE LEFT INTENTIONALLY BLANK

CHAPTER 6

INFECTIOUS DISEASES, IMMUNE DISORDERS, AND NUTRITIONAL DEFICIENCIES

Quick Reference:

CODE	CATEGORY	PAGE
6300	Cholera, Asiatic	89
6301	Visceral Leishmaniasis	89
6302	Leprosy (Hansen's Disease)	90
6304	Malaria	90
6305	Lymphatic Filariasis	90
6306	Bartonellosis	90
6307	Plague	90
6308	Relapsing Fever	90
6309	Rheumatic fever	90
6310	Syphilis, and other treponemal infections	91
6311	Tuberculosis, miliary	91
6313	Avitaminosis	91
6314	Beriberi	91
6315	Pellagra	91
6316	Brucellosis	92
6317	Typhus, scrub	92
6318	Melioidosis	92
6319	Lyme Disease	92
6320	Parasitic diseases otherwise not specified	92
6350	Lupus erythematosus, systemic (disseminated)	92
6351	HIV-Related Illness	93
6354	Chronic Fatigue Syndrome (CFS)	94

Rating

- 6300   Cholera, Asiatic:
  - As active disease, and for 3 months convalescence 100%
  - Thereafter rate residuals such as renal necrosis under the appropriate system.

- 6301   Visceral Leishmaniasis:
  - During treatment for active disease 100%

  - Note: A 100 percent evaluation shall continue beyond the cessation of treatment for active disease. Six months after discontinuance of such treatment, the appropriate disability rating shall be determined by mandatory VA examination. Rate residuals such as liver damage or lymphadenopathy under the appropriate system.

- 6302   Leprosy (Hansen's Disease):
  - As active disease.. 100%

  - Note: A 100 percent evaluation shall continue beyond the date that an examining physician has determined that this has become inactive. Six months after the date of inactivity, the appropriate disability rating shall be determined by mandatory VA examination. Rate residuals such as skin lesions or peripheral neuropathy under the appropriate system.

- 6304   Malaria:
  - As active disease.. 100%
  - Thereafter rate residuals such as liver or spleen damage under the appropriate system.

  - Note: The diagnosis of malaria depends on the identification of the malarial parasites in blood smears. If the veteran served in an endemic area and presents signs and symptoms compatible with malaria, the diagnosis may be based on clinical grounds alone. Relapses must be confirmed by the presence of malarial parasites in blood smears

- 6305   Lymphatic Filariasis:
  - As active disease.. 100%
  - Thereafter rate residuals such as epididymitis or lymphangitis under the appropriate system.

- 6306   Bartonellosis:
  - As active disease, and for 3 months convalescence 100%
  - Thereafter rate residuals such as skin lesions under the appropriate system.

- 6307   Plague:
  - As active disease.. 100%
  - Thereafter rate residuals such as lymphadenopathy under the appropriate system.

- 6308   Relapsing Fever:
  - As active disease.. 100%
  - Thereafter rate residuals such as liver or spleen damage or central nervous system involvement under the appropriate system.

- 6309   Rheumatic fever:
  - As active disease.. 100%
  - Thereafter rate residuals such as heart damage under the appropriate system.

- 6310 Syphilis, and other treponemal infections:
  -Rate the complications of nervous system, vascular system, eyes or ears.
  (See DC 7004, syphilitic heart disease, DC 8013, cerebrospinal syphilis,
  DC 8014, meningovascular syphilis, DC 8015, tabes dorsalis, and
  DC 9301, dementia associated with central nervous system syphilis).

- 6311 Tuberculosis, miliary:
  - As active disease.. 100%
  - Inactive: VA will rate based upon residuals.

- 6313 Avitaminosis:
  - Marked mental changes, moist dermatitis, inability to retain
  adequate nourishment, exhaustion, and cachexia 100%
  - With all of the symptoms listed below, plus mental symptoms
  and impaired bodily vigor 60%
  - With stomatitis, diarrhea, and symmetrical dermatitis.................................. 40%
  - With stomatitis, or achlorhydria, or diarrhea.. 20%
  - Confirmed diagnosis with nonspecific symptoms such as:
  decreased appetite, weight loss, abdominal discomfort, weakness,
  inability to concentrate and irritability.. 10%

- 6314 Beriberi:
  o As active disease:
  - With congestive heart failure, anasarca, or
  Wernicke-Korsakoff syndrome.. 100%
  - With cardiomegaly, or; with peripheral neuropathy with footdrop or
  atrophy of thigh or calf muscles.. 60%
  - With peripheral neuropathy with absent knee or ankle jerks and
  loss of sensation, or; with symptoms such as weakness, fatigue,
  anorexia, dizziness, heaviness and stiffness of legs, headache or
  sleep disturbance 30%
  - Thereafter rate residuals under the appropriate body system.

- 6315 Pellagra:
  - Marked mental changes, moist dermatitis, inability to retain
  adequate nourishment, exhaustion, and cachexia 100%
  - With all of the symptoms listed below, plus mental symptoms
  and impaired bodily vigor 60%
  - With stomatitis, diarrhea, and symmetrical dermatitis.................................. 40%
  - With stomatitis, or achlorhydria, or diarrhea.. 20%
  - Confirmed diagnosis with nonspecific symptoms such as:
  decreased appetite, weight loss, abdominal discomfort, weakness,
  inability to concentrate and irritability.. 10%

- 6316 Brucellosis:
  - As active disease.. 100%
  - Thereafter rate residuals such as liver or spleen damage or
  meningitis under the appropriate system.

- 6317 Typhus, scrub:
  - As active disease.. 100%
  - Thereafter rate residuals such as spleen damage or skin
  conditions under the appropriate system.

- 6318 Melioidosis:
  - As active disease, and for 3 months convalescence 100%
  - Thereafter rate residuals such as arthritis, lung lesions or
  meningitis under the appropriate system.

- 6319 Lyme Disease:
  - As active disease.. 100%
  - Thereafter rate residuals such as arthritis under the appropriate system.

- 6320 Parasitic diseases otherwise not specified:
  - As active disease.. 100%
  - Thereafter rate residuals such as spleen or liver damage
  under the appropriate system.

- 6350 Lupus erythematosus, systemic (disseminated):
  - Not to be combined with ratings under DC 7809
  - Acute, with frequent exacerbations, producing severe impairment
  of health 100%
  - Exacerbations lasting a week or more, 2 or 3 times per year 60%
  - Exacerbations once or twice a year or symptomatic during the
  past 2 years... 10%

  - Note: Evaluate this condition either by combining the evaluations for residuals under the appropriate system, or by evaluating DC 6350, whichever method results in a higher evaluation.

- 6351 HIV-Related Illness:

     - AIDS with recurrent opportunistic infections or with secondary diseases afflicting multiple body systems; HIV-related illness with debility and progressive weight loss, without remission, or few or brief remissions 100%

     - Refractory constitutional symptoms, diarrhea, and pathological weight loss, or; minimum rating following development of AIDS-related opportunistic infection or neoplasm 60%

     - Recurrent constitutional symptoms, intermittent diarrhea, and on approved medication(s), or; minimum rating with T4 cell count less than 200, or Hairy Cell Leukoplakia, or Oral Candidiasis 30%

     - Following development of definite medical symptoms, T4 cell of 200 or more and less than 500, and on approved medication(s), or; with evidence of depression or memory loss with employment limitations 10%

     - Asymptomatic, following initial diagnosis of HIV infection, with or without lymphadenopathy or decreased T4 cell count 0%

     - Note (1): The term "approved medication(s)" includes medications prescribed as part of a research protocol at an accredited medical institution.

     - Note (2): Psychiatric or central nervous system manifestations, opportunistic infections, and neoplasms may be rated separately under appropriate codes if higher overall evaluation results, but not in combination with percentages otherwise assignable above.

- 6354 Chronic Fatigue Syndrome (CFS):
  - Debilitating fatigue, cognitive impairments (such as inability to concentrate, forgetfulness, confusion), or a combination of other signs and symptoms:

    - Which are nearly constant and so severe as to restrict routine daily activities almost completely and which may occasionally preclude self-care 100%

    - Which are nearly constant and restrict routine daily activities to less than 50 percent of the pre-illness level, or; which wax and wane, resulting in periods of incapacitation of at least six weeks total duration per year 60%

    - Which are nearly constant and restrict routine daily activities to 50 to 75 percent of the pre-illness level, or; which wax and wane, resulting in periods of incapacitation of at least four but less than six weeks total duration per year 40%

    - Which are nearly constant and restrict routine daily activities by less than 25 percent of the pre-illness level, or; which wax and wane, resulting in periods of incapacitation of at least two but less than four weeks total duration per year 20%

    - Which wax and wane but result in periods of incapacitation of at least one but less than two weeks total duration per year, or; symptoms controlled by continuous medication 10%

    - Note: For the purpose of evaluating this disability, the condition will be considered incapacitating only while it requires bed rest and treatment by a physician.

CHAPTER 7

RESPIRATORY SYSTEM

Quick Reference:

DISEASES OF THE NOSE AND THROAT

Rating

- 6502   Septum, nasal, deviation of:
  - Traumatic only, With 50-percent obstruction of the nasal passage on both sides or complete obstruction on one side 10%

- 6504   Nose, loss of part of, or scars:
  - Exposing both nasal passages 30%
  - Loss of part of one ala, or other obvious disfigurement 10%

  - Note: Or evaluate as DC 7800, scars, disfiguring, head, face, or neck.

General Rating Formula for Sinusitis (DC's 6510 through 6514)

- 6510   Sinusitis, pansinusitis, chronic.
- 6511   Sinusitis, ethmoid, chronic.
- 6512   Sinusitis, frontal, chronic.
- 6513   Sinusitis, maxillary, chronic.
- 6514   Sinusitis, sphenoid, chronic.

  - Following radical surgery with chronic osteomyelitis, or; near constant sinusitis characterized by headaches, pain and tenderness of affected sinus, and purulent discharge or crusting after repeated surgeries 50%
  - Three or more incapacitating episodes per year of sinusitis requiring prolonged (lasting four to six weeks) antibiotic treatment, or; more than six non-incapacitating episodes per year of sinusitis characterized by headaches, pain, and purulent discharge or crusting 30%
  - One or two incapacitating episodes per year of sinusitis requiring prolonged (lasting four to six weeks) antibiotic treatment, or; three to six non-incapacitating episodes per year of sinusitis characterized by headaches, pain, and purulent discharge or crusting 10%
  - Detected by X-ray only 0%
  - Note: An incapacitating episode of sinusitis means one that requires bed rest and treatment by a physician.

- 6515   Laryngitis, tuberculous, active or inactive.
  - VA will evaluate and determine which is appropriate.

- 6516   Laryngitis, chronic:
  - Hoarseness, with thickening or nodules of cords, polyps,
  submucous infiltration, or pre-malignant changes on biopsy 30%
  - Hoarseness, with inflammation of cords or mucous membrane 10%

- 6518   Laryngectomy, total. 100%*
  - Rate the residuals of partial laryngectomy as laryngitis (DC 6516),
  aphonia (DC 6519), or stenosis of larynx (DC 6520).

- 6519   Aphonia, complete organic:
  - Constant inability to communicate by speech 100%*
  - Constant inability to speak above a whisper 60%

  Note: Evaluate incomplete aphonia as laryngitis, chronic (DC 6516).

  *Review for entitlement to special monthly compensation

- 6520   Larynx, stenosis of, including residuals of laryngeal trauma (unilateral or bilateral):
  - Forced expiratory volume in one second (FEV-1) less than
  40 percent of predicted value, with Flow-Volume Loop
  compatible with upper airway obstruction, or; permanent
  tracheostomy 100%
  - FEV-1 of 40- to 55-percent predicted, with Flow-Volume Loop
  compatible with upper airway obstruction 60%
  - FEV-1 of 56- to 70-percent predicted, with Flow-Volume Loop
  compatible with upper airway obstruction 30%
  FEV-1 of 71- to 80-percent predicted, with Flow-Volume Loop
  compatible with upper airway obstruction 10%

  Note: Or evaluate as aphonia (DC 6519).

- 6521   Pharynx, injuries to:
  - Stricture or obstruction of pharynx or nasopharynx, or; absence of
  soft palate secondary to trauma, chemical burn, or granulomatous
  disease, or; paralysis of soft palate with swallowing difficulty
  (nasal regurgitation) and speech impairment 50%

- 6522   Allergic or vasomotor rhinitis:
  - With polyps 30%
  -Without polyps, but with greater than 50-percent obstruction of nasal
  passage on both sides or complete obstruction on one side 10%

- 6523 Bacterial rhinitis:
  - Rhinoscleroma 50%
  -With permanent hypertrophy of turbinates and with greater
  than 50-percent obstruction of nasal passage on both sides or
  complete obstruction on one side 10%

- 6524 Granulomatous rhinitis:
  - Wegener's granulomatosis, lethal midline granuloma 100%
  - Other types of granulomatous infection 20%

  *Review for entitlement to special monthly compensation.

DISEASES OF THE TRACHEA AND BRONCHI

- 6600 Bronchitis, chronic:
  - FEV-1 less than 40 percent of predicted value, or; the ratio of
  Forced Expiratory Volume in one second to Forced Vital Capacity
  (FEV-1/FVC) less than 40 percent, or; Diffusion Capacity of the
  Lung for Carbon Monoxide by the Single Breath Method (DLCO
  (SB)) less than 40-percent predicted, or; maximum exercise capacity
  less than 15 ml/kg/min oxygen consumption (with cardiac or
  respiratory limitation), or; cor pulmonale (right heart failure), or;
  right ventricular hypertrophy, or; pulmonary hypertension (shown
  by Echo or cardiac catheterization), or; episode(s) of acute
  respiratory failure, or; requires outpatient oxygen therapy 100%
  - FEV-1 of 40- to 55-percent predicted, or; FEV-1/FVC of 40 to 55
  percent, or; DLCO (SB) of 40- to 55-percent predicted, or;
  maximum oxygen consumption of 15 to 20 ml/kg/min (with
  cardiorespiratory limit) 60%
  - FEV-1 of 56- to 70-percent predicted, or; FEV-1/FVC of 56 to 70
  percent, or; DLCO (SB) 56- to 65-percent predicted 30%
  - FEV-1 of 71- to 80-percent predicted, or; FEV-1/FVC of 71 to 80
  percent, or; DLCO (SB) 66- to 80-percent predicted 10%

▪ 6601 Bronchiectasis:
- With incapacitating episodes of infection of at least six weeks total
duration per year 100%
- With incapacitating episodes of infection of four to six weeks total
duration per year, or; near constant findings of cough with
purulent sputum associated with anorexia, weight loss, and frank
hemoptysis and requiring antibiotic usage almost continuously 60%
- With incapacitating episodes of infection of two to four weeks total
duration per year, or; daily productive cough with sputum that is
at times purulent or blood-tinged and that requires prolonged (lasting
four to six weeks) antibiotic usage more than twice a year 30%
- Intermittent productive cough with acute infection requiring a course
of antibiotics at least twice a year 10%
- Or rate according to pulmonary impairment as for chronic bronchitis (DC 6600).

Note: An incapacitating episode is one that requires bedrest and treatment by a
physician.

▪ 6602 Asthma, bronchial:
- FEV-1 less than 40-percent predicted, or; FEV-1/FVC less than
40 percent, or; more than one attack per week with episodes of
respiratory failure, or; requires daily use of systemic (oral or
parenteral) high dose corticosteroids or immuno-suppressive
medications 100%
- FEV-1 of 40- to 55-percent predicted, or; FEV-1/FVC of 40 to 55
percent, or; at least monthly visits to a physician for required
care of exacerbations, or; intermittent (at least three per year)
courses of systemic (oral or parenteral) corticosteroids 60%
- FEV-1 of 56- to 70-percent predicted, or; FEV-1/FVC of 56 to 70
percent, or; daily inhalational or oral bronchodilator therapy,
or; inhalational anti-inflammatory medication 30%
- FEV-1 of 71- to 80-percent predicted, or; FEV-1/FVC of 71 to 80
percent, or; intermittent inhalational or oral bronchodilator therapy 10%

Note: In the absence of clinical findings of asthma at time of examination, a verified
history of asthmatic attacks must be of record.

- 6603   Emphysema, pulmonary:
  - FEV-1 less than 40 percent of predicted value, or; the ratio of Forced Expiratory Volume in one second to Forced Vital Capacity (FEV-1/FVC) less than 40 percent, or; Diffusion Capacity of the Lung for Carbon Monoxide by the Single Breath Method (DLCO (SB)) less than 40-percent predicted, or; maximum exercise capacity less than 15 ml/kg/min oxygen consumption (with cardiac or respiratory limitation), or; cor pulmonale (right heart failure), or; right ventricular hypertrophy, or; pulmonary hypertension (shown by Echo or cardiac catheterization), or; episode(s) of acute respiratory failure, or; requires outpatient oxygen therapy. 100%
  - FEV-1 of 40- to 55-percent predicted, or; FEV-1/FVC of 40 to 55 percent, or; DLCO (SB) of 40- to 55-percent predicted, or; maximum oxygen consumption of 15 to 20 ml/kg/min (with cardiorespiratory limit) 60%
  - FEV-1 of 56- to 70-percent predicted, or; FEV-1/FVC of 56 to 70 percent, or; DLCO (SB) 56- to 65-percent predicted 30%
  - FEV-1 of 71- to 80-percent predicted, or; FEV-1/FVC of 71 to 80 percent, or; DLCO (SB) 66- to 80-percent predicted 10%

- 6604   Chronic obstructive pulmonary disease:
  - FEV-1 less than 40 percent of predicted value, or; the ratio of Forced Expiratory Volume in one second to Forced Vital Capacity (FEV-1/FVC) less than 40 percent, or; Diffusion Capacity of the Lung for Carbon Monoxide by the Single Breath Method (DLCO (SB)) less than 40-percent predicted, or; maximum exercise capacity less than 15 ml/kg/min oxygen consumption (with cardiac or respiratory limitation), or; cor pulmonale (right heart failure), or; right ventricular hypertrophy, or; pulmonary hypertension (shown by Echo or cardiac catheterization), or; episode(s) of acute respiratory failure, or; requires outpatient oxygen therapy. 100%
  - FEV-1 of 40- to 55-percent predicted, or; FEV-1/FVC of 40 to 55 percent, or; DLCO (SB) of 40- to 55-percent predicted, or; maximum oxygen consumption of 15 to 20 ml/kg/min (with cardiorespiratory limit) 60%
  - FEV-1 of 56- to 70-percent predicted, or; FEV-1/FVC of 56 to 70 percent, or; DLCO (SB) 56- to 65-percent predicted 30%
  - FEV-1 of 71- to 80-percent predicted, or; FEV-1/FVC of 71 to 80 percent, or; DLCO (SB) 66- to 80-percent predicted 10%

Rating

- 6701   Tuberculosis, pulmonary, chronic, far advanced, active 100%
- 6702   Tuberculosis, pulmonary, chronic, moderately advanced, active 100%
- 6703   Tuberculosis, pulmonary, chronic, minimal, active.. 100%
- 6704   Tuberculosis, pulmonary, chronic, active, advancement unspecified 100%

General Rating Formula for Inactive Pulminary Tuberculosis (DC's 6721 through 6724)

- 6721   Tuberculosis, pulmonary, chronic, far advanced, inactive
- 6722   Tuberculosis, pulmonary, chronic, moderately advanced, inactive
- 6723   Tuberculosis, pulmonary, chronic, minimal, inactive
- 6724   Tuberculosis, pulmonary, chronic, inactive, advancement unspecified

- For two years after date of inactivity, following active tuberculosis,
which was clinically identified during service or subsequently 100%
- Thereafter for four years, or in any event, to six years after date
of inactivity 50%
- Thereafter, for five years, or to eleven years after date of inactivity 30%
- Following far advanced lesions diagnosed at any time while the
disease process was active, minimum... 30%
- Following moderately advanced lesions, provided there is continued
disability, emphysema, dyspnea on exertion, impairment of
health, etc. 20%
- Otherwise 0%

Note (1): The 100-percent rating under codes 6701 through 6724 is not subject to a requirement of precedent hospital treatment. It will be reduced to 50 percent for failure to submit to examination or to follow prescribed treatment upon report to that effect from the medical authorities. When a veteran is placed on the 100-percent rating for inactive tuberculosis, the medical authorities will be appropriately notified of the fact, and of the necessity, which has been repealed by Public Law 90-493), to notify the Veterans Service Center in the event of failure to submit to examination or to follow treatment.

Note (2): The graduated 50-percent and 30-percent ratings and the permanent 30 percent and 20 percent ratings for inactive pulmonary tuberculosis are not to be combined with ratings for other respiratory disabilities. Following thoracoplasty the rating will be for removal of ribs combined with the rating for collapsed lung. Resection of the ribs incident to thoracoplasty will be rated as removal.

Ratings for Pulmonary Tuberculosis Initially Evaluated After August 19, 1968

- 6730   Tuberculosis, pulmonary, chronic, active 100%

    - Note: Active pulmonary tuberculosis will be considered permanently and totally disabling for non-service-connected pension purposes in the following circumstances:
    (a) Associated with active tuberculosis involving other than the respiratory system.
    (b) With severe associated symptoms or with extensive cavity formation.
    (c) Reactivated cases, generally.
    (d) With advancement of lesions on successive examinations or while under treatment.
    (e) Without retrogression of lesions or other evidence of material improvement at the end of six months hospitalization or without change of diagnosis from "active" at the end of 12 months hospitalization. Material improvement means lessening or absence of clinical symptoms, and X-ray findings of a stationary or retrogressive lesion.

- 6731   Tuberculosis, pulmonary, chronic, inactive:
    - Depending on the specific findings, rate residuals as interstitial lung disease, restrictive lung disease, or, when obstructive lung disease is the major residual, as chronic bronchitis (DC 6600). Rate thoracoplasty as removal of ribs under DC 5297.

    - Note: A mandatory examination will be requested immediately following notification that active tuberculosis evaluated under DC 6730 has become inactive.

- 6732   Pleurisy, tuberculous, active or inactive:
    - VA will rate and determine which is appropriate.

Rating

- 6817 Pulmonary Vascular Disease:

    - Primary pulmonary hypertension, or; chronic pulmonary thrombo-
    embolism with evidence of pulmonary hypertension, right
    ventricular hypertrophy, or cor pulmonale, or; pulmonary
    hypertension secondary to other obstructive disease of pulmonary
    arteries or veins with evidence of right ventricular hypertrophy or
    cor pulmonale.. 100%
    - Chronic pulmonary thromboembolism requiring anticoagulant therapy,
    or; following inferior vena cava surgery without evidence of
    pulmonary hypertension or right ventricular dysfunction 60%
    - Symptomatic, following resolution of acute pulmonary embolism 30%
    - Asymptomatic, following resolution of pulmonary thromboembolism 0%

    - Note: Evaluate other residuals following pulmonary embolism under the most
    appropriate diagnostic code, such as chronic bronchitis (DC 6600) or chronic
    pleural effusion or fibrosis (DC 6844), but do not combine that evaluation with any
    of the above evaluations.

- 6819 Neoplasms, malignant, any specified part of respiratory system exclusive
    of skin growths:... 100%

    - Note: A rating of 100 percent shall continue beyond the cessation of any surgical,
    X-ray, antineoplastic chemotherapy or other therapeutic procedure. Six months
    after discontinuance of such treatment, the appropriate disability rating shall be
    determined by mandatory VA examination. If there has been no local recurrence or
    metastasis, rate on residuals.

- 6820 Neoplasms, benign, any specified part of respiratory system:
    - Evaluate using an appropriate respiratory analogy.

General Rating Formula for Bacterial Infections of the Lung (DC's 6822 through 6824)

- 6822   Actinomycosis.
- 6823   Nocardiosis.
- 6824   Chronic lung abscess.

- Active infection with systemic symptoms such as fever, night sweats, weight loss, or hemoptysis.. 100%
- Depending on the specific findings, rate residuals as interstitial lung disease, restrictive lung disease, or, when obstructive lung disease is the major residual, as chronic bronchitis (DC 6600).

INTERSTITIAL LUNG DISEASE

General Rating Formula for Interstitial Lung Disease (DC's 6825 through 6833)

- 6825   Diffuse interstitial fibrosis (interstitial pneumonitis, fibrosing alveolitis).
- 6826   Desquamative interstitial pneumonitis.
- 6827   Pulmonary alveolar proteinosis.
- 6828   Eosinophilic granuloma of lung.
- 6829   Drug-induced pulmonary pneumonitis and fibrosis.
- 6830   Radiation-induced pulmonary pneumonitis and fibrosis.
- 6831   Hypersensitivity pneumonitis (extrinsic allergic alveolitis).
- 6832   Pneumoconiosis (silicosis, anthracosis, etc.).
- 6833   Asbestosis.

- Forced Vital Capacity (FVC) less than 50-percent predicted, or; Diffusion Capacity of the Lung for Carbon Monoxide by the Single Breath Method (DLCO (SB)) less than 40-percent predicted, or; maximum exercise capacity less than 15 ml/kg/min oxygen consumption with cardiorespiratory limitation, or; cor pulmonale or pulmonary hypertension, or; requires outpatient oxygen therapy 100%
- FVC of 50- to 64-percent predicted, or; DLCO (SB) of 40- to 55-percent predicted, or; maximum exercise capacity of 15 to 20 ml/kg/min oxygen consumption with cardiorespiratory limitation 60%
- FVC of 65- to 74-percent predicted, or; DLCO (SB) of 56- to 65-percent predicted.. 30%
- FVC of 75- to 80-percent predicted, or; DLCO (SB) of 66- to 80-percent predicted.. 10%

General Rating Formula for Mycotic Lung Disease (DC's 6834 through 6839)

- 6834   Histoplasmosis of lung.
- 6835   Coccidioidomycosis.
- 6836   Blastomycosis.
- 6837   Cryptococcosis.
- 6838   Aspergillosis.
- 6839   Mucormycosis.

- Chronic pulmonary mycosis with persistent fever, weight loss,
night sweats, or massive hemoptysis 100%
- Chronic pulmonary mycosis requiring suppressive therapy with
no more than minimal symptoms such as occasional minor
hemoptysis or productive cough 50%
- Chronic pulmonary mycosis with minimal symptoms such as
occasional minor hemoptysis or productive cough... 30%
- Healed and inactive mycotic lesions, asymptomatic 0%

-Note: Coccidioidomycosis has an incubation period up to 21 days, and the disseminated phase is ordinarily manifest within six months of the primary phase. However, there are instances of dissemination delayed up to many years after the initial infection which may have been unrecognized. Accordingly, when service connection is under consideration in the absence of record or other evidence of the disease in service, service in southwestern United States where the disease is endemic and absence of prolonged residence in this locality before or after service will be the deciding factor.

General Rating Formula for Mycotic Lung Disease (DC's 6840 through 6845)

- 6840   Diaphragm paralysis or paresis.
- 6841   Spinal cord injury with respiratory insufficiency.
- 6842   Kyphoscoliosis, pectus excavatum, pectus carinatum.
- 6843   Traumatic chest wall defect, pneumothorax, hernia, etc.
- 6844   Post-surgical residual (lobectomy, pneumonectomy, etc.).
- 6845   Chronic pleural effusion or fibrosis.

- FEV-1 less than 40 percent of predicted value, or; the ratio of Forced Expiratory Volume in one second to Forced Vital Capacity (FEV-1/FVC) less than 40 percent, or; Diffusion Capacity of the Lung for Carbon Monoxide by the Single Breath Method (DLCO (SB)) less than 40-percent predicted, or; maximum exercise capacity less than 15 ml/kg/min oxygen consumption (with cardiac or respiratory limitation), or; cor pulmonale (right heart failure), or; right ventricular hypertrophy, or; pulmonary hypertension (shown by Echo or cardiac catheterization), or; episode(s) of acute respiratory failure, or; requires outpatient oxygen therapy............................. 100%
- FEV-1 of 40- to 55-percent predicted, or; FEV-1/FVC of 40 to 55 percent, or; DLCO (SB) of 40- to 55-percent predicted, or; maximum oxygen consumption of 15 to 20 ml/kg/min (with cardiorespiratory limit) 60%
- FEV-1 of 56- to 70-percent predicted, or; FEV-1/FVC of 56 to 70 percent, or; DLCO (SB) 56- to 65-percent predicted 30%
- FEV-1 of 71- to 80-percent predicted, or; FEV-1/FVC of 71 to 80 percent, or; DLCO (SB) 66- to 80-percent predicted 10%
- Or rate primary disorder.

- Note (1): A 100-percent rating shall be assigned for pleurisy with empyema, with or without pleurocutaneous fistula, until resolved.

- Note (2): Following episodes of total spontaneous pneumothorax, a rating of 100 percent shall be assigned as of the date of hospital admission and shall continue for three months from the first day of the month after hospital discharge.

- Note (3): Gunshot wounds of the pleural cavity with bullet or missile retained in lung, pain or discomfort on exertion, or with scattered rales or some limitation of excursion of diaphragm or of lower chest expansion shall be rated at least 20-percent disabling. Disabling injuries of shoulder girdle muscles (Groups I to IV) shall be separately rated and combined with ratings for respiratory involvement. Involvement of Muscle Group XXI (DC 5321), however, will not be separately rated.

- 6846   Sarcoidosis:
  - Cor pulmonale, or; cardiac involvement with congestive heart failure, or; progressive pulmonary disease with fever, night sweats, and weight loss despite treatment 100%
  - Pulmonary involvement requiring systemic high dose (therapeutic) corticosteroids for control 60%
  - Pulmonary involvement with persistent symptoms requiring chronic low dose (maintenance) or intermittent corticosteroids 30%
  - Chronic hilar adenopathy or stable lung infiltrates without symptoms or physiologic impairment 0%
  - Or rate active disease or residuals as chronic bronchitis (DC 6600) and extra-pulmonary involvement under specific body system involved.

- 6847   Sleep Apnea Syndromes (Obstructive, Central, Mixed):
  - Chronic respiratory failure with carbon dioxide retention or cor pulmonale, or; requires tracheostomy.. 100%
  - Requires use of breathing assistance device such as continuous airway pressure (CPAP) machine 50%
  - Persistent day-time hypersomnolence 30%
  - Asymptomatic but with documented sleep disorder breathing 0%

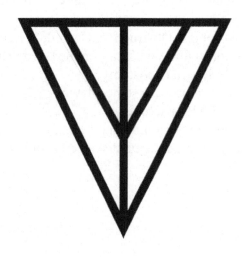

THIS PAGE LEFT INTENTIONALLY BLANK

CHAPTER 8

CARDIOVASCULAR SYSTEM

Quick Reference:

Note (1): Evaluate cor pulmonale, which is a form of secondary heart disease, as part of the pulmonary condition that causes it.

Note (2): One MET (metabolic equivalent) is the energy cost of standing quietly at rest and represents an oxygen uptake of 3.5 milliliters per kilogram of body weight per minute. When the level of METs at which dyspnea, fatigue, angina, dizziness, or syncope develops is required for evaluation, and a laboratory determination of METs by exercise testing cannot be done for medical reasons, an estimation by a medical examiner of the level of activity (expressed in METs and supported by specific examples, such as slow stair climbing or shoveling snow) that results in dyspnea, fatigue, angina, dizziness, or syncope may be used.

Rating

- 7000 Valvular heart disease (including rheumatic heart disease):
  -During active infection with valvular heart damage and for three
  months following cessation of therapy for the active infection 100%
  o Thereafter, with valvular heart disease (documented by findings on
  physical examination and either echocardiogram, Doppler
  echocardiogram, or cardiac catheterization) resulting in:
  - Chronic congestive heart failure, or; workload of 3 METs or less
  results in dyspnea, fatigue, angina, dizziness, or syncope, or; left
  ventricular dysfunction with an ejection fraction of
  less than 30 percent 100%
  - More than one episode of acute congestive heart failure in the past
  year, or; workload of greater than 3 METs but not greater than 5 METs
  results in dyspnea, fatigue, angina, dizziness, or syncope, or; left
  ventricular dysfunction with an ejection fraction of 30 to 50 percent 60%
  - Workload of greater than 5 METs but not greater than 7 METs results
  in dyspnea, fatigue, angina, dizziness, or syncope, or; evidence of
  cardiac hypertrophy or dilatation on electro-cardiogram,
  echocardiogram, or X-ray 30%
  - Workload of greater than 7 METs but not greater than 10 METs results
  in dyspnea, fatigue, angina, dizziness, or syncope, or; continuous
  medication required 10%

- 7001 Endocarditis:
  - For three months following cessation of therapy for active infection with cardiac involvement 100%
    - o Thereafter, with endocarditis (documented by findings on physical examination and either echocardiogram, Doppler echocardiogram, or cardiac catheterization) resulting in:
  - Chronic congestive heart failure, or; workload of 3 METs or less results in dyspnea, fatigue, angina, dizziness, or syncope, or; left ventricular dysfunction with an ejection fraction of less than 30 percent 100%
  - More than one episode of acute congestive heart failure in the past year, or; workload of greater than 3 METs but not greater than 5 METs results in dyspnea, fatigue, angina, dizziness, or syncope, or; left ventricular dysfunction with an ejection fraction of 30 to 50 percent 60%
  - Workload of greater than 5 METs but not greater than 7 METs results in dyspnea, fatigue, angina, dizziness, or syncope, or; evidence of cardiac hypertrophy or dilatation on electro-cardiogram, echocardiogram, or X-ray 30%
  - Workload of greater than 7 METs but not greater than 10 METs results in dyspnea, fatigue, angina, dizziness, or syncope, or; continuous medication required 10%

- 7002 Pericarditis:
  - For three months following cessation of therapy for active infection with cardiac involvement 100%
    - o Thereafter, with documented pericarditis resulting in:
  - Chronic congestive heart failure, or; workload of 3 METs or less results in dyspnea, fatigue, angina, dizziness, or syncope, or; left ventricular dysfunction with an ejection fraction of less than 30 percent 100%
  - More than one episode of acute congestive heart failure in the past year, or; workload of greater than 3 METs but not greater than 5 METs results in dyspnea, fatigue, angina, dizziness, or syncope, or; left ventricular dysfunction with an ejection fraction of 30 to 50 percent 60%
  - Workload of greater than 5 METs but not greater than 7 METs results in dyspnea, fatigue, angina, dizziness, or syncope, or; evidence of cardiac hypertrophy or dilatation on electro-cardiogram, echocardiogram, or X-ray 30%
  - Workload of greater than 7 METs but not greater than 10 METs results in dyspnea, fatigue, angina, dizziness, or syncope, or; continuous medication required 10%

111

- 7003 Pericardial adhesions:
  - Chronic congestive heart failure, or; workload of 3 METs or less results in dyspnea, fatigue, angina, dizziness, or syncope, or; left ventricular dysfunction with an ejection fraction of less than 30 percent 100%
  - More than one episode of acute congestive heart failure in the past year, or; workload of greater than 3 METs but not greater than 5 METs results in dyspnea, fatigue, angina, dizziness, or syncope, or; left ventricular dysfunction with an ejection fraction of 30 to 50 percent 60%
  - Workload of greater than 5 METs but not greater than 7 METs results in dyspnea, fatigue, angina, dizziness, or syncope, or; evidence of cardiac hypertrophy or dilatation on electro-cardiogram, echocardiogram, or X-ray 30%
  - Workload of greater than 7 METs but not greater than 10 METs results in dyspnea, fatigue, angina, dizziness, or syncope, or; continuous medication required 10%

- 7004 Syphilitic heart disease:
  - Chronic congestive heart failure, or; workload of 3 METs or less results in dyspnea, fatigue, angina, dizziness, or syncope, or; left ventricular dysfunction with an ejection fraction of less than 30 percent 100%
  - More than one episode of acute congestive heart failure in the past year, or; workload of greater than 3 METs but not greater than 5 METs results in dyspnea, fatigue, angina, dizziness, or syncope, or; left ventricular dysfunction with an ejection fraction of 30 to 50 percent 60%
  - Workload of greater than 5 METs but not greater than 7 METs results in dyspnea, fatigue, angina, dizziness, or syncope, or; evidence of cardiac hypertrophy or dilatation on electro-cardiogram, echocardiogram, or X-ray 30%
  - Workload of greater than 7 METs but not greater than 10 METs results in dyspnea, fatigue, angina, dizziness, or syncope, or; continuous medication required 10%

  Note: Evaluate syphilitic aortic aneurysms under DC 7110 (aortic aneurysm).

- 7005 Arteriosclerotic heart disease (Coronary artery disease):
  - With documented coronary artery disease resulting in:
    -Chronic congestive heart failure, or; workload of 3 METs or less results in dyspnea, fatigue, angina, dizziness, or syncope, or; left ventricular dysfunction with an ejection fraction of less than 30 percent 100%
    - More than one episode of acute congestive heart failure in the past year, or; workload of greater than 3 METs but not greater than 5 METs results in dyspnea, fatigue, angina, dizziness, or syncope, or; left ventricular dysfunction with an ejection fraction of 30 to 50 percent 60%
    - Workload of greater than 5 METs but not greater than 7 METs results in dyspnea, fatigue, angina, dizziness, or syncope, or; evidence of cardiac hypertrophy or dilatation on electro-cardiogram, echocardiogram, or X-ray 30%
    - Workload of greater than 7 METs but not greater than 10 METs results in dyspnea, fatigue, angina, dizziness, or syncope, or; continuous medication required 10%

  Note: If nonservice-connected arteriosclerotic heart disease is superimposed on service-connected valvular or other non-arteriosclerotic heart disease, request a medical opinion as to which condition is causing the current signs and symptoms.

- 7006 Myocardial infarction:
  -During and for three months following myocardial infarction, documented by laboratory tests 100%
  - Thereafter, with history of documented myocardial infarction resulting in:
    -Chronic congestive heart failure, or; workload of 3 METs or less results in dyspnea, fatigue, angina, dizziness, or syncope, or; left ventricular dysfunction with an ejection fraction of less than 30 percent 100%
    -More than one episode of acute congestive heart failure in the past year, or; workload of greater than 3 METs but not greater than 5 METs results in dyspnea, fatigue, angina, dizziness, or syncope, or; left ventricular dysfunction with an ejection fraction of 30 to 50 percent 60%
    - Workload of greater than 5 METs but not greater than 7 METs results in dyspnea, fatigue, angina, dizziness, or syncope, or; evidence of cardiac hypertrophy or dilatation on electro-cardiogram, echocardiogram, or X-ray 30%
    - Workload of greater than 7 METs but not greater than 10 METs results in dyspnea, fatigue, angina, dizziness, or syncope, or; continuous medication required 10%

- 7007   Hypertensive heart disease:
  - Chronic congestive heart failure, or; workload of 3 METs or less results in dyspnea, fatigue, angina, dizziness, or syncope, or; left ventricular dysfunction with an ejection fraction of less than 30 percent 100%
  - More than one episode of acute congestive heart failure in the past year, or; workload of greater than 3 METs but not greater than 5 METs results in dyspnea, fatigue, angina, dizziness, or syncope, or; left ventricular dysfunction with an ejection fraction of 30 to 50 percent 60%
  - Workload of greater than 5 METs but not greater than 7 METs results in dyspnea, fatigue, angina, dizziness, or syncope, or; evidence of cardiac hypertrophy or dilatation on electro-cardiogram, echocardiogram, or X-ray 30%
  - Workload of greater than 7 METs but not greater than 10 METs results in dyspnea, fatigue, angina, dizziness, or syncope, or; continuous medication required 10%

- 7008   Hyperthyroid heart disease:
  -Rate under the appropriate cardiovascular diagnostic code, depending on particular findings.

- 7010   Supraventricular arrhythmias:
  - Paroxysmal atrial fibrillation or other supraventricular tachycardia, with more than four episodes per year documented by ECG or Holter monitor 30%
  - Permanent atrial fibrillation (lone atrial fibrillation), or; one to four episodes per year of paroxysmal atrial fibrillation or other supraventricular stachycardia documented by ECG or Holter monitor 10%

- 7011   Ventricular arrhythmias (sustained):
  - For indefinite period from date of hospital admission for initial evaluation and medical therapy for a sustained ventricular arrhythmia, or; for indefinite period from date of hospital admission for ventricular aneurysmectomy, or; with an automatic implantable Cardioverter-Defibrillator (AICD) in place 100%
  - Chronic congestive heart failure, or; workload of 3 METs or less results in dyspnea, fatigue, angina, dizziness, or syncope, or; left ventricular dysfunction with an ejection fraction of less than 30 percent 100%

- More than one episode of acute congestive heart failure in the past year, or; workload of greater than 3 METs but not greater than 5 METs results in dyspnea, fatigue, angina, dizziness, or syncope, or; left ventricular dysfunction with an ejection fraction of 30 to 50 percent 60%
- Workload of greater than 5 METs but not greater than 7 METs results in dyspnea, fatigue, angina, dizziness, or syncope, or; evidence of cardiac hypertrophy or dilatation on electro-cardiogram, echocardiogram, or X-ray 30%
- Workload of greater than 7 METs but not greater than 10 METs results in dyspnea, fatigue, angina, dizziness, or syncope, or; continuous medication required 10%

- Note: A rating of 100 percent shall be assigned from the date of hospital admission for initial evaluation and medical therapy for a sustained ventricular arrhythmia or for ventricular aneurysmectomy. Six months following discharge, the appropriate disability rating shall be determined by mandatory VA examination.

- 7015   Atrioventricular block:
  - Chronic congestive heart failure, or; workload of 3 METs or less results in dyspnea, fatigue, angina, dizziness, or syncope, or; left ventricular dysfunction with an ejection fraction of less than 30 percent 100%
  - More than one episode of acute congestive heart failure in the past year, or; workload of greater than 3 METs but not greater than 5 METs results in dyspnea, fatigue, angina, dizziness, or syncope, or; left ventricular dysfunction with an ejection fraction of 30 to 50 percent 60%
  - Workload of greater than 5 METs but not greater than 7 METs results in dyspnea, fatigue, angina, dizziness, or syncope, or; evidence of cardiac hypertrophy or dilatation on electro-cardiogram, echocardiogram, or X-ray 30%
  - Workload of greater than 7 METs but not greater than 10 METs results in dyspnea, fatigue, angina, dizziness, or syncope, or; continuous medication or a pacemaker required 10%

- Note: Unusual cases of arrhythmia such as atrioventricular block associated with a supraventricular arrhythmia or pathological bradycardia should be submitted to the Director, Compensation Service. Simple delayed P-R conduction time, in the absence of other evidence of cardiac disease, is not a disability.

- 7016   Heart valve replacement (prosthesis):
    -For indefinite period following date of hospital admission for
    valve replacement 100%
    o   Thereafter:
    -Chronic congestive heart failure, or; workload of 3 METs or less
    results in dyspnea, fatigue, angina, dizziness, or syncope, or; left
    ventricular dysfunction with an ejection fraction of
    less than 30 percent 100%
    -More than one episode of acute congestive heart failure in the past
    year, or; workload of greater than 3 METs but not greater than 5 METs
    results in dyspnea, fatigue, angina, dizziness, or syncope, or; left
    ventricular dysfunction with an ejection fraction of 30 to 50 percent 60%
    - Workload of greater than 5 METs but not greater than 7 METs results
    in dyspnea, fatigue, angina, dizziness, or syncope, or; evidence of
    cardiac hypertrophy or dilatation on electro-cardiogram,
    echocardiogram, or X-ray 30%
    - Workload of greater than 7 METs but not greater than 10 METs results
    in dyspnea, fatigue, angina, dizziness, or syncope, or; continuous
    medication required 10%

    Note: A rating of 100 percent shall be assigned as of the date of hospital
    admission for valve replacement. Six months following discharge, the appropriate
    disability rating shall be determined by mandatory VA examination.

- 7017   Coronary bypass surgery:
    -For three months following hospital admission for surgery 100%
    o   Thereafter:
    -Chronic congestive heart failure, or; workload of 3 METs or less
    results in dyspnea, fatigue, angina, dizziness, or syncope, or; left
    ventricular dysfunction with an ejection fraction of
    less than 30 percent 100%
    -More than one episode of acute congestive heart failure in the past
    year, or; workload of greater than 3 METs but not greater than 5 METs
    results in dyspnea, fatigue, angina, dizziness, or syncope, or; left
    ventricular dysfunction with an ejection fraction of 30 to 50 percent 60%
    - Workload of greater than 5 METs but not greater than 7 METs results
    in dyspnea, fatigue, angina, dizziness, or syncope, or; evidence of
    cardiac hypertrophy or dilatation on electro-cardiogram,
    echocardiogram, or X-ray 30%
    - Workload of greater than 7 METs but not greater than 10 METs results
    in dyspnea, fatigue, angina, dizziness, or syncope, or; continuous
    medication required 10%

- **7018** Implantable cardiac pacemakers:
  -For two months following hospital admission for implantation
  or reimplantation 100%
  o Thereafter:
  -Evaluate as supraventricular arrhythmias (DC 7010), ventricular
  arrhythmias (DC 7011), or atrioventricular block (DC 7015)
  -Minimum 10%
  - Note: Evaluate implantable Cardioverter-Defibrillators (AICDs) under DC 7011.

- **7019** Cardiac transplantation:
  -For indefinite period following date of hospital admission for
  cardiac transplantation 100%
  o Thereafter:
  -Chronic congestive heart failure, or; workload of 3 METs or less
  results in dyspnea, fatigue, angina, dizziness, or syncope, or; left
  ventricular dysfunction with an ejection fraction of
  less than 30 percent 100%
  -More than one episode of acute congestive heart failure in the past
  year, or; workload of greater than 3 METs but not greater than 5 METs
  results in dyspnea, fatigue, angina, dizziness, or syncope, or; left
  ventricular dysfunction with an ejection fraction of 30 to 50 percent 60%
  - Minimum 30%

  - Note: A rating of 100 percent shall be assigned as of the date of hospital
  admission for cardiac transplantation. One year following discharge, the
  appropriate disability rating shall be determined by mandatory VA examination.

- **7020** Cardiomyopathy:
  - Chronic congestive heart failure, or; workload of 3 METs or less
  results in dyspnea, fatigue, angina, dizziness, or syncope, or; left
  ventricular dysfunction with an ejection fraction of
  less than 30 percent 100%
  - More than one episode of acute congestive heart failure in the past
  year, or; workload of greater than 3 METs but not greater than 5 METs
  results in dyspnea, fatigue, angina, dizziness, or syncope, or; left
  ventricular dysfunction with an ejection fraction of 30 to 50 percent 60%
  - Workload of greater than 5 METs but not greater than 7 METs results
  in dyspnea, fatigue, angina, dizziness, or syncope, or; evidence of
  cardiac hypertrophy or dilatation on electro-cardiogram,
  echocardiogram, or X-ray 30%
  - Workload of greater than 7 METs but not greater than 10 METs results
  in dyspnea, fatigue, angina, dizziness, or syncope, or; continuous
  medication required 10%

Rating

- 7101 Hypertensive vascular disease (hypertension and isolated systolic hypertension):
  - Diastolic pressure predominantly 130 or more...60%
  - Diastolic pressure predominantly 120 or more...40%
  - Diastolic pressure predominantly 110 or more, or; systolic pressure
  predominantly 200 or more..20%
  - Diastolic pressure predominantly 100 or more, or; systolic pressure
  predominantly 160 or more, or; minimum evaluation for an
  individual with a history of diastolic pressure predominantly 100
  or more who requires continuous medication for control..................................10%

  - Note (1): Hypertension or isolated systolic hypertension must be confirmed by readings taken two or more times on at least three different days. For purposes of this section, the term hypertension means that the diastolic blood pressure is predominantly 90mm. or greater, and isolated systolic hypertension means that the systolic blood pressure is predominantly 160mm. or greater with a diastolic blood pressure of less than 90mm.

  - Note (2): Evaluate hypertension due to aortic insufficiency or hyperthyroidism, which is usually the isolated systolic type, as part of the condition causing it rather than by a separate evaluation.

  - Note (3): Evaluate hypertension separately from hypertensive heart disease and other types of heart disease.

- 7110 Aortic aneurysm:
  - If five centimeters or larger in diameter, or; if symptomatic, or; for
  indefinite period from date of hospital admission for surgical
  correction (including any type of graft insertion) 100%
  - Precluding exertion...60%
  - Evaluate residuals of surgical correction according to organ systems affected.

  - Note: A rating of 100 percent shall be assigned as of the date of admission for surgical correction. Six months following discharge, the appropriate disability rating shall be determined by mandatory VA examination.

- 7111 Aneurysm, any large artery:
  - If symptomatic, or; for indefinite period from date of hospital admission for surgical correction 100%
  - o Following surgery:
    - Ischemic limb pain at rest, and; either deep ischemic ulcers or ankle/ brachial index of 0.4 or less 100%
    - Claudication on walking less than 25 yards on a level grade at 2 miles per hour, and; persistent coldness of the extremity, one or more deep ischemic ulcers, or ankle/brachial index of 0.5 or less 60%
    - Claudication on walking between 25 and 100 yards on a level grade at 2 miles per hour, and; trophic changes (thin skin, absence of hair, dystrophic nails), or ankle/brachial index of 0.7 or less 40%
    - Claudication on walking more than 100 yards, and; diminished peripheral pulses or ankle/brachial index of 0.9 or less 20%

  - Note (1): The ankle/brachial index is the ratio of the systolic blood pressure at the ankle (determined by Doppler study) divided by the simultaneous brachial artery systolic blood pressure. The normal index is 1.0 or greater.

  - Note (2): These evaluations are for involvement of a single extremity. If more than one extremity is affected, evaluate each extremity separately and combine using the bilateral factor, if applicable.

  - Note (3): A rating of 100 percent shall be assigned as of the date of hospital admission for surgical correction. Six months following discharge, the appropriate disability rating shall be determined by mandatory VA examination.

- 7112 Aneurysm, any small artery:
  - Asymptomatic 0%

  - Note: If symptomatic, evaluate according to body system affected. Following surgery, evaluate residuals under the body system affected.

- 7113 Arteriovenous fistula, traumatic:
  - o With high output heart failure 100%
  - o Without heart failure but with enlarged heart, wide pulse pressure, and tachycardia 60%
  - o Without cardiac involvement but with edema, stasis dermatitis, and either ulceration or cellulitis:
    - Lower extremity 50%
    - Upper extremity 40%
  - o With edema or stasis dermatitis:
    - Lower extremity 30%
    - Upper extremity 20%

- 7114   Arteriosclerosis obliterans:
  - Ischemic limb pain at rest, and; either deep ischemic ulcers
  or ankle/ brachial index of 0.4 or less 100%
  - Claudication on walking less than 25 yards on a level grade
  at 2 miles per hour, and; persistent coldness of the extremity,
  or ankle/brachial index of 0.5 or less 60%
  - Claudication on walking between 25 and 100 yards on a level grade
  at 2 miles per hour, and; trophic changes (thin skin, absence of hair,
  dystrophic nails), or ankle/brachial index of 0.7 or less 40%
  - Claudication on walking more than 100 yards, and; diminished
  peripheral pulses or ankle/brachial index of 0.9 or less.................................... 20%

  - Note (1): The ankle/brachial index is the ratio of the systolic blood pressure at the ankle (determined by Doppler study) divided by the simultaneous brachial artery systolic blood pressure. The normal index is 1.0 or greater.

  - Note (2): Evaluate residuals of aortic and large arterial bypass surgery or arterial graft as arteriosclerosis obliterans.

  - Note (3): These evaluations are for involvement of a single extremity. If more than one extremity is affected, evaluate each extremity separately and combine using the bilateral factor, if applicable.

- 7115   Thrombo-angiitis obliterans (Buerger's Disease):
  - Ischemic limb pain at rest, and; either deep ischemic ulcers
  or ankle/ brachial index of 0.4 or less 100%
  - Claudication on walking less than 25 yards on a level grade
  at 2 miles per hour, and; persistent coldness of the extremity,
  or ankle/brachial index of 0.5 or less 60%
  - Claudication on walking between 25 and 100 yards on a level grade
  at 2 miles per hour, and; trophic changes (thin skin, absence of hair,
  dystrophic nails), or ankle/brachial index of 0.7 or less 40%
  - Claudication on walking more than 100 yards, and; diminished
  peripheral pulses or ankle/brachial index of 0.9 or less.................................... 20%

  - Note (1): The ankle/brachial index is the ratio of the systolic blood pressure at the ankle (determined by Doppler study) divided by the simultaneous brachial artery systolic blood pressure. The normal index is 1.0 or greater.

  -Note (2): These evaluations are for involvement of a single extremity. If more than one extremity is affected, evaluate each extremity separately and combine using the bilateral factor, if applicable.

- 7117   Raynaud's syndrome:
    -With two or more digital ulcers plus autoamputation of one or more
    digits and history of characteristic attacks 100%
    -With two or more digital ulcers and history of characteristic attacks 60%
    -Characteristic attacks occurring at least daily 40%
    -Characteristic attacks occurring four to six time a week 20%
    -Characteristic attacks occurring one to three times a week 10%

    - Note: For purposes of this section, characteristic attacks consist of sequential
    color changes of the digits of one or more extremities lasting minutes to hours,
    sometimes with pain and paresthesias, and precipitated by exposure to cold or by
    emotional upsets. These evaluations are for the disease as a whole, regardless of
    the number of extremities involved or whether the nose and ears are involved.

- 7118   Angioneurotic edema:
    -Attacks without laryngeal involvement lasting one to seven days or
    longer and occurring more than eight times a year, or; attacks with
    laryngeal involvement of any duration occurring more than twice
    a year 40%
    -Attacks without laryngeal involvement lasting one to seven days
    and occurring five to eight times a year, or; attacks with laryngeal
    involvement of any duration occurring once or twice a year 20%
    -Attacks without laryngeal involvement lasting one to seven days
    and occurring two to four times a year 10%

- 7119   Erythromelalgia:
    -Characteristic attacks that occur more than once a day, last an average
    of more than two hours each, respond poorly to treatment, and that
    restrict most routine daily activities 100%
    -Characteristic attacks that occur more than once a day, last an average
    of more than two hours each, respond poorly to treatment, and that
    do not restrict most routine daily activities 60%
    -Characteristic attacks that occur daily or more but that respond to
    treatment 30%
    -Characteristic attacks that occur less than daily but at least three times
    a week and that respond to treatment 10%

    - Note: For purposes of this section, a characteristic attack of erythromelalgia
    consists of burning pain in the hands, feet, or both, usually bilateral and
    symmetrical, with increased skin temperature and redness, occurring at warm
    ambient temperatures. These evaluations are for the disease as a whole, regardless
    of the number of extremities involved.

- 7120 Varicose veins:
  - With the following findings attributed to the effects of varicose veins:

    Massive board-like edema with constant pain at rest 100%

    -Persistent edema or subcutaneous induration, stasis pigmentation or eczema, and persistent ulceration 60%

    - Persistent edema and stasis pigmentation or eczema, with or without intermittent ulceration 40%

    - Persistent edema, incompletely relieved by elevation of extremity, with or without beginning stasis pigmentation or eczema 20%

    - Intermittent edema of extremity or aching and fatigue in leg after prolonged standing or walking, with symptoms relieved by elevation of extremity or compression hosiery 10%

    - Asymptomatic palpable or visible varicose veins 0%

    - Note: These evaluations are for involvement of a single extremity. If more than one extremity is involved, evaluate each extremity separately and combine using the bilateral factor, if applicable.

- 7121 Post-phlebitic syndrome of any etiology:
  - With the following findings attributed to venous disease:

    Massive board-like edema with constant pain at rest 100%

    -Persistent edema or subcutaneous induration, stasis pigmentation or eczema, and persistent ulceration 60%

    - Persistent edema and stasis pigmentation or eczema, with or without intermittent ulceration 40%

    - Persistent edema, incompletely relieved by elevation of extremity, with or without beginning stasis pigmentation or eczema 20%

    - Intermittent edema of extremity or aching and fatigue in leg after prolonged standing or walking, with symptoms relieved by elevation of extremity or compression hosiery 10%

    - Asymptomatic palpable or visible varicose veins 0%

    - Note: These evaluations are for involvement of a single extremity. If more than one extremity is involved, evaluate each extremity separately and combine using the bilateral factor, if applicable.

- 7122 Cold injury residuals:
  - With the following in affected parts:
    -Arthralgia or other pain, numbness, or cold sensitivity plus two or more of the following: tissue loss, nail abnormalities, color changes, locally impaired sensation, hyperhidrosis, X-ray abnormalities (osteoporosis, subarticular punched out lesions, or osteoarthritis) 30%
    -Arthralgia or other pain, numbness, or cold sensitivity plus tissue loss, nail abnormalities, color changes, locally impaired sensation, hyperhidrosis, or X-ray abnormalities (osteoporosis, subarticular punched out lesions, or osteoarthritis) 20%
    -Arthralgia or other pain, numbness, or cold sensitivity.................................. 10%

    - Note (1): Separately evaluate amputations of fingers or toes, and complications such as squamous cell carcinoma at the site of a cold injury scar or peripheral neuropathy, under other diagnostic codes. Separately evaluate other disabilities that have been diagnosed as the residual effects of cold injury, such as Raynaud's phenomenon, muscle atrophy, etc., unless they are used to support an evaluation under diagnostic code 7122.

    - Note (2): Evaluate each affected part (e.g., hand, foot, ear, nose) separately and combine the ratings.

- 7123 Soft tissue sarcoma (of vascular origin).. 100%

  - Note: A rating of 100 percent shall continue beyond the cessation of any surgical, X-ray, antineoplastic chemotherapy or other therapeutic procedure. Six months after discontinuance of such treatment, the appropriate disability rating shall be determined by mandatory VA examination. If there has been no local recurrence or metastasis, rate on residuals.

THIS PAGE LEFT INTENTIONALLY BLANK

CHAPTER 9

DIGESTIVE SYSTEM

Quick Reference:

- Ratings under diagnostic codes 7301 to 7329, inclusive, 7331, 7342, and 7345 to 7348 inclusive will not be combined with each other. A single evaluation will be assigned under the diagnostic code which reflects the predominant disability picture, with elevation to the next higher evaluation where the severity of the overall disability warrants such elevation.

Rating

- 7200   Mouth, injuries of:
  - Rate as for disfigurement and impairment of function of mastication

- 7201   Lips, injuries of:
  - Rate as for disfigurement of the face

- 7202   Tongue, loss of whole or part:
  - With inability to communicate by speech 100%
  - One-half or more 60%
  - With marked speech impairment 30%

- 7203   Esophagus, stricture of:
  - Permitting passage of liquids only, with marked impairment of general health 80%
  - Severe, permitting liquids only 50%
  - Moderate 30%

- 7204   Esophagus, spasm of (cardiospasm):
  - If not amenable to dilation, rate as for the degree of obstruction (stricture).

126

- 7205   Esophagus, diverticulum of, acquired:
  Rate as for obstruction (stricture).

- 7301   Peritoneum, adhesions of:
  - Severe; definite partial obstruction shown by X-ray, with frequent
  and prolonged episodes of server colic distention, nausea or vomiting,
  following severe peritonitis, ruptured appendix, perforated ulcer, or
  operation with drainage.. 50%
  - Moderately severe; partial obstruction manifested by delayed motility
  of barium meal and less frequent and less prolonged episodes of pain............. 30%
  - Moderate; pulling pain on attempting to work or aggravated by movements
  of the body, or occasional episodes of colic pain, nausea, constipation
  (perhaps alternating with diarrhea) or abdominal distension........................... 10%
  - Mild 0%
  - Note: Ratings for adhesions will be considered when there is history of operative
  or other traumatic or infectious (intraabdominal) process, and at least two of the
  following: disturbance of motility, actual partial obstruction, reflex disturbances,
  presence of pain.

- 7304   Ulcer, gastric.

- 7305   Ulcer, duodenal:
  - Severe; pain only partially relieved by standard ulcer therapy, periodic
  vomiting, recurrent hematemesis or melena, with manifestations of
  anemia and weight loss productive of definite impairment of health............... 60%
  - Moderately severe; less than severe but with impairment of health
  manifested by anemia and weight loss; or recurrent incapacitating
  episodes averaging 10 days or more in duration at least four or more
  times a year 40%
  - Moderate; recurring episodes of severe symptoms two or three times a
  year averaging 10 days in duration; or with continuous moderate
  manifestations 20%
  - Mild; with recurring symptoms once or twice yearly..................................... 10%

- 7306   Ulcer, marginal (gastrojejunal):
  - Pronounced; periodic or continuous pain unrelieved by standard ulcer
  therapy with periodic vomiting, recurring melena or hematemesis,
  and weight loss. Totally incapacitating... 100%
  - Severe; same as pronounced with less pronounced and less continuous
  symptoms with definite impairment of health 60%
  - Moderately severe; intercurrent episodes of abdominal pain at least once
  a month partially or completely relieved by ulcer therapy, mild and
  transient episodes of vomiting or melena 40%
  - Moderate; with episodes of recurring symptoms several times a year............ 20%
  - Mild; with brief episodes of recurring symptoms once or twice yearly 10%

- 7307 Gastritis, hypertrophic (identified by gastroscope):
  - Chronic; with severe hemorrhages, or large ulcerated or eroded areas 60%
  - Chronic; with multiple small eroded or ulcerated areas, and symptoms 30%
  - Chronic; with small nodular lesions, and symptoms 10%

  Gastritis, atrophic.
  - A complication of a number of diseases, including pernicious anemia.
  - Rate the underlying condition.

- 7308 Postgastrectomy syndromes:
  - Severe; associated with nausea, sweating, circulatory disturbance after meals, diarrhea, hypoglycemic symptoms, and weight loss with malnutrition and anemia 60%
  - Moderate; less frequent episodes of epigastric disorders with characteristic mild circulatory symptoms after meals but with diarrhea and weight loss 40%
  - Mild; infrequent episodes of epigastric distress with characteristic mild circulatory symptoms or continuous mild manifestations 20%

- 7309 Stomach, stenosis of:
  - Rate as for gastric ulcer.

- 7310 Stomach, injury of, residuals:
  - Rate as peritoneal adhesions.

- 7311 Residuals of injury of the liver:
  - Depending on the specific residuals, separately evaluate as adhesions of peritoneum (diagnostic code 7301), cirrhosis of liver (diagnostic code 7312), and chronic liver disease without cirrhosis (diagnostic code 7345).

- 7312 Cirrhosis of the liver, primary biliary cirrhosis, or cirrhotic phase of sclerosing cholangitis:
  - Generalized weakness, substantial weight loss, and persistent jaundice, or; with one of the following refractory to treatment: ascites, hepatic encephalopathy, hemorrhage from varices or portal gastropathy (erosive gastritis) 100%
  - History of two or more episodes of ascites, hepatic encephalopathy, or hemorrhage from varices or portal gastropathy (erosive gastritis), but with periods of remission between attacks 70%
  - History of one episode of ascites, hepatic encephalopathy, or hemorrhage from varices or portal gastropathy (erosive gastritis) 50%
  - Portal hypertension and splenomegaly, with weakness, anorexia, abdominal pain, malaise, and at least minor weight loss 30%
  - Symptoms such as weakness, anorexia, abdominal pain, and malaise 10%
  - Note: For evaluation under diagnostic code 7312, documentation of cirrhosis (by biopsy or imaging) and abnormal liver function tests must be present.

- 7314   Cholecystitis, chronic:
  - Severe; frequent attacks of gall bladder colic 30%
  - Moderate; gall bladder dyspepsia, confirmed by X-ray technique, and with infrequent attacks (not over two or three a year) of gall bladder colic, with or without jaundice 10%
  - Mild 0%

- 7315   Cholelithiasis, chronic:
  - Rate as for chronic cholecystitis.

- 7316   Cholangitis, chronic:
  - Rate as for chronic cholecystitis.

- 7317   Gall bladder, injury of:
  - Rate as for peritoneal adhesions.

- 7318   Gall bladder, removal of:
  - With severe symptoms 30%
  - With mild symptoms 10%
  - Nonsymptomatic 0%
  - Spleen, disease or injury of: See Hemic and Lymphatic Systems.

- 7319   Irritable colon syndrome (spastic colitis, mucous colitis, etc.):
  - Severe; diarrhea, or alternating diarrhea and constipation, with more or less constant abdominal distress 30%
  - Moderate; frequent episodes of bowel disturbance with abdominal distress 10%
  - Mild, disturbances of bowel function with occasional episodes of abdominal distress 0%

- 7321   Amebiasis:
  - Mild gastrointestinal disturbances, lower abdominal cramps, nausea, gaseous distention, chronic constipation interrupted by diarrhea 10%
  - Asymptomatic 0%

  - Note: Amebiasis with or without liver abscess is parallel in symptomatology with ulcerative colitis and should be rated on the scale provided for the latter. Similarly, lung abscess due to amebiasis will be rated under the respiratory system schedule, diagnostic code 6809.

- 7322   Dysentery, bacillary:
  - Rate as for ulcerative colitis.

- 7323   Colitis, ulcerative:
  - Pronounced; resulting in marked malnutrition, anemia, and general debility, or with serious complication as liver abscess 100%
  - Severe; with numerous attacks a year and malnutrition, the health only fair during remissions. 60%
  - Moderately severe; with frequent exacerbations 30%
  - Moderate; with infrequent exacerbations 10%

- 7324   Distomiasis, intestinal or hepatic:
  - Severe symptoms 30%
  - Moderate symptoms 10%
  - Mild or no symptoms.. 0%

- 7325   Enteritis, chronic:
  - Rate as for irritable colon syndrome.

- 7326   Enterocolitis, chronic:
  - Rate as for irritable colon syndrome.

- 7327   Diverticulitis:
  - Rate as for irritable colon syndrome, peritoneal adhesions, or colitis, ulcerative, depending upon the predominant disability picture.

- 7328   Intestine, small, resection of:
  - With marked interference with absorption and nutrition, manifested by severe impairment of health objectively supported by examination findings including material weight loss 60%
  - With definite interference with absorption and nutrition, manifested by impairment of health objectively supported by examination findings including definite weight loss... 40%
  - Symptomatic with diarrhea, anemia and inability to gain weight 20%

  - Note: Where residual adhesions constitute the predominant disability, rate under diagnostic code 7301.

- 7329   Intestine, large, resection of:
  - With severe symptoms, objectively supported by examination findings 40%
  - With moderate symptoms.. 20%
  - With slight symptoms... 10%

  - Note: Where residual adhesions constitute the predominant disability, rate under diagnostic code 7301.

- 7330 Intestine, fistula of, persistent, or after attempt at operative closure:
  - Copious and frequent, fecal discharge... 100%
  - Constant or frequent, fecal discharge 60%
  - Slight infrequent, fecal discharge 30%
  - Healed: rate for peritoneal adhesions.

- 7331 Peritonitis, tuberculous, active or inactive:
  - Active.. 100%
  - Inactive: VA will rate based upon residuals.

- 7332 Rectum and anus, impairment of sphincter control:
  - Complete loss of sphincter control 100%
  - Extensive leakage and fairly frequent involuntary bowel movements............. 60%
  - Occasional involuntary bowel movements, necessitating wearing of pad 30%
  - Constant slight, or occasional moderate leakage. 10%
  - Healed or slight, without leakage 0%

- 7333 Rectum and anus, stricture of:
  - Requiring colostomy.. 100%
  - Great reduction of lumen, or extensive leakage 50%
  - Moderate reduction of lumen, or moderate constant leakage......................... 30%

- 7334 Rectum, prolapse of:
  - Severe (or complete), persistent 50%
  - Moderate, persistent or frequently recurring 30%
  - Mild with constant slight or occasional moderate leakage............................. 10%

- 7335 Ano, fistula in:
  - Rate as for impairment of sphincter control.

- 7336 Hemorrhoids, external or internal:
  - With persistent bleeding and with secondary anemia, or with fissures........... 20%
  - Large or thrombotic, irreducible, with excessive redundant tissue,
  evidencing frequent recurrences 10%
  - Mild or moderate 0%

- 7337 Pruritus ani:
  - Rate for the underlying condition.

- 7338   Hernia, inguinal:
  - Large, postoperative, recurrent, not well supported under ordinary conditions and not readily reducible, when considered inoperable 60%
  - Small, postoperative recurrent, or unoperated irremediable, not well supported by truss, or not readily reducible 30%
  - Postoperative recurrent, readily reducible and well supported by truss or belt 10%
  - Not operated, but remediable 0%
  - Small, reducible, or without true hernia protrusion 0%

  - Note: Add 10 percent for bilateral involvement, provided the second hernia is compensable. This means that the more severely disabling hernia is to be evaluated, and 10 percent, only, added for the second hernia, if the latter is of compensable degree.

- 7339   Hernia, ventral, postoperative:
  - Massive, persistent, severe diastasis of recti muscles or extensive diffuse destruction or weakening of muscular and fascial support of abdominal wall so as to be inoperable 100%
  - Large, not well supported by belt under ordinary conditions 40%
  - Small, not well supported by belt under ordinary conditions, or healed ventral hernia or postoperative wounds with weakening of abdominal wall and indication for a supporting belt 20%
  - Wounds, postoperative, healed, no disability, belt not indicated 0%

- 7340   Hernia, femoral:
  - Rate as for inguinal hernia.

- 7342   Visceroptosis, symptomatic, marked 10%

- 7343   Malignant neoplasms of the digestive system, exclusive of skin growths 100%

  - Note: A rating of 100 percent shall continue beyond the cessation of any surgical, X-ray, antineoplastic chemotherapy or other therapeutic procedure. Six months after discontinuance of such treatment, the appropriate disability rating shall be determined by mandatory VA examination. If there has been no local recurrence or metastasis, rate on residuals.

- 7344   Benign neoplasms, exclusive of skin growths:
  - Evaluate under an appropriate diagnostic code, depending on the predominant disability or the specific residuals after treatment.

- 7345 Chronic liver disease without cirrhosis (including hepatitis B, chronic active hepatitis, autoimmune hepatitis, hemochromatosis, drug-induced hepatitis, etc., but excluding bile duct disorders and hepatitis C):

- Near-constant debilitating symptoms (such as fatigue, malaise, nausea, vomiting, anorexia, arthralgia, and right upper quadrant pain) 100%

- Daily fatigue, malaise, and anorexia, with substantial weight loss (or other indication of malnutrition), and hepatomegaly, or; incapacitating episodes (with symptoms such as fatigue, malaise, nausea, vomiting, anorexia, arthralgia, and right upper quadrant pain) having a total duration of at least six weeks during the past 12- month period, but not occurring constantly 60%

- Daily fatigue, malaise, and anorexia, with minor weight loss and hepatomegaly, or; incapacitating episodes (with symptoms such as fatigue, malaise, nausea, vomiting, anorexia, arthralgia, and right upper quadrant pain) having a total duration of at least four weeks, but less than six weeks, during the past 12-month period 40%

- Daily fatigue, malaise, and anorexia (without weight loss or hepatomegaly), requiring dietary restriction or continuous medication, or; incapacitating episodes (with symptoms such as fatigue, malaise, nausea, vomiting, anorexia, arthralgia, and right upper quadrant pain) having a total duration of at least two weeks, but less than four weeks, during the past 12-month period 20%

- Intermittent fatigue, malaise, and anorexia, or; incapacitating episodes (with symptoms such as fatigue, malaise, nausea, vomiting, anorexia, arthralgia, and right upper quadrant pain) having a total duration of at least one week, but less than two weeks, during the past 12-month period 10%

- Nonsymptomatic 0%

- Note (1): Evaluate sequelae, such as cirrhosis or malignancy of the liver, under an appropriate diagnostic code, but do not use the same signs and symptoms as the basis for evaluation under DC 7354 and under a diagnostic code for sequelae.

- Note (2): For purposes of evaluating conditions under diagnostic code 7345, "incapacitating episode" means a period of acute signs and symptoms severe enough to require bed rest and treatment by a physician.

- Note (3): Hepatitis B infection must be confirmed by serologic testing in order to evaluate it under diagnostic code 7345.

- 7346   Hernia hiatal:
  - Symptoms of pain, vomiting, material weight loss and hematemesis
  or melena with moderate anemia; or other symptom combinations
  productive of severe impairment of health 60%
  - Persistently recurrent epigastric distress with dysphagia, pyrosis, and
  regurgitation, accompanied by substernal or arm or shoulder pain,
  productive of considerable impairment of health 30%
  - With two or more of the symptoms for the 30 percent evaluation of
  less severity 10%

- 7347   Pancreatitis:
  - With frequently recurrent disabling attacks of abdominal pain with few
  pain free intermissions and with steatorrhea, malabsorption, diarrhea
  and severe malnutrition 100%
  - With frequent attacks of abdominal pain, loss of normal body weight
  and other findings showing continuing pancreatic insufficiency
  between acute attacks 60%
  - Moderately severe; with at least 4-7 typical attacks of abdominal pain
  per year with good remission between attacks 30%
  - With at least one recurring attack of typical severe abdominal pain
  in the past year 10%

  - Note 1: Abdominal pain in this condition must be confirmed as resulting from pancreatitis by appropriate laboratory and clinical studies.

  - Note 2: Following total or partial pancreatectomy, rate under above, symptoms, minimum rating 30 percent.

- 7348   Vagotomy with pyloroplasty or gastroenterostomy:
  - Followed by demonstrably confirmative postoperative complications
  of stricture or continuing gastric retention 40%
  - With symptoms and confirmed diagnosis of alkaline gastritis, or of
  confirmed persisting diarrhea 30%
  - Recurrent ulcer with incomplete vagotomy 20%

  - Note: Rate recurrent ulcer following complete vagotomy under diagnostic code 7305, minimum rating 20 percent; and rate dumping syndrome under DC 7308.

- 7351   Liver transplant:
  - For an indefinite period from the date of hospital admission for
  transplant surgery 100%
  - Minimum 30%

  - Note: A rating of 100 percent shall be assigned as of the date of hospital admission for transplant surgery and shall continue. One year following discharge, the appropriate disability rating shall be determined by mandatory VA examination.

- 7354   Hepatitis C (or non-A, non-B hepatitis):
  o   With serologic evidence of hepatitis C infection and the following signs and symptoms due to hepatitis C infection:
  - Near-constant debilitating symptoms (such as fatigue, malaise, nausea, vomiting, anorexia, arthralgia, and right upper quadrant pain) 100%
  - Daily fatigue, malaise, and anorexia, with substantial weight loss (or other indication of malnutrition), and hepatomegaly, or; incapacitating episodes (with symptoms such as fatigue, malaise, nausea, vomiting, anorexia, arthralgia, and right upper quadrant pain) having a total duration of at least six weeks during the past 12-month period, but not occurring constantly........................ 60%
  - Daily fatigue, malaise, and anorexia, with minor weight loss and hepatomegaly, or; incapacitating episodes (with symptoms such as fatigue, malaise, nausea, vomiting, anorexia, arthralgia, and right upper quadrant pain) having a total duration of at least four weeks, but less than six weeks, during the past 12-month period 40%
  - Daily fatigue, malaise, and anorexia (without weight loss or hepatomegaly), requiring dietary restriction or continuous medication, or; incapacitating episodes (with symptoms such as fatigue, malaise, nausea, vomiting, anorexia, arthralgia, and right upper quadrant pain) having a total duration of at least two weeks, but less than four weeks, during the past 12-month period 20%
  - Intermittent fatigue, malaise, and anorexia, or; incapacitating episodes (with symptoms such as fatigue, malaise, nausea, vomiting, anorexia, arthralgia, and right upper quadrant pain) having a total duration of at least one week, but less than two weeks, during the past 12-month period.. 10%
  - Nonsymptomatic... 0%

- Note (1): Evaluate sequelae, such as cirrhosis or malignancy of the liver, under an appropriate diagnostic code, but do not use the same signs and symptoms as the basis for evaluation under DC 7354 and under a diagnostic code for sequelae.

- Note (2): For purposes of evaluating conditions under diagnostic code 7354, "incapacitating episode" means a period of acute signs and symptoms severe enough to require bed rest and treatment by a physician.

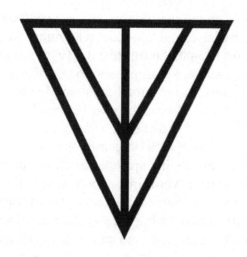

THIS PAGE LEFT INTENTIONALLY BLANK

CHAPTER 10

GENITOURINARY SYSTEM

Quick Reference:

CODE	CATEGORY	PAGE
7500	Kidney, removal of one	139
7501	Kidney, abscess of	139
7502	Nephritis, chronic	139
7504	Pyelonephritis, chronic	139
7505	Kidney, tuberculosis of	139
7507	Nephrosclerosis, arteriolar	140
7508	Nephrolithiasis	140
7509	Hydronephrosis	140
7510	Ureterolithiasis	140
7511	Ureter, stricture of	140
7512	Cystitis, chronic, includes interstitial and all etiologies, infectious and non-infectious	140
7515	Bladder, calculus in, with symptoms interfering with function	140
7516	Bladder, fistula of	140
7517	Bladder, injury of	141
7518	Urethra, stricture of	141
7519	Urethra, fistula of	141
7520	Penis, removal of half or more	141
7521	Penis, removal of glans	141
7522	Penis, deformity, with loss of erectile power	141
7523	Testis, atrophy complete	141
7524	Testis, removal	141
7525	Epididymo-orchitis, chronic only	141
7527	Prostate gland injuries, infections, hypertrophy, post-operative residuals	141
7528	Malignant neoplasms of the genitourinary system	142
7529	Benign neoplasms of the genitourinary system	142
7530	Chronic renal disease requiring regular dialysis	142
7531	Kidney transplant	142
7532	Renal tubular disorders (such as renal glycosurias, aminoacidurias, renal tubular acidosis, Fanconi's syndrome, Bartter's syndrome, related disorders of Henle's loop and proximal or distal nephron function, etc.)	142
7533	Cystic diseases of the kidneys (polycystic disease, uremic medullary cystic disease, Medullary sponge kidney, and similar conditions)	142
7534	Atherosclerotic renal disease (renal artery stenosis or atheroembolic renal disease)	142
7535	Toxic nephropathy (antibotics, radiocontrast agents, nonsteroidal anti-inflammatory agents, heavy metals, and similar agents)	142

CODE	CATEGORY	PAGE
7536	Glomerulonephritis	142
7537	Interstitial nephritis	142
7538	Papillary necrosis	143
7539	Renal amyloid disease	143
7540	Disseminated intravascular coagulation with renal cortical necrosis	143
7541	Renal involvement in diabetes mellitus, sickle cell anemia, systemic lupus erythematosus, vasculitis, or other systemic disease processes	143
7542	Neurogenic bladder	143

Note: When evaluating any claim involving loss or loss of use of one or more creative organs, determine whether the veteran may be entitled to special monthly compensation. Footnotes in the schedule indicate conditions which potentially establish entitlement to special monthly compensation; however, there are other conditions in this section which under certain circumstances also establish entitlement to special monthly compensation.

General Ratings of the Genitourinary Sytems- Dysfunctions

Rating

Renal Dysfunction:

- Requiring regular dialysis, or precluding more than sedentary activity from one of the following: Persistent edema and albuminuria; or, BUN more than 80mg%; or, creatinine more than 8mg%; or, markedly decreased function of kidney or other organ systems, especially cardiovascular 100%
- Persistent edema and albuminuria with BUN 40 to 80mg%; or, creatinine 4 to 8mg%; or, generalized poor health characterized by lethargy, weakness, anorexia, weight loss, or limitation of exertion.. 80%
- Constant albuminuria with some edema; or, definite decrease in kidney function; or, hypertension at least 40 percent disabling under diagnostic code 7101 .... 60%
- Albumin constant or recurring with hyaline and granular casts or red blood cells; or, transient or slight edema or hypertension at least 10 percent disabling under diagnostic code 7101 .... 30%
- Albumin and casts with history of acute nephritis; or, hypertension non-compensable under diagnostic code 7101 .... 0%

Voiding Dysfunction: Rate particular condition as urine leakage, frequency, or obstructed voiding. Continual Urine Leakage, Post Surgical Urinary Diversion, Urinary Incontinence, or Stress Incontinence:

- Requiring the use of an appliance or the wearing of absorbent materials which must be changed more than 4 times per day 60%
- Requiring the wearing of absorbent materials which must be changed 2 to 4 times per day 40%
- Requiring the wearing of absorbent materials which must be changed less than 2 times per day 20%

Urinary Frequency:
    - Daytime voiding interval less than one hour, or; awakening to void five or more times per night.. 40%
    - Daytime voiding interval between one and two hours, or; awakening to void three to four times per night.. 20%
    - Daytime voiding interval between two and three hours, or; awakening to void two times per night.. 10%

Obstructed Voiding:
    - Urinary retention requiring intermittent or continuous catheterization...................... 30%
    - Marked obstructive symptomatology (hesitancy, slow or weak stream, decreased force of stream) with any one or combination of the following: 10%
        - Post void residuals greater than 150cc.
        - Uroflowmetry; markedly diminished peak flow rate (less than 10cc/sec).
        - Recurrent urinary tract infections secondary to obstruction.
        - Stricture disease requiring periodic dilatation every 2 to 3 months.
    - Obstructive symptomatology with or without stricture disease requiring dilatation 1 to 2 times per year... 0%

Urinary Tract Infection: Poor renal function: Rate as renal dysfunction.
    - Recurrent symptomatic infection requiring drainage/frequent hospitalization (greater than two times/year), and/or requiring continuous intensive management 30%
    - Long-term drug therapy, 1-2 hospitalizations per year and/or requiring intermittent intensive management 10%

-   7500   Kidney, removal of one:
        - Minimum evaluation.. 30%
        - Or rate as renal dysfunction if there is nephritis, infection, or pathology of the other.

-   7501   Kidney, abscess of:
        - Rate as urinary tract infection.

-   7502   Nephritis, chronic:
        - Rate as renal dysfunction.

-   7504   Pyelonephritis, chronic:
        - Rate as renal dysfunction or urinary tract infection, whichever is predominant.

-   7505   Kidney, tuberculosis of:
        - VA will rate and determine which is appropriate.

- 7507   Nephrosclerosis, arteriolar:
  - Rate according to predominant symptoms as renal dysfunction, hypertension or heart disease. If rated under the cardiovascular schedule, however, the percentage rating which would otherwise be assigned will be elevated to the next higher evaluation.

- 7508   Nephrolithiasis:
  - Rate as hydronephrosis, *except for* recurrent stone formation requiring one or more of the following:
  - Diet therapy
  - Drug therapy
  - Invasive or non-invasive procedures more than two times/year 30%

- 7509   Hydronephrosis:
  - Severe; Rate as renal dysfunction.
  - Frequent attacks of colic with infection (pyonephrosis), kidney function impaired 30%
  - Frequent attacks of colic, requiring catheter drainage.................................. 20%
  - Only an occasional attack of colic, not infected and not requiring catheter drainage 10%

- 7510   Ureterolithiasis:
  - Rate as hydronephrosis, *except for* recurrent stone formation requiring one or more of the following:
  - Diet therapy
  - Drug therapy
  - Invasive or non-invasive procedures more than two times/year 30%

- 7511   Ureter, stricture of:
  - Rate as hydronephrosis, *except for* recurrent stone formation requiring one or more of the following:
  - Diet therapy
  - Drug therapy
  - Invasive or non-invasive procedures more than two times/year 30%

- 7512   Cystitis, chronic, includes interstitial and all etiologies, infectious and non-infectious:
  - Rate as voiding dysfunction.

- 7515   Bladder, calculus in, with symptoms interfering with function:
  - Rate as voiding dysfunction.

- 7516   Bladder, fistula of:
  - Rate as voiding dysfunction or or urinary tract infection, whichever is predominant.
  - Postoperative, superapubic cystotomy 100%

- 7517   Bladder, injury of:
  - Rate as voiding dysfunction.

- 7518   Urethra, stricture of:
  - Rate as voiding dysfunction.

- 7519   Urethra, fistula of:
  - Rate as voiding dysfunction.
  - Multiple urethroperineal fistulae 100%

- 7520   Penis, removal of half or more.. 30%
  - Or rate as voiding dysfunction.

- 7521   Penis, removal of glans 20%
  - Or rate as voiding dysfunction.

- 7522   Penis, deformity, with loss of erectile power.................................... 20%*

- 7523   Testis, atrophy complete:
  - Both 20%*
  - One... 0%*

- 7524   Testis, removal:
  - Both 30%*
  - One... 0%*

  *Review for entitlement to special monthly compensation.

  - Note: In cases of the removal of one testis as the result of a service-incurred injury or disease, other than an undescended or congenitally undeveloped testis, with the absence or nonfunctioning of the other testis unrelated to service, an evaluation of 30 percent will be assigned for the service-connected testicular loss. Testis, undescended, or congenitally undeveloped is not a ratable disability.

- 7525   Epididymo-orchitis, chronic only:
  - Rate as urinary tract infection.
  - For tubercular infections: VA will rate and determine which is appropriate.

- 7527   Prostate gland injuries, infections, hypertrophy, post-operative residuals:
  - Rate as voiding dysfunction or urinary tract infection, whichever is predominant.

- 7528 Malignant neoplasms of the genitourinary system: 100%

  - Note: Following the cessation of surgical, X-ray, antineoplastic chemotherapy or other therapeutic procedure, the rating of 100 percent shall continue with a mandatory VA examination at the expiration of six months. If there has been no local recurrence or metastasis, rate on residuals as voiding dysfunction or renal dysfunction, whichever is predominant.

- 7529 Benign neoplasms of the genitourinary system:
  - Rate as voiding dysfunction or renal dysfunction, whichever is predominant.

- 7530 Chronic renal disease requiring regular dialysis:
  - Rate as renal dysfunction.

- 7531 Kidney transplant:
  - Following transplant surgery 100%
  - Thereafter: Rate on residuals as renal dysfunction, minimum rating 30%

  - Note: The 100 percent evaluation shall be assigned as of the date of hospital admission for transplant surgery and shall continue with a mandatory VA examination one year following hospital discharge.

- 7532 Renal tubular disorders (such as renal glycosurias, aminoacidurias, renal tubular acidosis, Fanconi's syndrome, Bartter's syndrome, related disorders of Henle's loop and proximal or distal nephron function, etc.):
  - Minimum rating for symptomatic condition 20%
  - Or rate as renal dysfunction.

- 7533 Cystic diseases of the kidneys (polycystic disease, uremic medullary cystic disease, Medullary sponge kidney, and similar conditions):
  - Rate as renal dysfunction.

- 7534 Atherosclerotic renal disease (renal artery stenosis or atheroembolic renal disease):
  - Rate as renal dysfunction.

- 7535 Toxic nephropathy (antibotics, radiocontrast agents, nonsteroidal anti-inflammatory agents, heavy metals, and similar agents):
  - Rate as renal dysfunction.

- 7536 Glomerulonephritis:
  - Rate as renal dysfunction.

- 7537 Interstitial nephritis:
  - Rate as renal dysfunction.

- 7538   Papillary necrosis:
          - Rate as renal dysfunction.

- 7539   Renal amyloid disease:
          - Rate as renal dysfunction.

- 7540   Disseminated intravascular coagulation with renal cortical necrosis:
          - Rate as renal dysfunction.

- 7541   Renal involvement in diabetes mellitus, sickle cell anemia, systemic
          lupus erythematosus, vasculitis, or other systemic disease processes:
          - Rate as renal dysfunction.

- 7542   Neurogenic bladder:
          - Rate as voiding dysfunction.

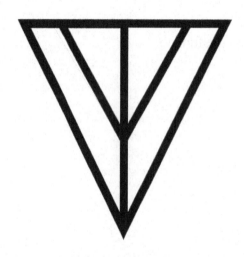

THIS PAGE LEFT INTENTIONALLY BLANK

CHAPTER 11

GYNECOLOGICAL CONDITIONS AND DISORDERS OF THE BREAST

Quick Reference:

CODE	CATEGORY	PAGE
7610	Vulva or clitorus, disease or injury of (including vulvovaginitis)	146
7611	Vagina, disease or injury of	146
7612	Cervix, disease or injury of	146
7613	Uterus, disease, injury, or adhesions of	146
7614	Fallopian tube, disease, injury, or adhesions of (including pelvic inflammatory disease (PID))	146
7615	Ovary, disease, injury, or adhesions of	146
7617	Uterus and both ovaries, removal of, complete	146
7618	Uterus, removal of, including corpus	146
7619	Ovary, removal of	146
7620	Ovaries, atrophy of both, complete	146
7621	Complete or incomplete pelvic organ prolapse due to injury, disease, or surgical complications of pregnancy	147
7624	Fistula, rectovaginal	147
7625	Fistula, urethrovaginal	147
7626	Breast, surgery of	147-8
7627	Malignant neoplasms of gynecological system	148
7628	Benign neoplasms of the gynecological system	148
7629	Endometriosis	148
7630	Malignant neoplasms of the breast	148
7631	Benign neoplasms of the breast and other injuries of the breast	149
7632	Female Sexual Arousal Disorder (FSAD)	149

- Note (1): Natural menopause, primary amenorrhea, and pregnancy and childbirth are not disabilities for rating purposes. Chronic residuals of medical or surgical complications of pregnancy may be disabilities for rating purposes.

- Note (2): When evaluating any claim involving loss or loss of use of one or more creative organs or anatomical loss of one or both breasts, determine whether the veteran may be entitled to special monthly compensation. Footnotes in the schedule indicate conditions which potentially establish entitlement to special monthly compensation; however, almost any condition in this section might, under certain circumstances, establish entitlement to special monthly compensation.

General Rating Formula for Disease, Injury, or Adhesions of Female Reproductive Organs (diagnostic codes 7610 – 7615):

Rating

- 7610   Vulva, disease or injury of (including vulvovaginitis).
- 7611   Vagina, disease or injury of.
- 7612   Cervix, disease or injury of.
- 7613   Uterus, disease, injury, or adhesions of.
- 7614   Fallopian tube, disease, injury, or adhesions of (including pelvic inflammatory disease (PID)).

- 7615   Ovary, disease, injury, or adhesions of.
  - Symptoms not controlled by continuous treatment 30%
  - Symptoms that require continuous treatment 10%
  - Symptoms that do not require continuous treatment .... 0%.
  - Note: For purposes of VA disability evaluation, a disease, injury, or adhesions of the ovaries resulting in ovarian dysfunction affecting the menstrual cycle, such as dysmenorrhea and secondary amenorrhea, are rated under diagnostic code 7615.

- 7617   Uterus and both ovaries, removal of, complete:
  - For three months after removal 100%*
  - Thereafter 50%*

- 7618   Uterus, removal of, including corpus:
  - For three months after removal 100%*
  - Thereafter 30%*

- 7619   Ovary, removal of:
  - For three months after removal 100%*
  - Thereafter:
    - Complete removal of both ovaries... 30%*
    - Removal of one with or without partial removal of the other 0%*
    - Note: In cases of the removal of one ovary as the result of a service-connected injury or disease, with the absence or nonfunctioning of the second ovary unrelated to service, an evaluation of 30 percent will be assigned for the service-connected ovarian loss.

- 7620   Ovaries, atrophy of both, complete..20%*

*Also review for special monthly compensation

- 7621 Complete or incomplete pelvic organ prolapse due to injury, disease, or surgical complications of pregnancy 10%
  - Note: Pelvic organ prolapse occurs when a pelvic organ such as bladder, urethra, uterus, vagina, small bowel, or rectum drops (prolapse) from its normal place in the abdomen. Conditions associated with pelvic organ prolapse include: uterine or vaginal vault prolapse, cystocele, urethrocele, rectocele, enterocele, or any combination thereof. Evaluate pelvic organ prolapse under DC 7621. Evaluate separately any genitourinary, digestive, or skin symptoms under the appropriate diagnostic code(s) and combine all with an evaluation of 10% under DC 7621.

- 7624 Fistula, rectovaginal:
  - Vaginal fecal leakage at least once a day requiring wearing a pad 100%
  - Vaginal fecal leakage four or more times per week, but less than daily, requiring wearing a pad 60%
  - Vaginal fecal leakage one to three times per week requiring wearing a pad 30%
  - Vaginal fecal leakage less than once a week 10%
  - Without leakage 0%

- 7625 Fistula, urethrovaginal:
  - Multiple urethrovaginal fistulae 100%
  - Requiring the use of an appliance or the wearing of absorbent materials which must be changed more than four times per day 60%
  - Requiring the wearing of absorbent materials which must be changed two to four times per day 40%
  - Requiring the wearing of absorbent materials which must be changed less than two times per day 20%

- 7626 Breast, surgery of:
  - o Following radical mastectomy:
    - Both 80%*
    - One... 50%*
  - o Following modified radical mastectomy:
    - Both 60%*
    - One... 40%*
  - o Following simple mastectomy or wide local excision with significant alteration of size or form:
    - Both 50%*
    - One... 30%*
  - o Following wide local excision without significant alteration of size or form:
    - Both or one 0%
    - Note (1): *Radical mastectomy* means removal of the entire breast, underlying pectoral muscles, and regional lymph nodes up to the coracoclavicular ligament.

- Note (2): *Modified radical mastectomy* means removal of the entire breast and axillary lymph nodes (in continuity with the breast). Pectoral muscles are left intact.
- Note (3): *Simple (or total) mastectomy* means removal of all of the breast tissue, nipple, and a small portion of the overlying skin, but lymph nodes and muscles are left intact.
- Note (4): *Wide local excision* (including partial mastectomy, lumpectomy, tylectomy, segmentectomy, and quadrantectomy) means removal of a portion of the breast tissue.

*Also review for special monthly compensation

Rating

- 7627 Malignant neoplasms of gynecological system 100%
    - Note: A rating of 100 percent shall continue beyond the cessation of any surgical, radiation, antineoplastic chemotherapy or other therapeutic procedure. Six months after discontinuance of such treatment, the appropriate disability rating shall be determined by mandatory VA examination. Rate chronic residuals to include scars, lymphedema, disfigurement, and/or other impairment of function under the appropriate diagnostic code(s) within the appropriate body system.

- 7628 Benign neoplasms of gynecological system:
    - Rate chronic residuals to include scars, lymphedema, disfigurement, and/or other impairment of function under the appropriate diagnostic code(s) within the appropriate body system.

- 7629 Endometriosis:
    -Lesions involving bowel or bladder confirmed by laproscopy, pelvic pain or heavy or irregular bleeding not controlled by treatment, and bowel or bladder symptoms 50%
    -Pelvic pain or heavy or irregular bleeding not controlled by treatment 30%
    -Pelvic pain or heavy or irregular bleeding requiring continuous treatment for control 10%
    - Note: Diagnosis of endometriosis must be substantiated by laparoscopy.

- 7630 Malignant neoplasms of the breast 100%
    - Note: A rating of 100 percent shall continue beyond the cessation of any surgical, radiation, antineoplastic chemotherapy or other therapeutic procedure. Six months after discontinuance of such treatment, the appropriate disability rating shall be determined by mandatory VA examination. Rate chronic residuals according to impairment of function due to scars, lymphedema, or disfigurement (e.g., limitation of arm, shoulder, and wrist motion, or loss of grip strength, or loss of sensation, or residuals from harvesting of muscles for reconstructive purposes), and/or under diagnostic code 7626.

- 7631   Benign neoplasms of the breasts and other injuries of the breasts. Rate chronic residuals according to impairment of function due to scars, lymphedema, or disfigurement (e.g., limitation of arm, shoulder, and wrist motion, or loss of grip strength, or loss of sensation, or residuals from harvesting of muscles for reconstructive purposes), and/or under diagnostic code 7626.

- 7632   Female Sexual Arousal Disorder (FSAD) 0%*

    *Also review for special monthly compensation

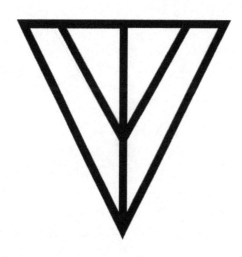

THIS PAGE LEFT INTENTIONALLY BLANK

CHAPTER 12

THE HEMIC AND LYMPHATIC SYSTEMS

Quick Reference:

Rating

- 7702   Agranulocytosis, acuired:
  - Requiring bone marrow transplant; or infections recurring, on average, at least once every six weeks per 12-month period 100%
  - Requiring intermittent myeloid growth factors (granulocyte colony-stimulating factor (G-CSF) or granulocyte-macrophage colony-stimulating factor (GM-CSF) or continuous immunosuppressive therapy such as cyclosporine to maintain absolute neutrophil count (ANC) greater than 500/microliter (µl) but less than 1000/µl; or infections recurring, on average, at least once every three months per 12-month period 60%
  - Requiring intermittent myeloid growth factors to maintain ANC greater than 1000/µl; or infections recurring, on average, at least once per 12-month period but less than once every three months per 12-month period 30%
  - Requiring continuous medication (e.g., antibiotics) for control; or requiring intermittent use of a myeloid growth factor to maintain ANC greater than or equal to 1500/µl 10%

- Note: The 100 percent rating for bone marrow transplant shall be assigned as of the date of hospital admission and shall continue with a mandatory VA examination six months following hospital discharge.

Rating

- **7703** Leukemia (except for chronic myelogenous leukemia):
  - With there is active disease or during a treatment phase............................ 100%
  - Otherwise rate residuals under the appropriate diagnostic code(s).
  - Chronic lymphocytic leukemia or monoclonal B-cell lymphocytosis (MBL), asymptomatic, Rai Stage 0 .... 0%.

  - Note (1): The 100 percent rating shall continue beyond the cessation of any surgical, radiation therapy, antineoplastic chemotherapy, or other therapeutic procedures. Six months after discontinuance of such treatment, the appropriate disability rating shall be determined by mandatory VA examination. If there has been no recurrence, rate on residuals.
  - Note (2): Evaluate symptomatic chronic lymphocytic leukemia that is at Rai Stage I, II, III, or IV the same as any other leukemia evaluated under this diagnostic code.
  - Note (3): Evaluate the residuals of leukemia or leukemia therapy under the appropriate diagnostic code(s). Myeloproliferative Disorders: (Diagnostic Codes 7704, 7718, 7719).

- **7704** Polycythemia vera:
  - Requiring peripheral blood or bone marrow stem-cell transplant or chemotherapy (including myelosuppressants) for the purpose of ameliorating the symptom burden 100%
  - Requiring phlebotomy 6 or more times per 12-month period or molecularly targeted therapy for the purpose of controlling RBC count 60%
  - Requiring phlebotomy 4-5 times per 12-month period, or if requiring continuous biologic therapy or myelosuppressive agents, to include interferon, to maintain platelets <200,000 or white blood cells (WBC) <12,000 .... 30%
  - Requiring phlebotomy 3 or fewer times per 12-month period or if requiring biologic therapy or interferon on an intermittent basis as needed to maintain all blood values at reference range levels.......................... 10%

  - Note (1): Rate complications such as hypertension, gout, stroke or thrombotic disease separately.
  - Note (2): If the condition undergoes leukemic transformation, evaluate as leukemia under diagnostic code 7703.
  - Note (3): A 100 percent evaluation shall be assigned as of the date of hospital admission for peripheral blood or bone marrow stem cell transplant; or during the period of treatment with chemotherapy (including myelosuppressants). Six months following hospital discharge or, in the case of chemotherapy treatment, six months after completion of treatment, the appropriate disability rating shall be determined by mandatory VA examination.

- 7705   Immune thrombocytopenia:
  - Requiring chemotherapy for chronic refractory thrombocytopenia;
  or a platelet count 30,000 or below despite treatment 100%
  - Requiring immunosuppressive therapy; or for a platelet count higher
  than 30,000 but not higher than 50,000, with history of hospitalization
  because of severe bleeding requiring intravenous immune globulin,
  high-dose parenteral corticosteroids, and platelet transfusions 70%
  - Platelet count higher than 30,000 but not higher than 50,000, with
  either immune thrombocytopenia or mild mucous membrane
  bleeding which requires oral corticosteroid therapy or intravenous
  immune globulin 30%
  - Platelet count higher than 30,000 but not higher than 50,000,
  not requiring treatment 10%
  - Platelet count above 50,000 and asymptomatic; or for immune
  thrombocytopenia in remission 0%
  - Note (1): Separately evaluate splenectomy under diagnostic code 7706 and
  combine with an evaluation under this diagnostic code.
  - Note (2): A 100 percent evaluation shall continue beyond the cessation of
  chemotherapy. Six months after discontinuance of such treatment, the appropriate
  disability rating shall be determined by mandatory VA examination.

- 7706   Splenectomy: 20%

  - Note: Separately rate complications such as systemic infections with encapsulated
  bacteria.

- 7707   Spleen, injury of, healed:
  - Rate for any residuals.

- 7709   Hodgkin's lymphoma:
  - With active disease or during a treatment phase 100%

  - Note: The 100 percent rating shall continue beyond the cessation of any surgical
  therapy, radiation therapy, antineoplastic chemotherapy or other therapeutic
  procedures. Six months after discontinuance of such treatment, the appropriate
  disability rating shall be determined by mandatory VA examination. If there has
  been no local recurrence or metastasis, rate on residuals under the appropriate
  diagnostic code(s).

- 7710   Adenitis, tuberculous, active or inactive:
  - VA will rate and determine which is appropriate.

- 7712 Multiple myeloma:
  - Symptomatic multiple myeloma 100%
  - Asymptomatic, smoldering, or monoclonal gammopathy of
  Undetermined significance (MGUS) 0%

  - Note (1): Current validated biomarkers of symptomatic multiple myeloma and asymptomatic multiple myeloma, smoldering, or monoclonal gammopathy of undetermined significance (MGUS) are acceptable for the diagnosis of multiple myeloma as defined by the American Society of Hematology (ASH) and International Myeloma Working Group (IMWG).
  - Note (2): The 100 percent evaluation shall continue for five years after the diagnosis of symptomatic multiple myeloma, at which time the appropriate disability evaluation shall be determined by mandatory VA examination.

- 7714 Sickle cell anemia:
  - With at least 4 or more painful episodes per 12-month period, occurring in skin, joints, bones, or any major organs, caused by hemolysis and sickling of red blood cells, with anemia, thrombosis, and infarction, with residual symptoms precluding even light manual labor 100%
  - With 3 painful episodes per 12-month period or with symptoms precluding other than light manual labor 60%
  - With 1 or 2 painful episodes per 12-month period 30%
  - Asymptomatic, established case in remission, but with identifiable organ impairment 10%

  Note: Sickle cell trait alone, without a history of directly attributable pathological findings, is not a ratable disability. Cases of symptomatic sickle cell trait will be forwarded to the Director, Compensation Service, for consideration.

- 7715 Non-Hodgkin's lymphoma:
  - When there is active disease, during treatment phase, or with indolent and non-contiguous phase of low-grade NHL 100%

  - Note: A 100 percent evaluation shall continue beyond the cessation of any surgical therapy, radiation therapy, antineoplastic chemotherapy, or other therapeutic procedures. Two years after discontinuance of such treatment, the appropriate disability rating shall be determined by mandatory VA examination. If there has been no recurrence, rate on residuals under the appropriate diagnostic code(s).

- 7716   Aplastic anemia:
  - Requiring peripheral blood or bone marrow stem cell transplant;
  or requiring transfusion of platelets or red cells, on average, at least
  once every six weeks per 12-month period; or infections recurring,
  on average, at least once every six weeks per 12-month period 100%
  - Requiring transfusion of platelets or red cells, on average, at least once
  every three months per 12-month period; or infections recurring,
  on average, at least once every three months per 12-month period;
  or using continuous therapy with immunosuppressive agent or
  newer platelet stimulating factors 60%
  - Requiring transfusion of platelets or red cells, on average, at least
  once per 12-month period; or infections recurring, on average,
  at least once per 12-month period 30%
  - Note (1): A 100 percent evaluation for peripheral blood or bone marrow stem cell
  transplant shall be assigned as of the date of hospital admission and shall continue
  with a mandatory VA examination six months following hospital discharge.
  - Note (2): The term "newer platelet stimulating factors" includes medication,
  factors, or other agents approved by the United States Food and Drug
  Administration.

- 7717   AL amyloidosis (primary amyloidosis) 100%

- 7718   Essential thrombocythemia and primary myelofibrosis:
  - Requiring either continuous myelosuppressive therapy or, for
  six months following hospital admission, peripheral blood or bone
  marrow stem cell transplant, or chemotherapy, or interferon treatment 100%
  - Requiring continuous or intermittent myelosuppressive therapy, or
  chemotherapy, or interferon treatment to maintain platelet
  count <500×10^9/L 70%
  - Requiring continuous or intermittent myelosuppressive therapy, or
  chemotherapy, or interferon treatment to maintain platelet count
  of 200,000-400,000, or white blood cell (WBC) count of 4,000-10,000 .... 30%
  - Asymptomatic.. 0%
  - Note (1): If the condition undergoes leukemic transformation, evaluate as
  leukemia under diagnostic code 7703.
  - Note (2): A 100 percent evaluation shall be assigned as of the date of hospital
  admission for peripheral blood or bone marrow stem cell transplant; or during the
  period of treatment with chemotherapy (including myelosuppressants). Six months
  following hospital discharge or, in the case of chemotherapy treatment, six months
  after completion of treatment, the appropriate disability rating shall be determined
  by mandatory VA examination.

- 7719   Chronic myelogenous leukemia (CML) (chronic myeloid leukemia or chronic granulocytic leukemia):
  - Requiring peripheral blood or bone marrow stem cell transplant, or continuous myelosuppressive or immunosuppressive therapy treatment 100%
  - Requiring intermittent myelosuppressive therapy, or molecularly targeted therapy with tyrosine kinase inhibitors, or interferon treatment when not in apparent remission 60%
  - In apparent remission on continuous molecularly targeted therapy with tyrosine kinase inhibitors 30%
  - Note (1): If the condition undergoes leukemic transformation, evaluate as leukemia under diagnostic code 7703.
  - Note (2): A 100 percent evaluation shall be assigned as of the date of hospital admission for peripheral blood or bone marrow stem cell transplant; or during the period of treatment with chemotherapy (including myelosuppressants). Six months following hospital discharge or, in the case of chemotherapy treatment, six months after completion of treatment, the appropriate disability rating shall be determined by mandatory VA examination.

- 7720   Iron deficiency anemia:
  - Requiring intravenous iron infusions 4 or more times per 12-month period 30%
  - Requiring intravenous iron infusions at least 1 time but less than 4 times per 12-month period, or requiring continuous treatment with oral supplementation 10%
  - Asymptomatic or requiring treatment only by dietary modification 0%
  - Note: Do not evaluate iron deficiency anemia due to blood loss under this diagnostic code. Evaluate iron deficiency anemia due to blood loss under the criteria for the condition causing the blood loss.

- 7721   Folic acid deficiency:
  - Requiring continuous treatment with high-dose oral supplementation 10%
  - Asymptomatic or requiring treatment only by dietary modification 0%

- 7722   Pernicious anemia and Vitamin B_{12} deficiency anemia:
  - For initial diagnosis requiring transfusion due to severe anemia, or if there are signs or symptoms related to central nervous system impairment, such as encephalopathy, myelopathy, or severe peripheral neuropathy, requiring parenteral B_{12} therapy... 100%
  - Requiring continuous treatment with Vitamin B_{12} injections, Vitamin B_{12} sublingual or high-dose oral tablets, or Vitamin B_{12} nasal spray or gel... 10%

- Note: A 100 percent evaluation for pernicious anemia and Vitamin B_{12} deficiency shall be assigned as of the date of the initial diagnosis requiring transfusion due to severe anemia or parenteral B_{12} therapy and shall continue with a mandatory VA examination six months following hospital discharge or cessation of parenteral B_{12} therapy. Thereafter, evaluate at 10 percent and separately evaluate any residual effects of pernicious anemia, such as neurologic involvement causing peripheral neuropathy, myelopathy, dementia, or related gastrointestinal residuals, under the most appropriate diagnostic code.

Rating

- 7723   Acquired hemolytic anemia:
  - Requiring a bone marrow transplant or continuous intravenous or immunosuppressive therapy (e.g., prednisone, Cytoxan, azathioprine, or rituximab) 100%
  - Requiring immunosuppressive medication 4 or more times per 12-month period.. 60%
  - Requiring at least 2 but less than 4 courses of immunosuppressive therapy per 12-month period.. 30%
  - Requiring one course of immunosuppressive therapy per 12-month period... 10%
  - Asymptomatic... 0%
  - Note (1): A 100 percent evaluation for bone marrow transplant shall be assigned as of the date of hospital admission and shall continue for six months after hospital discharge with a mandatory VA examination six months following hospital discharge.
  - Note (2): Separately evaluate splenectomy under diagnostic code 7706 and combine with an evaluation under diagnostic code 7723.

- 7724   Solitary plasmacytoma:
  - Solitary plasmacytoma, when there is active disease or during a treatment phase 100%
  - Note (1): A 100 percent evaluation shall continue beyond the cessation of any surgical therapy, radiation therapy, antineoplastic chemotherapy, or other therapeutic procedures (including autologous stem cell transplantation). Six months after discontinuance of such treatment, the appropriate disability rating shall be determined by mandatory VA examination. If there has been no recurrence, rate residuals under the appropriate diagnostic codes.
  - Note (2): Rate a solitary plasmacytoma that has developed into multiple myeloma as symptomatic multiple myeloma.
  - Note (3): Rate residuals of plasma cell dysplasia (e.g., thrombosis) and adverse effects of medical treatment (e.g., neuropathy) under the appropriate diagnostic codes.

- 7725   Myelodysplastic syndromes:
  - Requiring peripheral blood or bone marrow stem cell transplant; or requiring chemotherapy 100%
  - Requiring 4 or more blood or platelet transfusions per 12-month period; or infections requiring hospitalization 3 or more times per 12-month period... 60%
  - Requiring at least 1 but no more than 3 blood or platelet transfusions per 12-month period; infections requiring hospitalization at least 1 but no more than 2 times per 12-month period; or requiring biologic therapy on an ongoing basis or erythropoiesis stimulating agent (ESA) for 12 weeks or less per 12-month period.. 30%
  - Note (1): If the condition progresses to leukemia, evaluate as leukemia under diagnostic code 7703.
  - Note (2): A 100 percent evaluation shall be assigned as of the date of hospital admission for peripheral blood or bone marrow stem cell transplant, or during the period of treatment with chemotherapy, and shall continue with a mandatory VA examination six months following hospital discharge or, in the case of chemotherapy treatment, six months after completion of treatment. If there has been no recurrence, residuals will be rated under the appropriate diagnostic codes.

CHAPTER 13

THE SKIN

Quick Reference:

CODE	CATEGORY	PAGE
7828	Acne	168
7829	Chloracne	168
7830	Scarring alopecia	168
7831	Alopecia areata	168
7832	Hyperhidrosis	168
7833	Malignant melanoma	169

- A veteran whose scars were rated by VA under a prior version of diagnostic codes 7800, 7801, 7802, 7803, 7804, or 7805, as in effect before October 23, 2008, may request review under diagnostic codes 7800, 7801, 7802, 7804, and 7805, irrespective of whether his or her disability has worsened since the last review. VA will review that veteran's disability rating to determine whether the veteran may be entitled to a higher disability rating under diagnostic codes 7800, 7801, 7802, 7804, and 7805. A request for review pursuant to this rulemaking will be treated as a claim for an increased rating for purposes of determining the effective date of an increased rating awarded as a result of such review; however, in no case will the award be effective before October 23, 2008.

Rating

- 7800 Burn scar(s) of the head, face, or neck; scar(s) of the head, face, or neck due to other causes; or other disfigurement of the head, face, or neck:
  - With visible or palpable tissue loss and either gross distortion or asymmetry of three or more features or paired sets of features (nose, chin, forehead, eyes (including eyelids), ears (auricles), cheeks, lips), or; with six or more characteristics of disfigurement 80%
  - With visible or palpable tissue loss and either gross distortion or asymmetry of two features or paired sets of features (nose, chin, forehead, eyes (including eyelids), ears (auricles), cheeks, lips), or; with four or five characteristics of disfigurement 50%
  - With visible or palpable tissue loss and either gross distortion or asymmetry of one feature or paired set of features (nose, chin, forehead, eyes (including eyelids), ears (auricles), cheeks, lips), or; with two or three characteristics of disfigurement 30%
  With one characteristic of disfigurement 10%
  -Note (1): The 8 characteristics of disfigurement, for purposes of evaluation are:
  - Scar 5 or more inches (13 or more cm.) in length.
  - Scar at least one-quarter inch (0.6 cm.) wide at widest part.
  - Surface contour of scar elevated or depressed on palpation.
  - Scar adherent to underlying tissue.
  - Skin hypo-or hyper-pigmented in an area exceeding six square inches (39 sq. cm.).
  - Skin texture abnormal (irregular, atrophic, shiny, scaly, etc.) in an area exceeding six square inches (39 sq. cm.).
  - Underlying soft tissue missing in an area exceeding six square inches (39 sq. cm.).

- Skin indurated and inflexible in an area exceeding six square inches (39 sq. cm.).

-Note (2): Rate tissue loss of the auricle under DC 6207 (loss of auricle) and anatomical loss of the eye under DC 6061 (anatomical loss of both eyes) or DC 6063 (anatomical loss of one eye), as appropriate.

-Note (3): Take into consideration unretouched color photographs when evaluating under these criteria.

-Note (4): Separately evaluate disabling effects other than disfigurement that are associated with individual scar(s) of the head, face, or neck, such as pain, instability, and residuals of associated muscle or nerve injury, under the appropriate diagnostic code(s) and combine the evaluation(s) with the evaluation assigned under this diagnostic code.

-Note (5): The characteristic(s) of disfigurement may be caused by one scar or by multiple scars; the characteristic(s) required to assign a particular evaluation need not be caused by a single scar in order to assign that evaluation.

Rating

- 7801   Burn scar(s) or scar(s) due to other causes, not of the head, face, or neck, that are deep and nonlinear:
  - Area or areas of 144 square inches (929 sq. cm.) or greater 40%
  - Area or areas of at least 72 square inches (465 sq. cm.) but less than 144 square inches (929 sq. cm.) 30%
  - Area or areas of at least 12 square inches (77 sq. cm.) but less than 72 square inches (465 sq. cm.) 20%
  - Area or areas of at least 6 square inches (39 sq. cm.) but less than
  - 12 square inches (77 sq. cm.) 10%

Note (1): For the purposes of DCs 7801 and 7802, the six (6) zones of the body are defined as each extremity, anterior trunk, and posterior trunk. The midaxillary line divides the anterior trunk from the posterior trunk.

Note (2): A separate evaluation may be assigned for each affected zone of the body under this diagnostic code if there are multiple scars, or a single scar, affecting multiple zones of the body. Combine the separate evaluations. Alternatively, if a higher evaluation would result from adding the areas affected from multiple zones of the body, a single evaluation may also be assigned under this diagnostic code.

161

- 7802   Burn scar(s) or scar(s) due to other causes, not of the head, face, or neck, that are superficial and nonlinear:
  - Area or areas of 144 square inches (929 sq. cm.) or greater 10%

  - Note (1): For the purposes of DCs 7801 and 7802, the six (6) zones of the body are defined as each extremity, anterior trunk, and posterior trunk. The midaxillary line divides the anterior trunk from the posterior trunk.

  - Note (2): A separate evaluation may be assigned for each affected zone of the body under this diagnostic code if there are multiple scars, or a single scar, affecting multiple zones of the body. Combine the separate evaluations. Alternatively, if a higher evaluation would result from adding the areas affected from multiple zones of the body, a single evaluation may also be assigned under this diagnostic code.

- 7804   Scar(s), unstable or painful:
  - Five or more scars that are unstable or painful.. 30%
  - Three or four scars that are unstable or painful 20%
  - One or two scars that are unstable or painful 10%

  - Note (1): An unstable scar is one where, for any reason, there is frequent loss of covering of skin over the scar.

  - Note (2): If one or more scars are both unstable and painful, add 10 percent to the evaluation that is based on the total number of unstable or painful scars.

  - Note (3): Scars evaluated under diagnostic codes 7800, 7801, 7802, or 7805 may also receive an evaluation under this diagnostic code, when applicable.

- 7805   Scars, other (including linear scars) and other effects of scars evaluated under diagnostic codes 7800, 7801, 7802, and 7804:
  - Evaluate any disabling effect(s) not considered in a rating provided under diagnostic codes 7800-04 under an appropriate diagnostic code.

General Rating Formula for The Skin for diagnostic codes 7806, 7809, 7813-7816, 7820-7822, and 7824:

Rating

o At least one of the following:
- Characteristic lesions involving more than 40 percent of the entire body or more than 40 percent of exposed areas affected; or
- Constant or near-constant systemic therapy including, but not limited to, corticosteroids, phototherapy, retinoids, biologics, photochemotherapy, psoralen with long-wave ultraviolet-A light (PUVA), or other immunosuppressive drugs required over the past 12-month period..... 60%

o At least one of the following:
- Characteristic lesions involving 20 to 40 percent of the entire body or 20 to 40 percent of exposed areas affected; or Systemic therapy including, but not limited to, corticosteroids, phototherapy, retinoids, biologics, photochemotherapy, PUVA, or other immunosuppressive drugs required for a total duration of 6 weeks or more, but not constantly, over the past 12-month period.. 30%

o At least one of the following:
- Characteristic lesions involving at least 5 percent, but less than 20 percent, of the entire body affected; or
- At least 5 percent, but less than 20 percent, of exposed areas affected; or
- Intermittent systemic therapy including, but not limited to, corticosteroids, phototherapy, retinoids, biologics, photochemotherapy, PUVA, or other immunosuppressive drugs required for a total duration of less than 6 weeks over the past 12-month period 10%

o No more than topical therapy required over the past 12-month period and at least one of the following:
- Characteristic lesions involving less than 5 percent of the entire body affected; or
- Characteristic lesions involving less than 5 percent of exposed areas affected
- Or rate as disfigurement of the head, face, or neck (DC 7800) or scars (DCs 7801, 7802, 7804, or 7805), depending upon the predominant disability. This rating instruction does not apply to DC 7824 .... 0%

163

- 7806 Dermatitis or eczema:
  - Evaluate under the General Rating Formula for the Skin.

- 7807 American (New World) leishmaniasis (mucocutaneous, espundia):
  - Rate as disfigurement of the head, face, or neck (DC 7800), scars (DC's 7801, 7802, 7803, 7804, or 7805), or dermatitis (DC 7806), depending upon the predominant disability.
  - Note: Evaluate non-cutaneous (visceral) leishmaniasis under DC 6301 (visceral leishmaniasis).

- 7808 Old World leishmaniasis (cutaneous, Oriental sore):
  - Rate as disfigurement of the head, face, or neck (DC 7800), scars (DC's 7801, 7802, 7803, 7804, or 7805), or dermatitis (DC 7806), depending upon the predominant disability.
  - Note: Evaluate non-cutaneous (visceral) leishmaniasis under DC 6301 (visceral leishmaniasis).

- 7809 Discoid lupus erythematosus:
  - Evaluate under the General Rating Formula for the Skin.
  - Note: Do not combine with ratings under DC 6350.

- 7811 Tuberculosis luposa (lupus vulgaris), active or inactive:
  - VA will rate and determine which is appropriate.

- 7813 Dermatophytosis (ringworm: of body, tinea corporis; of head, tinea capitis; of feet, tinea pedis; of beard area, tinea barbae; of nails, tinea unguium (onychomycosis); of inguinal area (jock itch), tinea cruris; tinea vesicolor):
  - Evaluate under the General Rating Formula for the Skin.

- 7815 Bullous disorders (including pemphigus vulgaris, pemphigus foliaceous, bullous pemphigoid, dermatitis herpetiformis, epidermolysis bullosa acquisita, benign chronic familial pemphigus (Hailey-Hailey), and porphyri cutanea tarda):
  - Evaluate under the General Rating Formula for the Skin
  - Note. Rate complications and residuals of mucosal involvement (ocular, oral, gastrointestinal, respiratory, or genitourinary) separately under the appropriate diagnostic code.

- 7816 Psoriasis:
  - Evaluate under the General Rating Formula for the Skin
  - Note. Rate complications such as psoriatic arthritis and other clinical manifestations (*e.g.,* oral mucosa, nails) separately under the appropriate diagnostic code.

- 7817 Erythroderma:
  - Generalized involvement of the skin with systemic manifestations (such as fever, weight loss, or hypoproteinemia) AND one of the following 100%
  - Constant or near-constant systemic therapy such as therapeutic doses of corticosteroids, other immunosuppressive drugs, retinoids, PUVA (psoralen with long-wave ultraviolet-A light), UVB (ultraviolet-B light) treatments, biologics, or electron beam therapy required over the past 12 month period; or
  - No current treatment due to a documented history of treatment failure with 2 or more treatment regimens 100%
  - Generalized involvement of the skin without systemic manifestations and one of the following:
  - Constant or near-constant systemic therapy such as therapeutic doses of corticosteroids, other immunosuppressive drugs, retinoids, PUVA, UVB treatments, biologics, or electron beam therapy required over the past 12-month period; or
  - No current treatment due to a documented history of treatment failure with 1 treatment regimen 60%
  - Any extent of involvement of the skin, and any of the following therapies required for a total duration of 6 weeks or more, but not constantly, over the past 12-month period: systemic therapy such as therapeutic doses of corticosteroids, other immunosuppressive drugs, retinoids, PUVA, UVB treatments, biologics, or electron beam therapy 30%
  - Any extent of involvement of the skin, and any of the following therapies required for a total duration of less than 6 weeks over the past 12-month period: systemic therapy such as therapeutic doses of corticosteroids, other immunosuppressive drugs, retinoids, PUVA, UVB treatments, biologics, or electron beam therapy 10%
  - Any extent of involvement of the skin, and no more than topical therapy required over the past 12-month period 0%
  - Note: Treatment failure is defined as either disease progression, or less than a 25 percent reduction in the extent and severity of disease after four weeks of prescribed therapy, as documented by medical records.

- 7818   Malignant skin neoplasms (other than malignant melanoma):
  - Rate as disfigurement of the head, face, or neck (DC 7800), scars (DC's 7801, 7802, 7803, 7804, or7805), or impairment of function.
  Note: If a skin malignancy requires therapy that is comparable to that used for systemic malignancies, i.e., systemic chemotherapy, X-ray therapy more extensive than to the skin, or surgery more extensive than wide local excision, a 100-percent evaluation will be assigned from the date of onset of treatment, and will continue, with a mandatory VA examination six months following the completion of such antineoplastic treatment, and any change in evaluation based upon that or any subsequent examination will be subject review. If there has been no local recurrence or metastasis, evaluation will then be made on residuals. If treatment is confined to the skin, the provisions for a 100-percent evaluation do not apply.

Rating

- 7819   Benign skin neoplasms:
  - Rate as disfigurement of the head, face, or neck (DC 7800), scars (DC's 7801, 7802, 7803, 7804, or 7805), or impairment of function.

- 7820   Infections of the skin not listed elsewhere (including bacterial, fungal, viral, treponemal and parasitic diseases):
  - Evaluate under the General Rating Formula for the Skin.

- 7821   Cutaneous manifestations of collagen-vascular diseases not listed elsewhere (including scleroderma, calcinosis cutis, and dermatomyositis):
  - Evaluate under the General Rating Formula for the Skin.

- 7822   Papulosquamous disorders not listed elsewhere (including lichen planus, large or small plaque parapsoriasis, pityriasis lichenoides et varioliformis acuta (PLEVA) lymphomatoid papulosus, mycosis fungoids and pityriasis rubra pilaris (PRP)):
  - Evaluate under the General Rating Formula for the Skin.

- 7823   Vitiligo:
  - With exposed areas affected 10%
  - With no exposed areas affected 0%

- 7824   Diseases of keratinization (including icthyoses, Darier's disease, and palmoplantar keratoderma):
  - Evaluate under the General Rating Formula for the Skin

- 7825 Chronic urticaria:
  - For the purposes of this diagnostic code, chronic urticaria is defined as continuous urticaria at least twice per week, off treatment, for a period of six weeks or more.
  - Chronic refractory urticaria that requires third line treatment for control (e.g., plasmapheresis, immunotherapy, immunosuppressives) due to ineffectiveness with first and second line treatments 60%
  - Chronic urticaria that requires second line treatment (e.g., corticosteroids, sympathomimetics, leukotriene inhibitors, neutrophil inhibitors, thyroid hormone) for control 30%
  - Chronic urticaria that requires first line treatment (antihistamines) for control 10%

- 7826 Vasculitis, primary cutaneous:
  - Persistent documented vasculitis episodes refractory to continuous immunosuppressive therapy 60%
  - All of the following 30%
  - Recurrent documented vasculitic episodes occurring four or more times over the past 12-month period; and
  - Requiring intermittent systemic immunosuppressive therapy for control 30%
  - At least one of the following: 10%
  - Recurrent documented vasculitic episodes occurring one to three times over the past 12-month period, and requiring intermittent systemic immunosuppressive therapy for control; or
  - Without recurrent documented vasculitic episodes but requiring continuous systemic medication for control
  - Or rate as disfigurement of the head, face, or neck (DC 7800) or scars (DCs 7801, 7802, 7804, or 7805), depending upon the predominant disability.

- 7827 Erythema multiforme; Toxic epidermal necrolysis:
  - Recurrent mucosal, palmar, or plantar involvement impairing mastication, use of hands, or ambulation occurring four or more times over the past 12-month period despite ongoing immunosuppressive therapy 60%
  - All of the following: 30%
  - Recurrent mucosal, palmar, or plantar involvement not impairing mastication, use of hands, or ambulation, occurring four or more times over the past 12-month period; andrequiring intermittent systemic therapy
  - At least one of the following: 10%
  - One to three episodes of mucosal, palmar, or plantar involvement not impairing mastication, use of hands, or ambulation, occurring over the past 12-month period AND requiring intermittent systemic therapy; or
  - Without recurrent episodes, but requiring continuous systemic medication for control
  - Or rate as disfigurement of the head, face, or neck (DC 7800) or scars (DCs 7801, 7802, 7804, or 7805), depending upon the predominant disability
  - Note: For this DC only, systemic therapy may consist of one or more of the following treatment: immunosuppressives, antihistamines, or sympathomimetics.

- 7828   Acne:
  - Deep acne (deep inflamed nodules and pus-filled cysts) affecting 40 percent or more of the face and neck 30%
  - Deep acne (deep inflamed nodules and pus-filled cysts) affecting less than 40 percent of the face and neck, or; deep acne other than on the face and neck.. 10%
  - Superficial acne (comedones, papules, pustules) of any extent 0%
  Or rate as disfigurement of the head, face, or neck (DC 7800) or scars (DC's 7801, 7802, 7803, 7804, or 7805), depending upon the predominant disability.

- 7829   Chloracne:
  - Deep acne (deep inflamed nodules and pus-filled cysts) affecting 40 percent or more of the face and neck 30%
  -Deep acne (deep inflamed nodules and pus-filled cysts) affecting the intertriginous areas (the axilla of the arm, the anogenital region, skin folds of the breasts, or between digits) 20%
  - Deep acne (deep inflamed nodules and pus-filled cysts) affecting less than 40 percent of the face and neck; or deep acne affecting non-intertriginous areas of the body (other than the face and neck) 10%
  -Superficial acne (comedones, papules, pustules) of any extent 0%
  -Or rate as disfigurement of the head, face, or neck (DC 7800) or scars (DC's 7801, 7802, 7803, 7804, or 7805), depending upon the predominant disability.

- 7830   Scarring alopecia:
  - Affecting more than 40 percent of the scalp.. 20%
  - Affecting 20 to 40 percent of the scalp... 10%
  - Affecting less than 20 percent of the scalp.. 0%

- 7831   Alopecia areata:
  - With loss of all body hair 10%
  - With loss of hair limited to scalp and face 0%

- 7832   Hyperhidrosis:
  - Unable to handle paper or tools because of moisture, and unresponsive to therapy 30%
  - Able to handle paper or tools after therapy 0%

- 7833   Malignant melanoma:
  - Rate as scars (DC's 7801, 7802, 7803, 7804, or 7805), disfigurement of the head, face, or neck (DC 7800), or impairment of function (under the appropriate body system).

  - Note: If a skin malignancy requires therapy that is comparable to that used for systemic malignancies, i.e., systemic chemotherapy, X-ray therapy more extensive than to the skin, or surgery more extensive than wide local excision, a 100-percent evaluation will be assigned from the date of onset of treatment, and will continue, with a mandatory VA examination six months following the completion of such antineoplastic treatment, and any change in evaluation based upon that or any subsequent examination will be subject VA review. If there has been no local recurrence or metastasis, evaluation will then be made on residuals. If treatment is confined to the skin, the provisions for a 100-percent evaluation do not apply.

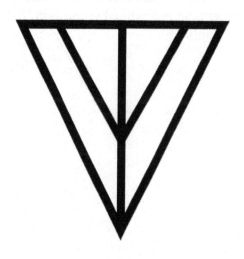

THIS PAGE LEFT INTENTIONALLY BLANK

CHAPTER 14

THE ENDOCRINE SYSTEM

Quick Reference:

CODE	CATEGORY	PAGE
7900	Hyperthyroidism, including, but not limited to, Graves' disease	171
7901	Thyroid enlargement, toxic	171
7902	Thyroid enlargement, nontoxic	172
7903	Hypothyroidism	172
7904	Hyperparathyroidism	172-3
7905	Hypoparathyroidism	173
7906	Thyroiditis	173
7907	Cushing's syndrome	173
7908	Acromegaly	173
7909	Diabetes insipidus	174
7911	Addison's disease (adrenocortical insufficiency)	174
7912	Polyglandular syndrome (multiple endocrine neoplasia, autoimmune polyglandular syndrome)	174
7913	Diabetes mellitus	175
7914	Neoplasm, malignant, any specified part of the endocrine system	175
7915	Neoplasm, benign, any specified part of the endocrine system	175
7916	Hyperpituitarism (prolactin secreting pituitary dysfunction)	175
7917	Hyperaldosteronism (benign or malignant)	175
7918	Pheochromocytoma (benign or malignant)	175
7919	C-cell hyperplasia of the thyroid	176

Rating

- 7900 Hyperthyroidism, including, but not limited to, Graves' disease:
  - For six months after initial diagnosis 30%
  - Thereafter, rate residuals of disease or complications of medical treatment within the appropriate diagnostic code(s) within the appropriate body system.
  - Note (1): If hyperthyroid cardiovascular or cardiac disease is present, separately evaluate under DC 7008 (hyperthyroid heart disease).
  - Note (2): Separately evaluate eye involvement occurring as a manifestation of Graves' Disease as diplopia (DC 6090); impairment of central visual acuity (DCs 6061-6066); or under the most appropriate DCs.

- 7901 Thyroid enlargement, toxic:
  - Note (1): Evaluate symptoms of hyperthyroidism under DC 7900, hyperthyroidism, including, but not limited to, Graves' disease.
  - Note (2): If disfigurement of the neck is present due to thyroid disease or enlargement, separately evaluate under DC 7800 (burn scar(s) of the head, face, or neck; scar(s) of the head, face, or neck due to other causes; or other disfigurement of the head, face, or neck).

- 7902   Thyroid enlargement, non-toxic:
    - Note (1): Evaluate symptoms due to pressure on adjacent organs (such as the trachea, larynx, or esophagus) under the appropriate diagnostic code(s) within the appropriate body system.
    - Note (2): If disfigurement of the neck is present due to thyroid disease or enlargement, separately evaluate under DC 7800 (burn scar(s) of the head, face, or neck; scar(s) of the head, face, or neck due to other causes; or other disfigurement of the head, face, or neck).

- 7903   Hypothyroidism:
    o   Hypothyroidism manifesting as myxedema (cold intolerance, muscular weakness, cardiovascular involvement (including, but not limited to hypotension, bradycardia, and pericardial effusion), and mental disturbance (including, but not limited to dementia, slowing of thought and depression)).. 100%
    - Note (1): This evaluation shall continue for six months beyond the date that an examining physician has determined crisis stabilization. Thereafter, the residual effects of hypothyroidism shall be rated under the appropriate diagnostic code(s) within the appropriate body system(s) (*e.g.,* eye, digestive, and mental disorders).

    o   Hypothyroidism without myxedema: 30%
    - Note (2): This evaluation shall continue for six months after initial diagnosis. Thereafter, rate residuals of disease or medical treatment under the most appropriate diagnostic code(s) under the appropriate body system (*e.g.,* eye, digestive, mental disorders).
    - Note (3): If eye involvement, such as exophthalmos, corneal ulcer, blurred vision, or diplopia, is also present due to thyroid disease, also separately evaluate under the appropriate diagnostic code(s) in Schedule of Ratings—Eye (such as diplopia (DC 6090) or impairment of central visual acuity (DCs 6061-6066)).

- 7904   Hyperparathyroidism:
    - For six months from date of discharge following surgery............................ 100%
    - Note (1): After six months, rate on residuals under the appropriate diagnostic code(s) within the appropriate body system(s) based on a VA examination.
    o   Hypercalcemia (indicated by at least one of the following: Total Ca greater than 12 mg/dL (3-3.5 mmol/L), Ionized Ca greater than 5.6 mg/dL (2-2.5 mmol/L), creatinine clearance less than 60 mL/min, bone mineral density T-score less than 2.5 SD (below mean) at any site or previous fragility fracture): 60%
    - Note (2): Where surgical intervention is indicated, this evaluation shall continue until the day of surgery, at which time the provisions pertaining to a 100-percent evaluation shall apply.
    - Note (3): Where surgical intervention is not indicated, this evaluation shall continue for six months after pharmacologic treatment begins. After six months, rate on residuals under the appropriate diagnostic code(s) within the appropriate body system(s) based on a VA examination.

- 7904 Hyperparathyroidism (Continued):
  - Symptoms such as fatigue, anorexia, nausea, or constipation that occur despite surgery; or in individuals who are not candidates for surgery but require continuous medication for control 10%
  - Asymptomatic 0%
  - Note (4): Following surgery or other treatment, evaluate chronic residuals, such as nephrolithiasis (kidney stones), decreased renal function, fractures, vision problems, and cardiovascular complications, under appropriate diagnostic codes.

- 7905 Hypoarathyroidism:
  - For three months after initial diagnosis 100%
  - Thereafter, evaluate chronic residuals, such as nephrolithiasis (kidney stones), cataracts, decreased renal function, and congestive heart failure under the appropriate diagnostic codes.

- 7906 Thyroiditis:
  - With normal thyroid function (euthyroid) 0%
  - Note: Manifesting as hyperthyroidism, evaluate as hyperthyroidism, including, but not limited to, Graves' disease (DC 7900); manifesting as hypothyroidism, evaluate as hypothyroidism (DC 7903).

- 7907 Cushing's syndrome:
  - As active, progressive disease, including areas of osteoporosis, hypertension, and proximal upper and lower extremity muscle wasting that results in inability to rise from squatting position, climb stairs, rise from a deep chair without assistance, or raise arms 100%
  - Proximal upper or lower extremity muscle wasting that results in inability to rise from squatting position, climb stairs, rise from a deep chair without assistance, or raise arms 60%
  - With striae, obesity, moon face, glucose intolerance, and vascular fragility .. 30%
  - Note: The evaluations specifically indicated under this diagnostic code shall continue for six months following initial diagnosis. After six months, rate on residuals under the appropriate diagnostic code(s) within the appropriate body system(s).

- 7908 Acomegaly:
  - Evidence of increased intracranial pressure (such as visual field defect), arthropathy, glucose intolerance, and either hypertension or cardiomegaly 100%
  - Arthropathy, glucose intolerance, and hypertension 60%
  - Enlargement of acral parts or overgrowth of long bones 30%

- 7909 Diabetes insipidus:
  - For three months after initial diagnosis 30%
  - Note: Thereafter, if diabetes insipidus has subsided, rate residuals under the appropriate diagnostic code(s) within the appropriate body system.
  - With persistent polyuria or requiring continuous hormonal therapy 10%

- 7911 Addison's disease (adrenocortical insufficiency):
  - Four or more crises during the past year 60%
  - Three crises during the past year, or; five or more episodes during the past year 40%
  - One or two crises during the past year, or; two to four episodes during the past year, or; weakness and fatigability, or; corticosteroid therapy required for control 20%
  - Note (1): An Addisonian "crisis" consists of the rapid onset of peripheral vascular collapse (with acute hypotension and shock), with findings that may include: anorexia; nausea; vomiting; dehydration; profound weakness; pain in abdomen, legs, and back; fever; apathy, and depressed mentation with possible progression to coma, renal shutdown, and death.
  - Note (2): An Addisonian "episode," for VA purposes, is a less acute and less severe event than an Addisonian crisis and may consist of anorexia, nausea, vomiting, diarrhea, dehydration, weakness, malaise, orthostatic hypotension, or hypoglycemia, but no peripheral vascular collapse.
  - Note (3): Tuberculous Addison's disease will be evaluated as active or inactive tuberculosis. If inactive, these evaluations are not to be combined with the graduated ratings of 50 percent or 30 percent for non-pulmonary tuberculosis. Assign the higher rating.

- 7912 Polyglandular syndrome (multiple endocrine neoplasia, autoimmune polyglandular syndrome):
  - Evaluate according to major manifestations to include, but not limited to, Type I diabetes mellitus, hyperthyroidism, hypothyroidism, hypoparathyroidism, or Addison's disease.

174

- 7913 Diabetes mellitus:
  - Requiring more than one daily injection of insulin, restricted diet, and regulation of activities (avoidance of strenuous occupational and recreational activities) with episodes of ketoacidosis or hypoglycemic reactions requiring at least three hospitalizations per year or weekly visits to a diabetic care provider, plus either progressive loss of weight and strength or complications that would be compensable if separately evaluated 100%
  - Requiring one or more daily injection of insulin, restricted diet, and regulation of activities with episodes of ketoacidosis or hypoglycemic reactions requiring one or two hospitalizations per year or twice a month visits to a diabetic care provider, plus complications that would not be compensable if separately evaluated 60%
  - Requiring one or more daily injection of insulin, restricted diet, and regulation of activities 40%
  - Requiring one or more daily injection of insulin and restricted diet, or; oral hypoglycemic agent and restricted diet 20%
  - Manageable by restricted diet only 10%

  - Note (1): Evaluate compensable complications of diabetes separately unless they are part of the criteria used to support a 100-percent evaluation. Noncompensable complications are considered part of the diabetic process under DC 7913.
  - Note (2): When diabetes mellitus has been conclusively diagnosed, do not request a glucose tolerance test solely for rating purposes.

- 7914 Neoplasm, malignant, any specified part of the endocrine system 100%
  - Note: A rating of 100 percent shall continue beyond the cessation of any surgical, X-ray, antineoplastic chemotherapy or other therapeutic procedure. Six months after discontinuance of such treatment, the appropriate disability rating shall be determined by mandatory VA examination. Any change in evaluation based upon that or any subsequent examination shall be subject to the provisions of this chapter. If there has been no local recurrence or metastasis, rate on residuals.

- 7915 Neoplasm, Neoplasm, benign, any specified part of the endocrine system:
  - Rate as residuals of endocrine dysfunction.

- 7916 Hyperpituitarism (prolactin secreting pituitary dysfunction):
  - Note: Evaluate as malignant or benign neoplasm, as appropriate.

- 7917 Hyperaldosteronism (benign or malignant):
  - Note: Evaluate as malignant or benign neoplasm, as appropriate.

- 7918 Pheochromocytoma (benign or malignant):
  - Note: Evaluate as malignant or benign neoplasm, as appropriate.

- 7919   C-cell hyperplasia of the thyroid:
  - If antineoplastic therapy is required, evaluate as a malignant neoplasm under DC 7914. If a prophylactic thyroidectomy is performed (based upon genetic testing) and antineoplastic therapy is not required, evaluate as hypothyroidism under DC 7903.

CHAPTER 15

NEUROLOGICAL CONDITIONS AND CONVULSIVE DISORDERS

With the exceptions noted, disability from the following diseases and their residuals may be rated from 10 percent to 100 percent in proportion to the impairment of motor, sensory, or mental function. Consider especially psychotic manifestations, complete or partial loss of use of one or more extremities, speech disturbances, impairment of vision, disturbances of gait, tremors, visceral manifestations, etc., referring to the appropriate bodily system of the schedule. With partial loss of use of one or more extremities from neurological lesions, rate by comparison with the mild, moderate, severe, or complete paralysis of peripheral nerves.

Quick Reference:

CODE	CATEGORY	PAGE
ORGANIC DISEASES OF THE CENTRAL NERVOUS SYSTEM		
8000	Encephalitis, epidemic, chronic	180
8002	Brain, new growth of: Malignant	180
8003	Brain, new growth of: Benign	180
8004	Paralysis agitans	180
8005	Bulbar palsy	180
8007	Brain, vessels, embolism of	181
8008	Brain, vessels, thrombosis of	181
8009	Brain, vessels, hemorrhage from	181
8010	Myelitis	181
8011	Poliomyelitis, anterior	181
8012	Hematomyelia	181
8013	Syphilis, cerebrospinal	181
8014	Syphilis, meningovascular	181
8015	Tabes dorsalis	181
8017	Amyotrophic lateral sclerosis	181
8018	Multiple sclerosis	181
8019	Meningitis, cerebrospinal, epidemic	181
8020	Brain, abscess of	181
8021	Spinal cord, new growths of: Malignant	182
8022	Spinal cord, new growths of: Benign	182
8023	Progressive muscular atrophy	182
8024	Syringomyelia	182
8025	Myasthenia gravis	182
8045	Residuals of traumatic brain injury (TBI)	182-3
8046	Cerebral Arteriosclerosis	190
MISCELLANEOUS DISEASES		
8100	Migraine	191
8103	Tic, convulsive	191
8104	Paramyoclonus multiplex (convulsive state, myoclonic type)	191
8105	Chorea, Sydenham's	191

MISCELLANEOUS DISEASES (Continued)		
8106	Chorea, Huntington's	191
8107	Athetosis, acquired	191
8108	Narcolepsy	191
DISEASES OF THE CRANIAL NERVES		
8205	Fifth (trigeminal) cranial nerve, Paralysis of	192
8305	Fifth (trigeminal) cranial nerve, Neuritis	192
8405	Fifth (trigeminal) cranial nerve, Neuralgia	192
8207	Seventh (facial) cranial nerve, Paralysis of	192
8307	Seventh (facial) cranial nerve, Neuritis	192
8407	Seventh (facial) cranial nerve, Neuralgia	192
8209	Ninth (glossopharyngeal) cranial nerve, Paralysis of	192
8309	Ninth (glossopharyngeal) cranial nerve, Neuritis	192
8409	Ninth (glossopharyngeal) cranial nerve, Neuralgia	192
8210	Tenth (pneumogastric, vagus) cranial nerve, Paralysis of	193
8310	Tenth (pneumogastric, vagus) cranial nerve, Neuritis	193
8410	Tenth (pneumogastric, vagus) cranial nerve, Neuralgia	193
8211	Eleventh (spinal accessory, external branch) cranial nerve, Paralysis of	193
8311	Eleventh (spinal accessory, external branch) cranial nerve, Neuritis	193
8411	Eleventh (spinal accessory, external branch) cranial nerve, Neuralgia	193
8212	Twelfth (hypoglossal) cranial nerve, Paralysis of	193
8312	Twelfth (hypoglossal) cranial nerve, Neuritis	193
8412	Twelfth (hypoglossal) cranial nerve, Neuralgia	193
DISEASES OF THE PERIPHERAL NERVES		
8510	Upper radicular group (fifth and sixth cervicals), Paralysis of	194
8610	Upper radicular group (fifth and sixth cervicals), Neuritis	194
8710	Upper radicular group (fifth and sixth cervicals), Neuralgia	194
8511	Middle radicular group, Paralysis of	194
8611	Middle radicular group, Neuritis	194
8711	Middle radicular group, Neuralgia	194
8512	Lower radicular group, Paralysis of	195
8612	Lower radicular group, Neuritis	195
8712	Lower radicular group, Neuralgia	195
8513	All radicular groups, Paralysis of	195
8613	All radicular groups, Neuritis	195
8713	All radicular groups, Neuralgia	195
8514	The musculospiral nerve (radial nerve), Paralysis of	196
8614	The musculospiral nerve (radial nerve), Neuritis	196
8714	The musculospiral nerve (radial nerve), Neuralgia	196
8515	The median nerve, Paralysis of	196
8615	The median nerve, Neuritis	196
8715	The median nerve, Neuralgia	196
8516	The ulnar nerve, Paralysis of	197
8616	The ulnar nerve, Neuritis	197

	DISEASES OF THE PERIPHERAL NERVES (Continued)	
8716	The ulnar nerve, Neuralgia	197
8517	Musculocutaneous nerve, Paralysis of	197
8617	Musculocutaneous nerve, Neuritis	197
8717	Musculocutaneous nerve, Neuralgia	197
8518	Circumflex nerve, Paralysis of	197
8618	Circumflex nerve, Neuritis	197
8718	Circumflex nerve, Neuralgia	197
8519	Long thoracic nerve, Paralysis of	198
8619	Long thoracic nerve, Neuritis	198
8719	Long thoracic nerve, Neuralgia	198
8520	Sciatic nerve, Paralysis of	198
8620	Sciatic nerve, Neuritis	198
8720	Sciatic nerve, Neuralgia	198
8521	External popliteal nerve (common peroneal), Paralysis of	199
8621	External popliteal nerve (common peroneal), Neuritis	199
8721	External popliteal nerve (common peroneal), Neuralgia	199
8522	Musculocutaneous nerve (superficial peroneal), Paralysis of	199
8622	Musculocutaneous nerve (superficial peroneal), Neuritis	199
8722	Musculocutaneous nerve (superficial peroneal), Neuralgia	199
8523	Anterior tibial nerve (deep peroneal), Paralysis of	199
8623	Anterior tibial nerve (deep peroneal), Neuritis	199
8723	Anterior tibial nerve (deep peroneal), Neuralgia	199
8524	Internal popliteal nerve (tibial), Paralysis of	200
8624	Internal popliteal nerve (tibial), Neuritis	200
8724	Internal popliteal nerve (tibial), Neuralgia	200
8525	Posterior tibial nerve, Paralysis of	200
8625	Posterior tibial nerve, Neuritis	200
8725	Posterior tibial nerve, Neuralgia	200
8526	Anterior crural nerve (femoral), Paralysis of	200
8626	Anterior crural nerve (femoral), Neuritis	200
8726	Anterior crural nerve (femoral), Neuralgia	200
8527	Internal saphenous nerve, Paralysis of	201
8627	Internal saphenous nerve, Neuritis	201
8727	Internal saphenous nerve, Neuralgia	201
8528	Obturator nerve, Paralysis of	201
8628	Obturator nerve, Neuritis	201
8728	Obturator nerve, Neuralgia	201
8529	External cutaneous nerve of thigh, Paralysis of	201
8629	External cutaneous nerve of thigh, Neuritis	201
8729	External cutaneous nerve of thigh, Neuralgia	201
8530	Ilio-inguinal nerve, Paralysis of	201
8630	Ilio-inguinal nerve, Neuritis	201
8730	Ilio-inguinal nerve, Neuralgia	201

	SARCOMA AND THE EPILEPSIES	
8540	Soft-tissue sarcoma (of neurogenic origin)	202
8910	Epilepsy, grand mal	202
8911	Epilepsy, petit mal	202
8912	Epilepsy, Jacksonian and focal motor or sensory	203
8913	Epilepsy, diencephalic	203
8914	Epilepsy, psychomotor	203

- Note: It is required for the minimum ratings for residuals under diagnostic codes 8000-8025, that there be ascertainable residuals. Determinations as to the presence of residuals not capable of objective verification, i.e., headaches, dizziness, fatigability, must be approached on the basis of the diagnosis recorded; subjective residuals will be accepted when consistent with the disease and not more likely attributable to other disease or no disease. It is of exceptional importance that when ratings in excess of the prescribed minimum ratings are assigned, the diagnostic codes utilized as bases of evaluation be cited, in addition to the codes identifying the diagnoses.

ORGANIC DISEASES OF THE CENTRAL NERVOUS SYSTEM

Rating

- 8000   Encephalitis, epidemic, chronic:
    - As active febrile disease 100%
    - Rate residuals, minimum 10%

Brain, new growth of:

- 8002   Malignant: 100%
    -Minimum rating 30%
    -Note: The rating in code 8002 will be continued for 2 years following cessation of surgical, chemotherapeutic or other treatment modality. At this point, if the residuals have stabilized, the rating will be made on neurological residuals according to symptomatology.

- 8003   Benign, minimum: 60%
    - Rate residuals, minimum 10%

- 8004   Paralysis agitans:
    -Minimum rating 30%

- 8005   Bulbar palsy: 100%

General Rating Formula for Vascular Conditions (DC's 8007 through 8009)

Rating

- 8007   Brain, vessels, embolism of:
- 8008   Brain, vessels, thrombosis of:
- 8009   Brain, vessels, thrombosis of:
  - Rate the vascular conditions under Codes 8007 through 8009,
  for 6 months 100%
  - Rate residuals, thereafter, minimum 10%

- 8010   Myelitis:
  -Minimum rating 10%

- 8011   Poliomyelitis, anterior:
  - As active febrile disease 100%
  - Rate residuals, minimum 10%

- 8012   Hematomyelia:
  - For 6 months 100%
  - Rate residuals, minimum 10%

General Rating Formula for Vascular Conditions (DC's 8013 through 8015)

- 8013   Syphilis, cerebrospinal:
- 8014   Syphilis, meningovascular:
- 8015   Tabes dorsalis:

  - Note: Rate upon the severity of convulsions, paralysis, visual impairment or psychotic involvement, etc.

- 8017   Amyotrophic lateral sclerosis:
  - Minimum rating 100%*

  * Note: Consider the need for special monthly compensation.

- 8018   Multiple sclerosis:
  - Minimum rating 30%

- 8019   Meningitis, cerebrospinal, epidemic:
  - As active febrile disease 100%
  - Rate residuals, minimum 10%

- 8020   Brain, abscess of:
  - As active febrile disease 100%
  - Rate residuals, minimum 10%

Spinal cord, new growths of:

- 8021 Malignant: 100%
  - Minimum rating... 30%

  -Note: The rating in code 8021 will be continued for 2 years following cessation of surgical, chemotherapeutic or other treatment modality. At this point, if the residuals have stabilized, the rating will be made on neurological residuals according to symptomatology.

- 8022 Benign, minimum rating: 60%
  - Rate residuals, minimum 10%

- 8023 Progressive muscular atrophy:
  - Minimum rating... 30%

- 8024 Syringomyelia:
  - Minimum rating... 30%

- 8025 Myasthenia gravis:
  - Minimum rating... 30%
  - Note. It is required for the minimum ratings for residuals under diagnostic codes 8000-8025, that there be ascertainable residuals. Determinations as to the presence of residuals not capable of objective verification, *i.e.*, headaches, dizziness, fatigability, must be approached on the basis of the diagnosis recorded; subjective residuals will be accepted when consistent with the disease and not more likely attributable to other disease or no disease. It is of exceptional importance that when ratings in excess of the prescribed minimum ratings are assigned, the diagnostic codes utilized as bases of evaluation be cited, in addition to the codes identifying the diagnoses.

- 8045 Residuals of traumatic brain injury (TBI):
  - There are three main areas of dysfunction that may result from TBI and have profound effects on functioning: cognitive (which is common in varying degrees after TBI), emotional/behavioral, and physical. Each of these areas of dysfunction may require evaluation.

  - Cognitive impairment is defined as decreased memory, concentration, attention, and executive functions of the brain. Executive functions are goal setting, speed of information processing, planning, organizing, prioritizing, self-monitoring, problem solving, judgment, decision making, spontaneity, and flexibility in changing actions when they are not productive. Not all of these brain functions may be affected in a given individual with cognitive impairment, and some functions may be affected more severely than others. In a given individual, symptoms may fluctuate in severity from day to day. Evaluate cognitive impairment under the table titled "Evaluation of Cognitive Impairment and Other Residuals of TBI Not Otherwise Classified."

- Subjective symptoms may be the only residual of TBI or may be associated with cognitive impairment or other areas of dysfunction. Evaluate subjective symptoms that are residuals of TBI, whether or not they are part of cognitive impairment, under the subjective symptoms facet in the table titled "Evaluation of Cognitive Impairment and Other Residuals of TBI Not Otherwise Classified." However, separately evaluate any residual with a distinct diagnosis that may be evaluated under another diagnostic code, such as migraine headache or Meniere's disease, even if that diagnosis is based on subjective symptoms, rather than under the "Evaluation of Cognitive Impairment and Other Residuals of TBI Not Otherwise Classified" table.

- Evaluate emotional/behavioral dysfunction when there is a diagnosis of a mental disorder. When there is no diagnosis of a mental disorder, evaluate emotional/behavioral symptoms under the criteria in the table titled "Evaluation of Cognitive Impairment and Other Residuals of TBI Not Otherwise Classified."

- Evaluate physical (including neurological) dysfunction based on the following list, under an appropriate diagnostic code: Motor and sensory dysfunction, including pain, of the extremities and face; visual impairment; hearing loss and tinnitus; loss of sense of smell and taste; seizures; gait, coordination, and balance problems; speech and other communication difficulties, including aphasia and related disorders, and dysarthria; neurogenic bladder; neurogenic bowel; cranial nerve dysfunctions; autonomic nerve dysfunctions; and endocrine dysfunctions.

- The preceding list of types of physical dysfunction does not encompass all possible residuals of TBI. For residuals not listed here that are reported on an examination, evaluate under the most appropriate diagnostic code. Evaluate each condition separately, as long as the same signs and symptoms are not used to support more than one evaluation, and combine the evaluations for each separately rated condition. The evaluation assigned based on the "Evaluation of Cognitive Impairment and Other Residuals of TBI Not Otherwise Classified" table will be considered the evaluation for a single condition for purposes of combining with other disability evaluations.

- Consider the need for special monthly compensation for such problems as loss of use of an extremity, certain sensory impairments, erectile dysfunction, the need for aid and attendance (including for protection from hazards or dangers incident to the daily environment due to cognitive impairment), being housebound, etc.

183

Evaluation of Cognitive Impairment and Subjective Symptoms

- The table titled "Evaluation of Cognitive Impairment and Other Residuals of TBI Not Otherwise Classified" contains 10 important facets of TBI related to cognitive impairment and subjective symptoms. It provides criteria for levels of impairment for each facet, as appropriate, ranging from 0 to 3, and a 5th level, the highest level of impairment, labeled "total." However, not every facet has every level of severity. The Consciousness facet, for example, does not provide for an impairment level other than "total," since any level of impaired consciousness would be totally disabling. Assign a 100-percent evaluation if "total" is the level of evaluation for one or more facets. If no facet is evaluated as "total," assign the overall percentage evaluation based on the level of the highest facet as follows: 0 = 0 percent; 1 = 10 percent; 2 = 40 percent; and 3 = 70 percent. For example, assign a 70 percent evaluation if 3 is the highest level of evaluation for any facet.

- Note (1): There may be an overlap of manifestations of conditions evaluated under the table titled "Evaluation Of Cognitive Impairment And Other Residuals Of TBI Not Otherwise Classified" with manifestations of a comorbid mental or neurologic or other physical disorder that can be separately evaluated under another diagnostic code. In such cases, do not assign more than one evaluation based on the same manifestations. If the manifestations of two or more conditions cannot be clearly separated, assign a single evaluation under whichever set of diagnostic criteria allows the better assessment of overall impaired functioning due to both conditions. However, if the manifestations are clearly separable, assign a separate evaluation for each condition.

- Note (2): Symptoms listed as examples at evaluation levels in the table are only examples; they are not symptoms that must be present in order to assign a particular evaluation.

- Note (3): "Instrumental activities of daily living" refers to activities other than self-care that are needed for independent living, such as meal preparation, doing housework and other chores, shopping, traveling, doing laundry, being responsible for one's own medications, and using a telephone. These activities are distinguished from "Activities of daily living," which refers to basic self-care and includes bathing or showering, dressing, eating, getting in or out of bed or a chair, and using the toilet.

- Note (4): The terms "mild," "moderate," and "severe" TBI, which may appear in medical records, refer to a classification of TBI made at, or close to, the time of injury rather than to the current level of functioning. This classification does not affect the rating assigned under diagnostic code 8045.

- Note (5): A veteran whose residuals of TBI are rated under a version of diagnostic code 8045, in effect before October 23, 2008 may request review under diagnostic code 8045, irrespective of whether his or her disability has worsened since the last review. VA will review that veteran's disability rating to determine whether the veteran may be entitled to a higher disability rating under diagnostic code 8045. A request for review pursuant to this note will be treated as a claim for an increased rating for purposes of determining the effective date of an increased rating awarded as a result of such review; however, in no case will the award be effective before October 23, 2008. For the purposes of determining the effective date of an increased rating awarded as a result of such review, VA will apply 38 CFR 3.114, if applicable.

EVALUATION OF COGNITIVE IMPAIRMENT AND OTHER RESIDUALS OF TBI NOT OTHERWISE CLASSIFIED

Facets of cognitive impairment and other residuals of TBI not otherwise classified	Level of impairment	Criteria
Memory, attention, concentration, executive functions.	0	No complaints of impairment of memory, attention, concentration, or executive functions.
	1	A complaint of mild loss of memory (such as having difficult following a conversation, recalling recent conversations, remembering names of new acquaintances, or finding words, or often misplacing items), attention, concentration, or executive functions, but without objective evidence on testing.
	2	Objective evidence on testing of mild impairment of memory, attention, concentration, or executive functions resulting in mild functional impairment.
	3	Objective evidence on testing of moderate impairment of memory, attention, concentration, or executive functions resulting in moderate functional impairment.
	Total	Objective evidence on testing of severe impairment of memory, attention, concentration, or executive functions resulting in severe functional impairment.

Judgment	0	Normal.
	1	Mildly impaired judgment. For complex or unfamiliar decisions, occasionally unable to identify, understand, and weigh the alternatives, understand the consequences of choices, and make a reasonable decision.
	2	Moderately impaired judgment. For complex or unfamiliar decisions, usually unable to identify, understand, and weigh the alternatives, understand the consequences of choices, and make a reasonable decision, although has little difficulty with simple decisions.
	3	Moderately severely impaired judgment. For even routine and familiar decisions, occasionally unable to identify, understand, and weigh the alternatives, understand the consequences of choices, and make a reasonable decision.
	Total	Severely impaired judgment. For even routine and familiar decisions, usually unable to identify, understand, and weigh the alternatives, understand the consequences of choices, and make a reasonable decision. For example, unable to determine appropriate clothing for current weather conditions or judge when to avoid dangerous situations or activities.
Social interaction	0	Social interaction is routinely appropriate.
	1	Social interaction is occasionally inappropriate.
	2	Social interaction is frequently inappropriate.
	3	Social interaction is inappropriate most or all of the time.

Orientation	0	Always oriented to person, time, place, and situation.
	1	Occasionally disoriented to one of the four aspects (person, time, place, situation) of orientation.
	2	Occasionally disoriented to two of the four aspects (person, time, place, situation) of orientation or often disoriented to one aspect of orientation.
	3	Often disoriented to two or more of the four aspects (person, time, place, situation) of orientation.
	Total	Consistently disoriented to two or more of the four aspects (person, time, place, situation) of orientation.
Motor activity (with intact motor and sensory system).	0	Motor activity normal.
	1	Motor activity normal most of the time, but mildly slowed at times due to apraxia (inability to perform previously learned motor activities, despite normal motor function).
	2	Motor activity mildly decreased or with moderate slowing due to apraxia.
	3	Motor activity moderately decreased due to apraxia.
	Total	Motor activity severely decreased due to apraxia.

Visual spatial orientation	0	Normal.
	1	Mildly impaired. Occasionally gets lost in unfamiliar surroundings, has difficulty reading maps or following directions. Is able to use assistive devices such as GPS (global positioning system).
	2	Moderately impaired. Usually gets lost in unfamiliar surroundings, has difficulty reading maps, following directions, and judging distance. Has difficulty using assistive devices such as GPS (global positioning system).
	3	Moderately severely impaired. Gets lost even in familiar surroundings, unable to use assistive devices such as GPS (global positioning system).
	Total	Severely impaired. May be unable to touch or name own body parts when asked by the examiner, identify the relative position in space of two different objects, or find the way from one room to another in a familiar environment.
Subjective symptoms	0	Subjective symptoms that do not interfere with work; instrumental activities of daily living; or work, family, or other close relationships. Examples are: mild or occasional headaches, mild anxiety.
	1	Three or more subjective symptoms that mildly interfere with work; instrumental activities of daily living; or work, family, or other close relationships. Examples of findings that might be seen at this level of impairment are: intermittent dizziness, daily mild to moderate headaches, tinnitus, frequent insomnia, hypersensitivity to sound, hypersensitivity to light.
	2	Three or more subjective symptoms that moderately interfere with work; instrumental activities of daily living; or work, family, or other close relationships. Examples of findings that might be seen at this level of impairment are: marked fatigability, blurred or double vision, headaches requiring rest periods during most days.

Neurobehavioral effects	0	One or more neurobehavioral effects that do not interfere with workplace interaction or social interaction. Examples of neurobehavioral effects are: Irritability, impulsivity, unpredictability, lack of motivation, verbal aggression, physical aggression, belligerence, apathy, lack of empathy, moodiness, lack of cooperation, inflexibility, and impaired awareness of disability. Any of these effects may range from slight to severe, although verbal and physical aggression are likely to have a more serious impact on workplace interaction and social interaction than some of the other effects.
	1	One or more neurobehavioral effects that occasionally interfere with workplace interaction, social interaction, or both but do not preclude them.
	2	One or more neurobehavioral effects that frequently interfere with workplace interaction, social interaction, or both but do not preclude them.
	3	One or more neurobehavioral effects that interfere with or preclude workplace interaction, social interaction, or both on most days or that occasionally require supervision for safety of self or others.
Consciousness	Total	Persistently altered state of consciousness, such as vegetative state minimally responsive state, coma.

Communication	0	Able to communicate by spoken and written language (expressive communication), and to comprehend spoken and written language.
	1	Comprehension or expression, or both, of either spoken language or written language is only occasionally impaired. Can communicate complex ideas.
	2	Inability to communicate either by spoken language, written language, or both, more than occasionally but less than half of the time, or to comprehend spoken language, written language, or both, more than occasionally but less than half of the time. Can generally communicate complex ideas.
	3	Inability to communicate either by spoken language, written language, or both, at least half of the time but not all of the time, or to comprehend spoken language, written language, or both, at least half of the time but not all of the time. May rely on gestures or other alternative modes of communication. Able to communicate basic needs.
	Total	Complete inability to communicate either by spoken language, written language, or both, or to comprehend spoken language, written language, or both. Unable to communicate basic needs.

- 8046   Cerebral arteriosclerosis:

- Purely neurological disabilities, such as hemiplegia, cranial nerve paralysis, etc., due to cerebral arteriosclerosis will be rated under the diagnostic codes dealing with such specific disabilities, with citation of a hyphenated diagnostic code (e.g., 8046-8207).

- Purely subjective complaints such as headache, dizziness, tinnitus, insomnia and irritability, recognized as symptomatic of a properly diagnosed cerebral arteriosclerosis, will be rated 10 percent and no more under diagnostic code 9305. This 10 percent rating will not be combined with any other rating for a disability due to cerebral or generalized arteriosclerosis. Ratings in excess of 10 percent for cerebral arteriosclerosis under diagnostic code 9305 are not assignable in the absence of a diagnosis of multi-infarct dementia with cerebral arteriosclerosis.

- Note: The ratings under code 8046 apply only when the diagnosis of cerebral arteriosclerosis is substantiated by the entire clinical picture and not solely on findings of retinal arteriosclerosis.

Rating

- 8100 Migraine:
  - With very frequent completely prostrating and prolonged attacks productive of severe economic inadaptability 50%
  - With characteristic prostrating attacks occurring on an average once a month over last several months.. 30%
  - With characteristic prostrating attacks averaging one in 2 months over last several months... 10%
  - With less frequent attacks 0%

- 8103 Tic, convulsive:
  - Severe 30%
  - Moderate 10%
  - Mild 0%

  - Note: Depending upon frequency, severity, muscle groups involved.

- 8104 Paramyoclonus multiplex (convulsive state, myoclonic type):
  - Rate as tic; convulsive; severe cases 60%

- 8105 Chorea, Sydenham's:
  - Pronounced, progressive grave types 100%
  - Severe 80%
  - Moderately severe... 50%
  - Moderate 30%
  - Mild 10%

  - Note: Consider rheumatic etiology and complications.

- 8106 Chorea, Huntington's:
  - Rate as Sydenham's chorea. This, though a familial disease, has its onset in late adult life, and is considered a ratable disability.

- 8107 Athetosis, acquired:
  - Rate as chorea.

- 8108 Narcolepsy:
  - Rate as for epilepsy, petit mal.

Disability from lesions of peripheral portions of first, second, third, fourth, sixth, and eighth nerves will be rated under the Organs of Special Sense. The ratings for the cranial nerves are for unilateral involvement; when bilateral, combine but without the bilateral factor.

Rating

Fifth (trigeminal) cranial nerve

- 8205   Paralysis of:
  - Complete.. 50%
  - Incomplete, severe 30%
  - Incomplete, moderate 10%
  - Note: Dependent upon relative degree of sensory manifestation or motor loss.

- 8305   Neuritis.

- 8405   Neuralgia.

  - Note: Tic douloureux may be rated in accordance with severity, up to complete paralysis.

Seventh (facial) cranial nerve

- 8207   Paralysis of:
  - Complete.. 30%
  - Incomplete, severe 20%
  - Incomplete, moderate 10%

  - Note: Dependent upon relative loss of innervation of facial muscles.

- 8307   Neuritis.

- 8407   Neuralgia.

Ninth (glossopharyngeal) cranial nerve

- 8209   Paralysis of:
  - Complete.. 30%
  - Incomplete, severe 20%
  - Incomplete, moderate 10%

  - Note: Dependent upon relative loss of ordinary sensation in mucous membrane of the pharynx, fauces, and tonsils.

- 8309   Neuritis.

- 8409   Neuralgia.

Tenth (pneumogastric, vagus) cranial nerve

- 8210 Paralysis of:
  - Complete... 50%
  - Incomplete, severe 30%
  - Incomplete, moderate 10%

  - Note: Dependent upon extent of sensory and motor loss to organs of voice, respiration, pharynx, stomach and heart.

- 8310 Neuritis.

- 8410 Neuralgia.

Eleventh (spinal accessory, external branch) cranial nerve.

- 8211 Paralysis of:
  - Complete... 30%
  - Incomplete, severe 20%
  - Incomplete, moderate 10%

  - Note: Dependent upon loss of motor function of sternomastoid and trapezius muscles.

- 8311 Neuritis.

- 8411 Neuralgia.

Twelfth (hypoglossal) cranial nerve.

- 8212 Paralysis of:
  - Complete... 50%
  - Incomplete, severe 30%
  - Incomplete, moderate 10%

  - Note: Dependent upon loss of motor function of tongue.

- 8312 Neuritis.

- 8412 Neuralgia.

The term "incomplete paralysis" with this and other peripheral nerve injuries indicates a degree of lost or impaired function substantially less than the type pictured for complete paralysis given with each nerve, whether due to varied level of the nerve lesion or to partial regeneration. When the involvement is wholly sensory, the rating should be for the mild, or at most, the moderate degree. The following ratings for the peripheral nerves are for unilateral involvement; when bilateral, combine with application of the bilateral factor.

Rating
Major Minor

Upper radicular group (fifth and sixth cervicals)

- 8510   Paralysis of:
  - o Complete; all shoulder and elbow movements lost or severely affected, hand and wrist movements not affected.................................70%.....60%
  - o Incomplete:
    - Severe ....50%.....40%
    - Moderate..40%.....30%
    - Mild ....20%.....20%

- 8610   Neuritis.

- 8710   Neuralgia.

Middle radicular group

- 8511   Paralysis of:
  - o Complete; adduction, abduction, and rotation of arm, flexion of elbow, and extension of wrist lost or severely affected........................70%.....60%
  - o Incomplete:
    - Severe ....50%.....40%
    - Moderate..40%.....30%
    - Mild ....20%.....20%

- 8611   Neuritis.

- 8711   Neuralgia.

Lower radicular group

- 8512 Paralysis of:
  - ○ Complete; all intrinsic muscles of hand, and some or all of flexors of wrist and fingers, paralyzed (substantial loss of use of hand) ....70%.....60%
  - ○ Incomplete:
    - Severe ....50%.....40%
    - Moderate..40%.....30%
    - Mild ....20%.....20%

- 8612 Neuritis.

- 8712 Neuralgia.

All radicular groups

- 8513 Paralysis of:
  - ○ Complete ....90%.....80%
  - ○ Incomplete:
    - Severe ....70%.....60%
    - Moderate..40%.....30%
    - Mild ....20%.....20%

- 8613 Neuritis.

- 8713 Neuralgia.

The musculospiral nerve (radial nerve)

- 8514   Paralysis of:
  - ○ Complete; drop of hand and fingers, wrist and fingers perpetually flexed, the thumb adducted falling within the line of the outer border of the index finger; cannot extend hand at wrist, extend proximal phalanges of fingers, extend thumb, or make lateral movement of wrist; supination of hand, extension and flexion of elbow weakened, the loss of synergic motion of extensors impairs the hand grip seriously; total paralysis of the triceps occurs only as the greatest rarity...70%.....60%
  - ○ Incomplete:
    - Severe ....50%.....40%
    - Moderate ....30%.....20%
    - Mild ....20%.....20%

- 8614   Neuritis.

- 8714   Neuralgia.
  - Note: Lesions involving only "dissociation of extensor communis digitorum" and "paralysis below the extensor communis digitorum," will not exceed the moderate rating under code 8514.

The median nerve

- 8515   Paralysis of:
  - ○ Complete; the hand inclined to the ulnar side, the index and middle fingers more extended than normally, considerable atrophy of the muscles of the thenar eminence, the thumb in the plane of the hand (ape hand); pronation incomplete and defective, absence of flexion of index finger and feeble flexion of middle finger, cannot make a fist, index and middle fingers remain extended; cannot flex distal phalanx of thumb, defective opposition and abduction of the thumb at right angles to palm; flexion of wrist weakened; pain with trophic disturbances...70%.....60%
  - ○ Incomplete:
    - Severe ....50%.....40%
    - Moderate ....30%.....20%
    - Mild ....10%.....10%

- 8615   Neuritis.

- 8715   Neuralgia.

The ulnar nerve

- 8516 Paralysis of:
  - Complete; the "griffin claw" deformity, due to flexor contraction of ring and little fingers, atrophy very marked in dorsal interspace and thenar and hypothenar eminences; loss of extension of ring and little fingers, cannot spread the fingers (or reverse), cannot adduct the thumb; flexion of wrist weakened ....60%.....50%
  - Incomplete:
    - Severe ....40%.....30%
    - Moderate ....30%.....20%
    - Mild ....10%.....10%

- 8616 Neuritis.

- 8716 Neuralgia.

Musculocutaneous nerve

- 8517 Paralysis of:
  - Complete; weakness but not loss of flexion of elbow and supination of forearm..30%.....20%
  - Incomplete:
    - Severe ....20%.....20%
    - Moderate ....10%.....10%
    - Mild ....0%.....0%

- 8617 Neuritis.

- 8717 Neuralgia.

Circumflex nerve

- 8518 Paralysis of:
  - Complete; abduction of arm is impossible, outward rotation is weakened; muscles supplied are deltoid and teres minor ....50%.....40%
  - Incomplete:
    - Severe ....30%.....20%
    - Moderate ....10%.....10%
    - Mild ....0%.....0%

- 8618 Neuritis.

- 8718 Neuralgia.

Long thoracic nerve

- 8519 Paralysis of:
  - Complete; inability to raise arm above shoulder level, winged scapula deformity..30%.....20%
  - Incomplete:
    - Severe ....20%.....20%
    - Moderate ....10%.....10%
    - Mild ....0%.....0%

    - Note: Not to be combined with lost motion above shoulder level.

- 8619 Neuritis.

- 8719 Neuralgia.

    Note: Combined nerve injuries should be rated by reference to the major involvement, or if sufficient in extent, consider radicular group ratings.

Sciatic nerve

- 8520 Paralysis of:
  - Complete: the foot dangles and drops, no active movement possible of muscles below the knee, flexion of knee weakened or (very rarely) lost 80%
  - Incomplete:
    - Severe, with marked muscular atrophy 60%
    - Moderately severe.. 40%
    - Moderate 20%
    - Mild 10%

- 8620 Neuralgia.

- 8720 Neuralgia.

External popliteal nerve (common peroneal)

- 8521   Paralysis of:
  - o   Complete; foot drop and slight droop of first phalanges of all toes, cannot dorsiflex the foot, extension (dorsal flexion) of proximal phalanges of toes lost; abduction of foot lost, adduction weakened; anesthesia covers entire dorsum of foot and toes... 40%
  - o   Incomplete:
    - - Severe 30%
    - - Moderate 20%
    - - Mild 10%

- 8621   Neuralgia.

- 8721   Neuralgia.

Musculocutaneous nerve (superficial peroneal)

- 8522   Paralysis of:
  - o   Complete; eversion of foot weakened.. 30%
  - o   Incomplete:
    - - Severe 20%
    - - Moderate 10%
    - - Mild 0%

- 8622   Neuralgia.

- 8722   Neuralgia.

Anterior tibial nerve (deep peroneal)

- 8523   Paralysis of:
  - o   Complete; dorsal flexion of foot lost 30%
  - o   Incomplete:
    - - Severe 20%
    - - Moderate 10%
    - - Mild 0%

- 8623   Neuralgia.

- 8723   Neuralgia.

Internal popliteal nerve (tibial)

- 8524   Paralysis of:
  - Complete; plantar flexion lost, frank adduction of foot impossible, flexion and separation of toes abolished; no muscle in sole can move; in lesions of the nerve high in popliteal fossa, plantar flexion of foot is lost 40%
  - Incomplete:
    - Severe 30%
    - Moderate 20%
    - Mild 10%

- 8624   Neuralgia.

- 8724   Neuralgia.

Posterior tibial nerve

- 8525   Paralysis of:
  - Complete; paralysis of all muscles of sole of foot, frequently with painful paralysis of a causalgic nature; toes cannot be flexed; adduction is weakened; plantar flexion is impaired 30%
  - Incomplete:
    - Severe 20%
    - Moderate 10%
    - Mild 10%

- 8625   Neuralgia.

- 8725   Neuralgia.

Anterior crural nerve (femoral)

- 8526   Paralysis of:
  - Complete; paralysis of quadriceps extensor muscles 40%
  - Incomplete:
    - Severe 30%
    - Moderate 20%
    - Mild 10%

- 8626   Neuralgia.

- 8726   Neuralgia.

Internal saphenous nerve

- 8527   Paralysis of:
  - Severe to Complete:.. 10%
  - Mild to Moderate 0%

- 8627   Neuralgia.

- 8727   Neuralgia.

Obturator nerve

- 8528   Paralysis of:
  - Severe to Complete:.. 10%
  - Mild to Moderate 0%

- 8628   Neuralgia.

- 8728   Neuralgia.

External cutaneous nerve of thigh

- 8529   Paralysis of:
  - Severe to Complete:.. 10%
  - Mild to Moderate 0%

- 8629   Neuralgia.

- 8729   Neuralgia.

Ilio-inguinal nerve

- 8530   Paralysis of:
  - Severe to Complete:.. 10%
  - Mild to Moderate 0%

- 8630   Neuralgia.

- 8730   Neuralgia.

- 8540   Soft-tissue sarcoma (of neurogenic origin)... 100%

    - Note: The 100 percent rating will be continued for 6 months following the cessa-
    tion of surgical, X-ray, antineoplastic chemotherapy or other therapeutic proce-
    dure. At this point, if there has been no local recurrence or metastases, the rating
    will be made on residuals.

THE EPILEPSIES

A thorough study of the preface and under the ratings for epilepsy is necessary prior to any
rating action.

- 8910   Epilepsy, grand mal.
    - Rate under the general rating formula for major seizures.

- 8911   Epilepsy, petit mal.
    - Rate under the general rating formula for minor seizures.

    - Note (1): A major seizure is characterized by the generalized tonic-clonic
    convulsion with unconsciousness.

    - Note (2): A minor seizure consists of a brief interruption in consciousness or
    conscious control associated with staring or rhythmic blinking of the eyes or
    nodding of the head ("pure" petit mal), or sudden jerking movements of the arms,
    trunk, or head (myoclonic type) or sudden loss of postural control (akinetic type).

General Rating Formula for Major and Minor Epileptic Seizures

Rating

- Averaging at least 1 major seizure per month over the last year................... 100%
- Averaging at least 1 major seizure in 3 months over the last year;
or more than 10 minor seizures weekly 80%
- Averaging at least 1 major seizure in 4 months over the last year;
or 9-10 minor seizures per week 60%
- At least 1 major seizure in the last 6 months or 2 in the last year;
or averaging at least 5 to 8 minor seizures weekly 40%
- At least 1 major seizure in the last 2 years; or at least 2 minor seizures
in the last 6 months 20%
- A confirmed diagnosis of epilepsy with a history of seizures 10%
- Note (1): When continuous medication is shown necessary for the control of
epilepsy, the minimum evaluation will be 10 percent. This rating will not be
combined with any other rating for epilepsy.
- Note (2): In the presence of major and minor seizures, rate the predominating type.
- Note (3): There will be no distinction between diurnal and nocturnal major
seizures.

- 8912   Epilepsy, Jacksonian and focal motor or sensory.

- 8913   Epilepsy, diencephalic.
  - Rate as minor seizures, except in the presence of major and minor seizures, rate the predominating type.

- 8914   Epilepsy, psychomotor.
  o Major seizures:
  - Psychomotor seizures will be rated as major seizures under the general rating formula when characterized by automatic states and/or generalized convulsions with unconsciousness.
  o Minor seizures:
  - Psychomotor seizures will be rated as minor seizures under the general rating formula when characterized by brief transient episodes of random motor movements, hallucinations, perceptual illusions, abnormalities of thinking, memory or mood, or autonomic disturbances.

Mental Disorders in Epilepsies: A nonpsychotic organic brain syndrome will be rated separately under the appropriate diagnostic code (e.g., 9304 or 9326). In the absence of a diagnosis of non-psychotic organic psychiatric disturbance (psychotic, psychoneurotic or personality disorder) if diagnosed and shown to be secondary to or directly associated with epilepsy will be rated separately. The psychotic or psychoneurotic disorder will be rated under the appropriate diagnostic code. The personality disorder will be rated as a dementia (e.g., diagnostic code 9304 or 9326).

Epilepsy and Unemployability:
  - Note (1): Rating specialists must bear in mind that the epileptic, although his or her seizures are controlled, may find employment and rehabilitation difficult of attainment due to employer reluctance to the hiring of the epileptic.
  - Note (2): Where a case is encountered with a definite history of unemployment, full and complete development should be undertaken to ascertain whether the epilepsy is the determining factor in his or her inability to obtain employment.
  - Note (3): The assent of the claimant should first be obtained for permission to conduct this economic and social survey. The purpose of this survey is to secure all the relevant facts and data necessary to permit of a true judgment as to the reason for his or her unemployment and should include information as to:
    - Education;
    - Occupations prior and subsequent to service;
    - Places of employment and reasons for termination;
    - Wages received;
    - Number of seizures.
  - Note (4): Upon completion of this survey and current examination, the case should have rating board consideration. Where in the judgment of the rating board the veteran's unemployability is due to epilepsy and jurisdiction is not vested in that body by reason of schedular evaluations, the case should be submitted to the Director, Compensation Service or the Director, Pension and Fiduciary Service.

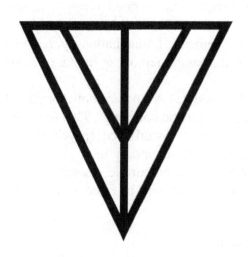

THIS PAGE LEFT INTENTIONALLY BLANK

CHAPTER 16

MENTAL DISORDERS

Quick Reference:

CODE	CATEGORY	PAGE
9201-9211	Schizophrenia and Other Psychotic Disorders	205
9300-9326	Delirium and Neurocognitive Disorders	205
9400-9413	Anxiety Disorders	206
9416-9417	Dissociative Disorders	206
9421-9425	Somatoform Disorders	206
9431-9435	Mood Disorders	206
9440	Chronic Adjustment Disorder	206
	General Rating Formula for Mental Disorders	207
9520-9521	Eating Disorders	208
	General Rating Formula for Eating Disorders	208

The nomenclature employed in this portion of the rating schedule is based upon the Diagnostic and Statistical Manual of Mental Disorders, Fifth Edition, of the American Psychiatric Association (DSM-V). Rating agencies must be thoroughly familiar with this manual to properly implement the directives to apply the general rating formula for mental disorders. The schedule for rating for mental disorders is set forth as follows:

SCHIZOPHRENIA AND OTHER PSYCHOTIC DISORDERS:
- 9201   Schizophrenia.
- 9208   Delusional disorder.
- 9210   Other specified and unspecified schizophrenia spectrum and other psychotic disorders.
- 9211   Schizoaffective disorder.

DELIRIUM, DEMENTIA, AND AMNESTIC AND OTHER COGNITIVE DISORDERS:
- 9300   Delirium.
- 9301   Major or mild neurocognitive disorder due to HIV or other infections.
- 9304   Major or mild neurocognitive disorder due to traumatic brain injury.
- 9305   Major or mild vascular neurocognitive disorder.
- 9310   Unspecified neurocognitive disorder.
- 9312   Major or mild neurocognitive disorder due to Alzheimer's disease.
- 9326   Major or mild neurocognitive disorder due to another medical condition or substance/ medication-induced major or mild neurocognitive disorder.

ANXIETY DISORDERS:

- 9400   Generalized anxiety disorder
- 9403   Specific phobia; social anxiety disorder (social phobia).
- 9404   Obsessive compulsive disorder
- 9410   Other specified anxiety disorder.
- 9411   Posttraumatic stress disorder (PTSD).
- 9412   Panic disorder and/or agoraphobia.
- 9413   Unspecified anxiety disorder.

DISSOCIATIVE DISORDERS:

- 9416   Dissociative amnesia; dissociative identity disorder.
- 9417   Depersonalization/Derealization disorder.

SOMATOFORM DISORDERS:

- 9421   Somatic symptom disorder.
- 9422   Other specified somatic symptom and related disorder.
- 9423   Unspecified somatic symptom and related disorder.
- 9424   Conversion disorder (functional neurological symptom disorder).
- 9425   Illness anxiety disorder.

MOOD DISORDERS:

- 9431   Cyclothymic disorder.
- 9432   Bipolar disorder.
- 9433   Persistent depressive disorder (dysthymia).
- 9434   Major depressive disorder.
- 9435   Unspecified depressive disorder.

CHRONIC ADJUSTMENT DISORDER:

- 9440   Chronic adjustment disorder.

General Rating Formula for Mental Disorders

Rating

- Total occupational and social impairment, due to such symptoms as: gross impairment in thought processes or communication; persistent delusions or hallucinations; grossly inappropriate behavior; persistent danger of hurting self or others; intermittent inability to perform activities of daily living (including maintenance of minimal personal hygiene); disorientation to time or place; memory loss for names of close relatives, own occupation, or own name 100%

- Occupational and social impairment, with deficiencies in most areas, such as work, school, family relations, judgment, thinking, or mood, due to such symptoms as: suicidal ideation; obsessional rituals which interfere with routine activities; speech intermittently illogical, obscure, or irrelevant; near-continuous panic or depression affecting the ability to function independently, appropriately and effectively; impaired impulse control (such as unprovoked irritability with periods of violence); spatial disorientation; neglect of personal appearance and hygiene; difficulty in adapting to stressful circumstances (including work or a worklike setting); inability to establish and maintain effective relationships 70%

- Occupational and social impairment with reduced reliability and productivity due to such symptoms as: flattened affect; circumstantial, circumlocutory, or stereotyped speech; panic attacks more than once a week; difficulty in understanding complex commands; impairment of short- and long-term memory (e.g., retention of only highly learned material, forgetting to complete tasks); impaired judgment; impaired abstract thinking; disturbances of motivation and mood; difficulty in establishing and maintaining effective work and social relationships 50%

- Occupational and social impairment with occasional decrease in work efficiency and intermittent periods of inability to perform occupational tasks (although generally functioning satisfactorily, with routine behavior, self-care, and conversation normal), due to such symptoms as: depressed mood, anxiety, suspiciousness, panic attacks (weekly or less often), chronic sleep impairment, mild memory loss (such as forgetting names, directions, recent events) 30%

- Occupational and social impairment due to mild or transient symptoms which decrease work efficiency and ability to perform occupational tasks only during periods of significant stress, or; symptoms controlled by continuous medication 10%

- A mental condition has been formally diagnosed, but symptoms are not severe enough either to interfere with occupational and social functioning or to require continuous medication 0%

207

EATING DISORDERS:
- 9520   Anorexia nervosa.
- 9521   Bulimia nervosa.

Rating Formula for Eating Disorders:

Rating

- Self-induced weight loss to less than 80 percent of expected minimum weight, with incapacitating episodes of at least six weeks total duration per year, and requiring hospitalization more than twice a year for parenteral nutrition or tube feeding.. 100%

- Self-induced weight loss to less than 85 percent of expected minimum weight with incapacitating episodes of six or more weeks total duration per year 60%

- Self-induced weight loss to less than 85 percent of expected minimum weight with incapacitating episodes of more than two but less than six weeks total duration per year 30%

Binge eating followed by self-induced vomiting or other measures to prevent weight gain, or resistance to weight gain even when below expected minimum weight, with diagnosis of an eating disorder and incapacitating episodes of up to two weeks total duration per year 10%

- Binge eating followed by self-induced vomiting or other measures to prevent weight gain, or resistance to weight gain even when below expected minimum weight, with diagnosis of an eating disorder but without incapacitating episodes 0%

- Note (1): An incapacitating episode is a period during which bed rest and treatment by a physician are required.
- Note (2): Ratings under diagnostic codes 9201 to 9440 will be evaluated using the General Rating Formula for Mental Disorders. Ratings under diagnostic codes 9520 and 9521 will be evaluated using the General Rating Formula for Eating Disorders.

CHAPTER 17

DENTAL AND ORAL CONDITIONS

Quick Reference:

Rating

- 9900   Maxilla or mandible, chronic osteomyelitis or osteoradionecrosis of:
  - Rate as osteomyelitis, chronic under diagnostic code 5000.

- 9901   Mandible, loss of, complete, between angles 100%

- 9902   Mandible, loss of, including ramus, unilaterally or bilaterally:
  - ○ Loss of one-half or more:
    - Involving temporomandibular articulation:
    - Not replaceable by prosthesis 70%
    - Replaceable by prosthesis 50%
    - Not-Involving temporomandibular articulation:
    - Not replaceable by prosthesis 40%
    - Replaceable by prosthesis 30%
  - ○ Loss of less than one-half:
    - Involving temporomandibular articulation:
    - Not replaceable by prosthesis 70%
    - Replaceable by prosthesis 50%
    - Not-Involving temporomandibular articulation:
    - Not replaceable by prosthesis 20%
    - Replaceable by prosthesis 10%

- **9903** Mandible, nonunion of confirmed by diagnostic imaging studies:
  - Severe with false motion 30%
  - Moderate, without false motion 10%

- **9904** Mandible, malunion of:
  - Displacement, causing severe anterior or posterior open bite 20%
  - Displacement, causing moderate anterior or posterior open bite 10%
  - Displacement, not causing anterior or posterior open bite 0%

- **9905** Temporomandibular articulation, limited motion of:
  - Inter-incisal Range:
  - 0-10 mm:
    - With dietary restrictions to all mechanically altered foods 50%
    - Without dietary restrictions to all mechanically altered foods 40%
  - 11-20 mm:
    - With dietary restrictions to all mechanically altered foods 40%
    - Without dietary restrictions to all mechanically altered foods 30%
  - 21-29 mm:
    - With dietary restrictions to full liquid and pureed foods 40%
    - With dietary restrictions to soft and semi-solid foods 30%
    - Without dietary restrictions to all mechanically altered foods 20%
  - 30-34 mm:
    - With dietary restrictions to full liquid and pureed foods 30%
    - With dietary restrictions to soft and semi-solid foods 20%
    - Without dietary restrictions to all mechanically altered foods 10%
  - Lateral excursion range of motion:
    - 0 to 4mm 10%
  - Note (1): Ratings for limited interincisal movement shall not be combined with ratings for limited lateral excursion.
  - Note (2): For VA compensation purposes, the normal maximum unassisted range of vertical jaw opening is from 35 to 50 mm
  - Note (3): For VA compensation purposes, mechanically altered foods are defined as altered by blending, chopping, grinding or mashing so that they are easy to chew and swallow. There are four levels of mechanically altered foods: full liquid, puree, soft, and semisolid foods. To warrant elevation based on mechanically altered foods, the use of texture-modified diets must be recorded or verified by a physician.

- **9908** Condyloid process, loss of, one or both sides 30%

- **9909** Coronoid process, loss of:
  - Bilateral 20%
  - Unilateral 10%

- 9911 Hard Palate, loss of
  - Loss of half or more, not replaceable by prosthesis 30%
  - Loss of less than half, not replaceable by prosthesis 20%
  - Loss of half or more, replacable by prosthesis 10%
  - Loss of less than half, replaceable by prosthesis 0%

- 9913 Teeth, loss of, due to loss of substance of body of maxilla or mandible without loss:
  - o Where the loss of masticatory surface cannot be restored by suitable prosthesis:
    - Loss of all teeth.. 40%
    - Loss of all upper teeth 30%
    - Loss of all lower teeth 30%
    - All upper and lower posterior teeth missing................................... 20%
    - All upper and lower anterior teeth missing 20%
    - All upper anterior teeth missing 10%
    - All lower anterior teeth missing 10%
    - All upper and lower teeth on one side missing................................ 10%
  - o Where the loss of masticatory surface can be restored by suitable prosthesis: ... 0%
    - Note: These ratings apply only to bone loss through trauma or disease such as osteomyelitis, and not to the loss of the alveolar process as a result of periodontal disease, since such loss is not considered disabling.

- 9914 Maxilla, loss of more than half:
  - Not replaceable by prosthesis 100%
  - Replaceable by prosthesis... 50%

- 9915 Maxilla, loss of half or less:
  - o Loss of 25 to 50 percent
    - Not replaceable by prosthesis 40%
    - Replaceable by prosthesis.. 30%
  - o Loss of less than 25 percent
    - Not replaceable by prosthesis 20%
    - Replaceable by prosthesis.. 0%

- 9916 Maxilla, malunion or nonunion of:
  - o Nonunion:
    - With false motion 30%
    - Without false motion 10%
  - o Malunion:
    - With displacement, causing severe anterior or posterior open bite................. 30%
    - With displacement, causing moderate anterior or posterior open bite 10%
    - With displacement, causing mild anterior or posterior open bite..................... 0%
    - Note: For VA compensation purposes, the severity of maxillary nonunion is dependent upon the degree of abnormal mobility of maxilla fragments following treatment (*i.e.*, presence or absence of false motion), and maxillary nonunion must be confirmed by diagnostic imaging studies.

- 9917 Neoplasm, hard and soft tissue, benign:
  - Rate as loss of supporting structures (bone or teeth) and/or functional impairment due to scarring.

- 9918 Neoplasm, hard and soft tissue, malignant: 100%
  - A rating of 100 percent shall continue beyond the cessation of any surgical, radiation, antineoplastic chemotherapy or other therapeutic procedure. Six months after discontinuance of such treatment, the appropriate disability rating shall be determined by mandatory VA examination. Any change in evaluation based upon that or any subsequent examination shall be subject to the provisions of this chapter. If there has been no local recurrence or metastasis, rate on residuals such as loss of supporting structures (bone or teeth) and/or functional impairment due to scarring.

CHAPTER 18

ALPHABETICAL LISTING OF AILMENTS, DISEASES, AND DISABILITIES

Ailment, Disease, or Disability	VA Code	Chapter	Page #
Abscess of: Brain	8020	15	181
Abscess of: Kidney	7501	10	139
Abscess of: Lung, Chronic	6824	7	104
Acne	7828	13	168
Acquired hemolytic anemia	7723	12	157
Acromegaly	7908	14	173
Actinomycosis	6822	7	104
Addison's disease (adrenocortical insufficiency)	7911	14	174
Adenitis, tuberculosis, active or inactive	7710	12	53
Agranulocystosis, acquired	7702	12	151-2
AL Amyloidosis (primary amyloidosis)	7717	12	155
Allergic or vasomotor rhinitis	6522	7	97
Alopecia Areata	7831	13	168
Amebiasis	7321	9	129
Amputation: Arm- Disarticulation	5120	1	41
Amputation: Arm- Above Insertion of Deltoid	5121	1	41
Amputation: Arm- Below Insertion of Deltoid	5122	1	41
Amputation: Digits- Five of One Hand	5126	1	42
Amputation: Digits- Four of One Hand- Thumb, Index, Long, Ring	5127	1	42
Amputation: Digits- Four of One Hand- Thumb, Index, Long, Little	5128	1	42
Amputation: Digits- Four of One Hand- Thumb, Index, Ring, Little	5129	1	42
Amputation: Digits- Four of One Hand- Thumb, Long, Ring, Little	5130	1	42
Amputation: Digits- Four of One Hand- Index, Long, Ring, Little	5131	1	42
Amputation: Digits- Three of One Hand- Thumb, Index, Long	5132	1	42
Amputation: Digits- Three of One Hand- Thumb, Index, Ring	5133	1	42
Amputation: Digits- Three of One Hand- Thumb, Index, Little	5134	1	42
Amputation: Digits- Three of One Hand- Thumb, Long, Ring	5135	1	42
Amputation: Digits- Three of One Hand- Thumb, Long, Little	5136	1	42
Amputation: Digits- Three of One Hand- Thumb, Ring, Little	5137	1	42
Amputation: Digits- Three of One Hand- Index, Long, Ring	5138	1	42
Amputation: Digits- Three of One Hand- Index, Long, Little	5139	1	42
Amputation: Digits- Three of One Hand- Index, Ring, Little	5140	1	42
Amputation: Digits- Three of One Hand- Long, Ring, Little	5141	1	42
Amputation: Digits- Two of One Hand- Thumb, Index	5142	1	42
Amputation: Digits- Two of One Hand- Thumb, Long	5143	1	42
Amputation: Digits- Two of One Hand- Thumb, Ring	5144	1	42
Amputation: Digits- Two of One Hand- Thumb, Little	5145	1	42
Amputation: Digits- Two of One Hand- Index, Long	5146	1	42
Amputation: Digits- Two of One Hand- Index, Ring	5147	1	42
Amputation: Digits- Two of One Hand- Index, Little	5148	1	42

Ailment, Disease, or Disability	VA Code	Chapter	Page #
Amputation: Digits- Two of One Hand- Long, Ring	5149	1	42
Amputation: Digits- Two of One Hand- Long, Little	5150	1	42
Amputation: Digits- Two of One Hand- Ring, Little	5151	1	42
Amputation: Digit- Single Finger- Thumb	5152	1	43-44
Amputation: Digit- Single Finger- Index	5153	1	43-44
Amputation: Digit- Single Finger- Long	5154	1	43-44
Amputation: Digit- Single Finger- Ring	5155	1	43-44
Amputation: Digit- Single Finger- Little	5156	1	43-44
Amputation: Forearm- Above Insertion of Pronator Teres	5123	1	41
Amputation: Forearm- Below Insertion of Pronator Teres	5124	1	41
Amputation: Leg- With Defective Stump	5163	1	44
Amputation: Leg- Not Improvable by Prosthesis controlled by natural knee action	5164	1	44
Amputation: Leg- At a lower level, permitting prosthesis	5165	1	44
Amputation: Leg- Forefoot- Proximal to metatarsal bones	5166	1	44
Amputation Thigh- Disarticulation	5160	1	44
Amputation Thigh- Upper Third	5161	1	44
Amputation Thigh- Middle or Lower Thirds	5162	1	44
Amputation: Toes, all without metatarsal bones	5170	1	44
Amputation: Toes, Great	5171	1	44
Amputation: Toes, Other than Great, with removal of metatarsal head	5172	1	44
Amputation: Toes- Three or More, without Metatarsal Head	5173	1	44
Amyotrophic Lateral Sclerosis	8017	15	181
Anatomical Loss of: Both Eyes	6061	3	80
Anatomical Loss of: Both Feet	5107	1	41
Anatomical Loss of: Both Hands	5106	1	41
Anatomical Loss of: One Hand and One Foot	5108	1	41
Anatomical Loss of: One Eye, with Visual Acuity of the other 5/200 (1.5/60)	6063	3	80
Anatomical Loss of: One Eye, with Visual Acuity of the other 10/200 (3/60); 15/200 (4.5/60); 20/200 (6/60)	6063	3	80
Anatomical Loss of: One Eye, with Visual Acuity of the other 20/100 (6/30); 20/70 (6/21); 20/50 (6/15)	6063	3	80
Anatomical Loss of: One Eye, with Visual Acuity of the other 20/40 (6/12)	6063	3	80
Anatomical Loss of: One Foot and Use of One Hand	5105	1	41
Anatomical Loss of: One Hand and Use of One Foot	5104	1	41
Aneurysm: Aortic	7110	8	118
Aneurysm: Large Artery	7111	8	119
Aneurysm: Small Artery	7112	8	119
Angioneurotic Adema	7118	8	121
Ankle replacement (prosthesis)	5056	1	40-41
Ankylosis: Ankle	5270	1	59

Ailment, Disease, or Disability	VA Code	Chapter	Page #
Ankylosis: Digits, Individual- Thumb	5224	1	51
Ankylosis: Digits, Individual- Index Finger	5225	1	51
Ankylosis: Digits, Individual- Long Finger	5226	1	51
Ankylosis: Digits, Individual- Ring or Little Finger	5227	1	51
Ankylosis: Elbow	5205	1	46
Ankylosis: Hand- Favorable: 5 digits on one hand	5220	1	50
Ankylosis: Hand- Favorable: 4 digits on one hand	5221	1	50
Ankylosis: Hand- Favorable: 3 digits on one hand	5222	1	50
Ankylosis: Hand- Favorable: 2 digits on one hand	5223	1	50
Ankylosis: Hand- Unfavorable: 5 digits on one hand	5216	1	50
Ankylosis: Hand- Unfavorable: 4 digits on one hand	5217	1	50
Ankylosis: Hand- Unfavorable: 3 digits on one hand	5218	1	50
Ankylosis: Hand- Unfavorable: 2 digits on one hand	5219	1	50
Ankylosis: Hip	5250	1	57
Ankylosis: Knee	5256	1	58
Ankylosis: Scapulohumeral Articulation	5200	1	45
Ankylosis: Subastragalar or tarsal joint	5272	1	59
Ankylosis: Wrist	5214	1	48
Ankylosing Spondylitis	5240	1	54
Ano, fistula in	7335	9	131
Aphakia or dislocation of crystalline lens	6029	3	79
Aphonia, Organic, complete	6519	7	97
Aplastic Anemia	7716	12	155
Arrhythmia: Supraventricular	7010	8	114
Arrhythmia: Ventricular	7011	8	114-5
Arteriosclerosis Obliterans	7114	8	120
Arteriosclerotic Heart Disease	7005	8	113
Arteriovenous Fistula, traumatic	7113	8	119
Arthritis: Degenerative (Hypertrophic or Osteoarthritis)	5003	1	37-38
Arthritis: Due to Trauma	5010	1	38
Arthritis: Gonorrheal	5004	1	38
Arthritis: Other Types	5009	1	38
Arthritis: Pneumococcic	5005	1	38
Arthritis: Rheumatoid (Atrophic)	5002	1	37
Arthritis: Spine, Degenerative	5242	1	54
Arthritis: Streptococcic	5008	1	38
Arthritis: Syphilitic	5007	1	38
Arthritis: Typhoid	5006	1	38
Asbestosis	6833	7	104
Aspergillosis	6838	7	105
Asthma, Bronchial	6602	7	99
Astragalectomy	5274	1	59
Atherosclerotic Renal Disease	7534	10	142
Athetosis, acquired	8107	15	191

Ailment, Disease, or Disability	VA Code	Chapter	Page #
Cerebral Arteriosclerosis	8046	15	190
Cervical Strain	5237	1	54
Cervix Disease or Injury	7612	11	146
Chorea: Huntington's	8106	15	191
Chorea: Sydenham's	8105	15	191
Chloracne	7829	13	168
Cholangitis, Chronic	7316	9	129
Cholecystitis, Chronic	7314	9	129
Cholelithiasis, Chronic	7315	9	129
Cholera, Asiatic	6300	6	89
Choroidopathy, including uveitis, iritis, cyclitis, or choroiditis	6000	3	76
Chronic Fatigue Syndrome (CFS)	6354	6	94
Chronic Lung Abscess	6824	7	104
Chronic myelogenous leukemia (CML) (chronic myeloid leukemia or chronic granulocytic leukemia)	7719	12	156
Chronic Obstructive Pulmonary Disease (COPD)	6604	7	100
Chronic Renal Disease requiring regular dialysis	7530	10	142
Cirrhosis of the liver, primary biliary cirrhosis, or cirrhotic phase of sclerosing cholangitis	7312	9	128
Clawfoot (pes cavus), acquired	5278	1	61
Coccidiodomycosis	6835	7	105
Cold Injury Residuals	7122	8	123
Colitis, Ulcerative	7323	9	130
Conjunctivitis: Trachomatous	6017	3	78
Conjunctivitis: Other	6018	3	78
Corneal Transplant, Status Post-Operative	6036	3	79
Coronary Bypass Surgery	7017	8	116
Cryptococcosis	6837	7	105
Cushing's syndrome	7907	14	173
Cutaneous Manifestations of Collagen-Vascular Diseases	7821	13	166
Cystitis, Chronic, Includes Interstitial and all Etiologies	7512	10	140
Dacrocystitis disorder of the lacrimal process	6025	3	78
Degenerative arthritis (hypertrophic or osteoarthritis)	5003	1	37-38
Dermatitis or Eczema	7806	13	155
Dermatophytosis (Ring Worm)	7813	13	164
Desquamative Interstitial Pneumonitis	6826	7	104
Diaphragm: Paralysis or Paresis	6840	7	106
Diabetes insipidus	7909	14	174
Diabetes mellitus	7913	14	175
Diabetic retinopathy	6040	3	79
Diaphragm: Rupture or, with herniation	5324	2	74
Diffuse interstitial fibrosis of the lung	6825	7	104
Diplopia: Limited Muscle Function, Eye	6090	3	83
Disease: Addison's (adrenocortical insufficiency)	7911	14	174

Ailment, Disease, or Disability	VA Code	Chapter	Page #
Disease: Buerger's	7115	8	120
Disease: Chaisson	5011	1	38
Disease: Chronic Obstructive Pulmonary Disease (COPD)	6604	7	100
Disease: Hansen's (Leprosy)	6302	6	90
Disease: Hodgkin's lymphoma	7709	12	153
Disease: Lyme	6319	6	92
Disease: Malaria	6304	6	90
Disease: Morton's	5279	1	61
Disease: Parasitic, Otherwise Not Specified	6320	6	92
Dislocation: Cartilage, Semilunar	5258	1	58
Dislocation: Lens, Crystalline	6029	3	79
Disorders of the lacrimal apparatus (epiphora, dacryocystitis, etc.)	6025	3	78
Disseminated Intravascular Coagulation with renal cortical necrosis	7540	10	143
Distomiasis, Intestinal or Hepatic	7324	9	130
Diverticulitis	7327	9	130
Dysentery, Bacillary	7322	9	129
Ectropion	6020	3	78
Elbow replacement (prosthesis)	5052	1	39
Embolism, Brain, vessels of	8007	15	181
Emphysema, Pulmonary	6603	7	100
Encephalitis, Epidemic, Chronic	8000	15	180
Endocarditis	7001	8	111
Endometriosis	7629	11	148
Enteritis, Chronic	7325	9	130
Enterocolitis, Chronic	7326	9	130
Entropion	6021	3	78
Eosinophilic Granuloma of Lung	6828	7	104
Epididymo-orchitis	7525	10	141
Epilepsy, Diencephalic	8913	15	203
Epilepsy, Grand Mal	8910	15	202
Epilepsy, Jacksonian and Focal Motor or Sensory	8912	15	203
Epilepsy, Petit Mal	8911	15	202
Epilepsy, Psychomotor	8914	15	203
Epiphora disorder of the lacrimal apparatus	6025	3	78
Erythema Multiforme; toxic epidermal necrolysis	7827	13	167
Erythroderma	7817	13	165
Erythromelalgia	7119	8	121
Esophagus: Diverticulum of, acquired	7205	9	127
Esophagus: Spasm of (cardiospasm)	7204	9	126
Esophagus: Stricture of	7203	9	126
Essential thrombocythemia and primary myelofibrosis	7718	12	155
Fallopian Tube: Disease, Injury, Including Pelvic Inflammatory Disease (PID)	7614	11	146
Female sexual arousal disorder (FSAD)	7632	11	149

Ailment, Disease, or Disability	VA Code	Chapter	Page #
Fever: Relapsing	6308	6	90
Fever: Rheumatic	6309	6	90
Fibrosis of Lung, Diffuse Interstitial	6825	7	104
Fibromyalgia (fibrositis, primary fibromyalgia syndrome)	5025	1	39
Fistula: in Ano	7335	9	131
Fistula: Intestine, persistent, or after attempt at operative closure	7330	9	131
Fistula: Rectovaginal	7624	11	147
Fistula: Urethra	7519	10	141
Fistula: Urethrovagial	7625	11	147
Flatfoot, Acquired	5276	1	60
Folic acid deficiency	7721	12	156
Gastritis, Hypertrophic	7307	9	128
Genu, Recurvatum	5263	1	58
Glaucoma: Angle Closure	6012	3	77
Glaucoma: Open Angle	6013	3	77
Glomerulonephritis	7536	10	142
Gout	5017	1	38
Granulomatous rhinitis	6524	7	98
Hallux: Rigidus, unilateral, severe	5281	1	61
Hallux: Valgus, unilateral	5280	1	61
Hammer Toe	5282	1	61
Hand, loss of use of	5125	1	41
Hansen's disease (leprosy)	6302	6	90
Heart Valve Replacement (Prosthesis)	7016	8	116
Hematomyelia	8012	15	181
Hemorrhage: Brain, vessels of	8009	15	181
Hemorrhage: Intraocular	6007	3	76
Hemorrhoids, external or internal	7336	9	131
Hepatitis C	7354	9	135
Hernia: Fermoral	7340	9	132
Hernia: Hiatal	7346	9	134
Hernia: Inguinal	7338	9	132
Hernia: Muscle, Extensive, without injury to the muscle	5326	2	74
Hernia: Ventral, post operative	7339	9	132
Hip: Degenerative Arthritis	5003	1	37-38
Hip: Flail Joint	5254	1	57
Hip replacement (prosthesis)	5054	1	40
Histoplasmosis of the Lung	6834	7	105
HIV-Related Illness	6351	6	93
Hodgkin's Disease	7709	12	153
Hydrarthrosis, Intermittent	5018	1	38
Hydronephrosis	7509	10	140
Hyperaldosteronism	7917	14	175
Hyperhidrosis	7832	13	168

Ailment, Disease, or Disability	VA Code	Chapter	Page #
Hyperparathyroidism	7904	14	172-73
Hyperpituitarism	7916	14	175
Hypersensitivity, Pneumonitis (extrinsic allergic alveolitis)	6831	7	104
Hypertensive Heart Disease	7007	8	114
Hypertensive Vascular Disease	7101	8	118
Hyperthyroidism, including, but not limited to, Graves' disease	7900	14	171
Hyperthyroid Heart Disease	7008	8	114
Hypoparathyroidism	7905	14	173
Hypothyroidism	7903	14	172
Immune thrombocytopenia	7705	12	153
Impairment of: Clavicle or Scapula	5203	1	45
Impairment of: Elbow, Flail Joint	5209	1	46
Impairment of: Humerus	5202	1	45
Impairment of: Thigh	5253	1	57
Impairment of: Femur	5255	1	57
Impairment of: Knee, Other	5257	1	58
Impairment of: Field Vision	6080	3	82
Impairment of: Radius	5212	1	47
Impairment of Shoulder- Supination and Pronation	5213	1	47
Impairment of Spincter Control: Rectum & Anus	7332	9	131
Impairment of: Tibia and Fibula	5262	1	58
Impairment of: Ulna	5211	1	46
Implantable Cardiac Pacemakers	7018	8	117
Infections of the Skin Not Listed Elsewhere	7820	13	166
Injury: Bladder	7517	10	141
Injury: Cervix, or disease of	7612	11	146
Injury: Clitorus or	7610	11	146
Injury: Eye, Unhealed	6009	3	76
Injury: Facial Muscles	5325	2	74
Injury: Foot, Other	5284	1	61
Injury: Gall Bladder	7317	9	129
Injury: Lips	7201	9	126
Injury: Liver, Unhealed Residuals	7311	9	128
Injury: Mouth	7200	9	126
Injury: Muscle Group 1- Upward Rotation of the Scapula	5301	2	67
Injury: Muscle Group 2- Depression of the Arm	5302	2	67
Injury: Muscle Group 3- Elevation and Abduction of the Arm	5303	2	67
Injury: Muscle Group 4- Stabilization of the Shoulder	5304	2	67
Injury: Muscle Group 5- Elbow Supination	5305	2	68
Injury: Muscle Group 6- Extension of the Elbow	5306	2	68
Injury: Muscle Group 7- Flexion of the Wrist and Fingers	5307	2	68
Injury: Muscle Group 8- Extension of the Wrist, Fingers, and Thumb	5308	2	68
Injury: Muscle Group 9- Forearm Muscles	5309	2	69
Injury: Muscle Group 10- Movement of the Forefoot and Toes	5310	2	70

Ailment, Disease, or Disability	VA Code	Chapter	Page #
Injury: Muscle Group 11- Propulsion of the Foot	5311	2	70
Injury: Muscle Group 12- Dorsiflexion	5312	2	70
Injury: Muscle Group 13- Extension of Hip and Flexion of the Knee	5313	2	71
Injury: Muscle Group 14- Extension of the Knee	5314	2	71
Injury: Muscle Group 15- Abduction of the Hip	5315	2	71
Injury: Muscle Group 16- Flexion of the Hip	5316	2	71
Injury: Muscle Group 17- Extension of the Hip	5317	2	72
Injury: Muscle Group 18- Outward Rotation of the Thigh	5318	2	72
Injury: Muscle Group 19- Abdominal Wall and Lower Thorax	5319	2	72
Injury: Muscle Group 20- Postural Support of the Body	5320	2	73
Injury: Muscle Group 21- Respiration	5321	2	73
Injury: Muscle Group 22- Rotary and Forward Movements, Head	5322	2	73
Injury: Muscle Group 23- Movements of the Head	5323	2	73
Injury: Pharynx	6521	7	97
Injury: Sacroiliac and injury	5236	1	54
Injury: Spinal Cord with Respiratory Insufficiency	6841	7	106
Injury: Stomach, Residuals of	7310	9	128
Injury: Vulva, or disease of (including vulvovaginitis)	7610	11	146
Interstitial Nephritis	7537	10	142
Intervertebral Disc Syndrome (IVDS)	5243	1	54
Intestine, Fistula of	7330	9	131
Iritis	6000	3	76
Iron deficiency anemia	7720	12	156
Irritable Colon Syndrome	7319	9	129
Keratinization, Diseases of	7824	13	166
Keratoconus	6035	3	79
Keratopathy	6001	3	76
Kidney: Abscess	7501	10	139
Kidney: Cycstic Diseases	7533	10	142
Kidney: Removal of one	7500	10	139
Kidney: Transplant	7531	10	142
Kidney: Tuberculosis of	7505	10	139
Knee replacement (prosthesis)	5055	1	40
Kyphoscoliosis, Pectus Excavatum, Pectus Carinatum	6842	7	106
Lagophthalmos	6022	3	78
Laryngectomy, total	6518	7	97
Laryngitis: Tuberculous, active or inactive	6515	7	96
Laryngitis: Chronic	6516	7	97
Larynx, Stenosis of	6520	7	97
Leishmaniasis: American (New World)	7807	13	164
Leishmaniasis: Old World (Cutaneous, Oriental Sore)	7808	13	164
Leprosy (Hansen's Disease)	6302	6	90
Leukemia (except for chronic myelogenous leukemia)	7703	12	152
Limitation of Extension: Forearm	5207	1	46

Ailment, Disease, or Disability	VA Code	Chapter	Page #
Limitation of Extension: Leg	5261	1	58
Limitation of Extension: Thigh	5251	1	57
Limitation of Extension and Flexion: Forearm	5208	1	46
Limitation of Flexion: Forearm	5206	1	46
Limitation of Flexion: Leg	5260	1	58
Limitation of Flexion: Thigh	5252	1	57
Limitation of Motion: Ankle	5271	1	59
Limitation of Motion: Arm	5201	1	45
Limitation of Motion: Index or Long Finger	5229	1	52
Limitation of Motion: Ring or Little Finger	5230	1	52
Limitation of Motion: Temporomandibular disorder (TMJ)	9905	17	210
Limitation of Motion: Thumb	5228	1	51
Limitation of Motion: Wrist	5215	1	48
Liver: Disease, Chronic, Without Cirrhosis	7345	9	133
Liver: Transplant	7351	9	134
Liver: Cirrhosis	7312	9	128
Loss of: Auricle	6207	4	86
Loss of: Condyloid Process	9908	17	210
Loss of: Coronoid Process	9909	17	210
Loss of: Eyebrows	6023	3	78
Loss of: Eyelashes	6024	3	78
Loss of: Eyelids	6032	3	79
Loss of: Feet, both	5107	1	41
Loss of: Hands, both	5106	1	41
Loss of: Mandible, complete between angles	9901	17	209
Loss of: Mandible, including ramus, unliterally or bilaterally	9902	17	209
Loss of: Maxilla, more than half	9914	17	211
Loss of: Maxilla, less than half	9915	17	211
Loss of: Nose, part of, scars	6504	7	96
Loss of: One Hand and One Foot	5108	1	41
Loss of: One Foot and Use of One Hand	5105	1	41
Loss of: One Hand and Use of One Foot	5104	1	41
Loss of: Palate, hard	9911	17	211
Loss of: Skull, part of, both inner and outer tables	5296	1	63
Loss of: Smell, sense of	6275	5	87
Loss of: Taste, sense of	6276	5	87
Loss of: Teeth, due to loss of substance of body of maxilla or mandible without loss of continuity	9913	17	211
Loss of: Tongue, whole or part	7202	9	126
Loss of Use of: Both Feet	5110	1	41
Loss of Use of: Both Hands	5109	1	41
Loss of Use of: Foot	5167	1	44
Loss of Use of: Hand	5125	1	41
Loss of Use of: One Hand and One Foot	5111	1	41

Ailment, Disease, or Disability	VA Code	Chapter	Page #
Lumbosacral or cervical strain	5237	1	54
Lupus: Erythematosus, systemic (disseminated)	6350	6	92
Lupus: Erythematosus, Discoid	7809	13	164
Lyme Disease	6319	6	92
Lymphatic Filariasis	6305	6	90
Malaria	6304	6	90
Malignant Melanoma	7833	13	169
Malunion: Mandible	9904	17	210
Malunion: Os Calcis or Astragalus	5273	1	59
Maxilla, Malunion or Non-Union	9916	17	211
Melioidosis	6318	6	92
Meniere's Syndrome	6205	4	86
Meningitis, Cerebrospinal, Epidemic	8019	15	181
Mental Disorders: Anorexia Nervosa	9520	16	208
Mental Disorders: Bipolar Disorder	9432	16	206
Mental Disorders: Bulimia Nervosa	9521	16	208
Mental Disorders: Chronic Adjustment Disorder	9440	16	206
Mental Disorders: Conversion Disorder (Functional Neurological Symptoms Disorder)	9424	16	206
Mental Disorders: Cyclothymic Disorder	9431	16	206
Mental Disorders: Delirium	9300	16	205
Mental Disorders: Delusional Disorder	9208	16	205
Mental Disorders: Depersonalization/Derealization Disorder	9417	16	206
Mental Disorders: Dissociative Amnesia; Dissociative Identity Disorder	9416	16	206
Mental Disorders: Generalized Anxiety Disorder	9400	16	206
Mental Disorders: Illness Anxiety Disorder	9425	16	206
Mental Disorders: Major Depressive Disorder	9434	16	206
Mental Disorders: Major or mild neurocognitive disorder due to Alzheimer's disease	9312	16	205
Mental Disorders: Major or mild neurocognitive disorder due to HIV or other infections	9301	16	205
Mental Disorders: Major or mild neurocognitive disorder due to traumatic brain injury	9304	16	205
Mental Disorders: Major or mild neurocognitive disorder due to another medical condition or substance/medication-induced major or mild neurocognitive disorder	9326	16	205
Mental Disorders: Major or mild vascular neurocognitive disorder	9305	16	205
Mental Disorders: Unspecified neurocognitive disorder	9310	16	205
Mental Disorders: Obsessive Compulsive Disorder	9404	16	206
Mental Disorders: Unspecified Anxiety Disorder	9413	16	206
Mental Disorders: Pain Disorder, Other Specified Somatic Symptom and Related Disorder	9422	16	206
Mental Disorders: Panic Disorder and/or Agoraphobia	9412	16	206

Ailment, Disease, or Disability	VA Code	Chapter	Page #
Mental Disorders: Persistent Depressive Disorder	9433	16	206
Mental Disorders: Posttraumatic Stress Disorder (PTSD)	9411	16	206
Mental Disorders: Schizoaffective Disorder	9211	16	205
Mental Disorders: Schizophrenia	9201	16	205
Mental Disorders: Somatic Symptom Disorder	9421	16	206
Mental Disorders: Unspecified Somatic symptom & related disorder	9423	16	206
Mental Disorders: Other Specified Anxiety Disorder	9410	16	206
Mental Disorders: Unspecified Depressive Disorder	9435	16	206
Metatarsalgia, Anterior- Unilateral or Bilateral	5279	1	61
Migraine	8100	15	191
Morton's Disease	5279	1	61
Mucormycosis	6839	7	105
Multiple myeloma	7712	12	154
Multiple Sclerosis	8018	15	181
Myasthenia Gravis	8025	15	182
Myelitis	8010	15	181
Myelodysplastic syndromes	7725	12	158
Myocardial Infarction	7006	8	113
Myositis Ossificans	5023	1	38
Myositis	5021	1	38
Narcolepsy	8108	15	191
Neoplasms: Benign, Breast and other injuries of the breast	7631	11	149
Neoplasms: Benign, Ear, other than skin only	6209	4	86
Neoplasms: Benign, Endocrine system	7915	14	175
Neoplasms: Benign, Exclusive of Skin Growths	7344	9	132
Neoplasms: Benign, Eye Orbit, and Adnexa	6015	3	77
Neoplasms: Benign, Genitourinary system	7529	10	142
Neoplasms: Benign, Gynecological system	7628	11	148
Neoplasms: Benign, Hard and Soft Tissue	9917	17	212
Neoplasms: Benign, Muscle, Post-Operative	5328	2	74
Neoplasms: Benign, Respiratory system	6820	7	103
Neoplasms: Benign, Skin	7819	13	166
Neoplasms: Malignant, Breast	7630	11	148
Neoplasms: Malignant, Digestive System, exclusive of skin growths	7343	9	132
Neoplasms: Malignant, Ear, Other Than Skin Only	6208	4	86
Neoplasms: Malignant, Endocrine system	7914	14	175
Neoplasms: Malignant, Eye, orbit, and adnexa (excluding skin)	6014	3	77
Neoplasms: Malignant, Genitourinary system	7528	10	142
Neoplasms: Malignant, Gynecological system	7627	11	148
Neoplasms: Malignant, Hard and Soft Tissue	9918	17	212
Neoplasms: Malignant, Muscle, Excluding Soft Tissue Sarcoma	5327	2	74
Neoplasms: Malignant, Respiratory	6819	7	103
Neoplasms: Malignant, Skin	7818	13	166
Nephritis, Chronic	7502	10	139

Ailment, Disease, or Disability	VA Code	Chapter	Page #
Nephrolithiasis	7508	10	140
Nephrosclerosis, Arteriolar	7507	10	140
Neuralgia: Cranial Nerves- Fifth (Trigeminal)	8405	15	192
Neuralgia: Cranial Nerves- Seventh (Facial)	8407	15	192
Neuralgia: Cranial Nerves- Ninth (Glossopharyngeal)	8409	15	192
Neuralgia: Cranial Nerves- Tenth (Pneumogastric, Vagus)	8410	15	193
Neuralgia: Cranial Nerves- Eleventh (Spinal Accessory, External Branch)	8411	15	193
Neuralgia: Cranial Nerves- Twelfth (Hypoglossal)	8412	15	193
Neuralgia: Peripheral Nerves- Upper Radicular Group	8710	15	194
Neuralgia: Peripheral Nerves- Middle Radicular Group	8711	15	194
Neuralgia: Peripheral Nerves- Lower Radicular Group	8712	15	195
Neuralgia: Peripheral Nerves- All Radicular Groups	8713	15	195
Neuralgia: Peripheral Nerves- Musculospiral (Radial)	8714	15	196
Neuralgia: Peripheral Nerves- Median	8715	15	196
Neuralgia: Peripheral Nerves- Ulnar	8716	15	197
Neuralgia: Peripheral Nerves- Musculocutaneous	8717	15	197
Neuralgia: Peripheral Nerves- Circumflex	8718	15	197
Neuralgia: Peripheral Nerves- Long Thoracic	8719	15	198
Neuralgia: Peripheral Nerves- Sciatic	8720	15	198
Neuralgia: Peripheral Nerves- External Popliteal (Common Peroneal)	8721	15	199
Neuralgia: Peripheral Nerves- Musculocutaneous (Superficial Peroneal)	8722	15	199
Neuralgia: Peripheral Nerves- Anterior Tibial (Deep Peroneal)	8723	15	199
Neuralgia: Peripheral Nerves- Internal Popliteal (Tibial)	8724	15	200
Neuralgia: Peripheral Nerves- Posterior Tibial	8725	15	200
Neuralgia: Peripheral Nerves- Anterior Crural (Femoral)	8726	15	200
Neuralgia: Peripheral Nerves- Interal Saphenous	8727	15	201
Neuralgia: Peripheral Nerves- Obturator	8728	15	201
Neuralgia: Peripheral Nerves- External Cutaneous Nerves of Thigh	8729	15	201
Neuralgia: Peripheral Nerves- Ilio-Inguinal	8730	15	201
Neuritis: Cranial Nerves- Fifth (Trigeminal)	8305	15	192
Neuritis: Cranial Nerves- Seventh (Facial)	8307	15	192
Neuritis: Cranial Nerves- Ninth (Glossopharyngeal)	8309	15	192
Neuritis: Cranial Nerves- Tenth (Pneumogastric, Vagus)	8310	15	193
Neuritis: Cranial Nerves- Eleventh (Spinal Accessory, External Branch)	8311	15	193
Neuritis: Cranial Nerves- Twelfth (Hypoglossal)	8312	15	193
Neuritis: Peripheral Nerves- Upper Radicular Group	8610	15	194
Neuritis: Peripheral Nerves- Middle Radicular Group	8611	15	194
Neuritis: Peripheral Nerves- Lower Radicular Group	8612	15	195
Neuritis: Peripheral Nerves- All Radicular Groups	8613	15	195
Neuritis: Peripheral Nerves- Musculospiral (Radial)	8614	15	196
Neuritis: Peripheral Nerves- Median	8615	15	196

Ailment, Disease, or Disability	VA Code	Chapter	Page #
Neuritis: Peripheral Nerves- Ulnar	8616	15	197
Neuritis: Peripheral Nerves- Musculocutaneous	8617	15	197
Neuritis: Peripheral Nerves- Circumflex	8618	15	197
Neuritis: Peripheral Nerves- Long Thoracic	8619	15	198
Neuritis: Peripheral Nerves- Sciatic	8620	15	198
Neuritis: Peripheral Nerves- External Popliteal (Common Peroneal)	8621	15	199
Neuritis: Peripheral Nerves- Musculocutaneous (Superficial Peroneal)	8622	15	199
Neuritis: Peripheral Nerves- Anterior Tibial (Deep Peroneal)	8623	15	199
Neuritis: Peripheral Nerves- Internal Popliteal (Tibial)	8624	15	200
Neuritis: Peripheral Nerves- Posterior Tibial	8625	15	200
Neuritis: Peripheral Nerves- Anterior Crural (Femoral)	8626	15	200
Neuritis: Peripheral Nerves- Interal Saphenous	8627	15	201
Neuritis: Peripheral Nerves- Obturator	8628	15	201
Neuritis: Peripheral Nerves- External Cutaneous Nerves of Thigh	8629	15	201
Neuritis: Peripheral Nerves- Ilio-Inguinal	8630	15	201
Neurogenic Bladder	7542	10	143
New Growths: Benign- Bones	5015	1	38
New Growths: Benign- Brain	8003	15	180
New Growths: Benign- Spinal Cord	8022	15	182
New Growths: Malignant- Bones	5012	1	38
New Growths: Malignant- Brain	8002	15	180
New Growths: Malignant- Spinal Cord	8021	15	182
Nocardiosis	6823	7	104
Non-Hodgkin's Lymphoma	7715	12	154
Non-Union: Mandible	9903	17	210
Non-Union: Radius and Ulna	5210	1	46
Nystagmus, Central	6016	3	77
Optic Neuropathy	6026	3	78
Os calcis or astragalus, malunion of	5273	1	59
Osteitis Deformans	5016	1	38
Osteomalacia	5014	1	38
Osteomyelitis	5000	1	36
Osteomyelitis, chronic, Maxilla or Mandible	9900	17	209
Osteonecrosis, chronic, Maxilla or Mandible	9900	17	209
Osteoradionecrosis, chronic, Maxilla or Mandible	9900	17	209
Osteoporosis, with Joint Manifestations	5013	1	38
Otitis Media: Externa, chronic	6210	4	86
Otitis Media: Chronic, Non-Suppurative, with effusion	6201	4	85
Otitis Media: Chronic, Suppurative, mastoiditis, or cholesteatoma	6200	4	85
Otosclerosis	6202	4	85
Ovaries, Atrophy of both, complete	7620	11	146
Ovary: Disease, injury or adhesions of	7615	11	146
Ovary: Removal of	7619	11	146
Palsy, Bulbar	8005	15	160

Ailment, Disease, or Disability	VA Code	Chapter	Page #
Pancreatitis	7347	9	134
Papillary Necrosis	7538	10	143
Papulosquamous Disorders	7822	13	166
Paralysis: Accommodation	6030	3	79
Paralysis: Agitans	8004	15	180
Paralysis, Nerve- Cranial Nerves: Fifth (Trigeminal)	8205	15	192
Paralysis, Nerve- Cranial Nerves: Seventh (Facial)	8207	15	192
Paralysis, Nerve- Cranial Nerves: Ninth (Glossopharyngeal)	8209	15	192
Paralysis, Nerve- Cranial Nerves: Tenth (Pneumogastric, Vagus)	8210	15	193
Paralysis, Nerve- Cranial Nerves: Eleventh (Spinal Accessory, External Branch)	8211	15	193
Paralysis, Nerve- Cranial Nerves: Twelfth (Hypoglossal)	8212	15	193
Paralysis, Nerve: Peripheral Nerves- Upper Radicular Group	8510	15	194
Paralysis, Nerve: Peripheral Nerves- Middle Radicular Group	8511	15	194
Paralysis, Nerve: Peripheral Nerves- Lower Radicular Group	8512	15	195
Paralysis, Nerve: Peripheral Nerves- All Radicular Groups	8513	15	195
Paralysis, Nerve: Peripheral Nerves- Musculospiral (Radial)	8514	15	196
Paralysis, Nerve: Peripheral Nerves- Median	8515	15	196
Paralysis, Nerve: Peripheral Nerves- Ulnar	8516	15	197
Paralysis, Nerve: Peripheral Nerves- Musculocutaneous	8517	15	197
Paralysis, Nerve: Peripheral Nerves- Circumflex	8518	15	197
Paralysis, Nerve: Peripheral Nerves- Long Thoracic	8519	15	198
Paralysis, Nerve: Peripheral Nerves- Sciatic	8520	15	198
Paralysis, Nerve: Peripheral Nerves- External Popliteal (Common Peroneal)	8521	15	199
Paralysis, Nerve: Peripheral Nerves- Musculocutaneous (Superficial Peroneal)	8522	15	199
Paralysis, Nerve: Peripheral Nerves- Anterior Tibial (Deep Peroneal)	8523	15	199
Paralysis, Nerve: Peripheral Nerves- Internal Popliteal (Tibial)	8524	15	200
Paralysis, Nerve: Peripheral Nerves- Posterior Tibial	8525	15	200
Paralysis, Nerve: Peripheral Nerves- Anterior Crural (Femoral)	8526	15	200
Paralysis, Nerve: Peripheral Nerves- Interal Saphenous	8527	15	201
Paralysis, Nerve: Peripheral Nerves- Obturator	8528	15	201
Paralysis, Nerve: Peripheral Nerves- External Cutaneous Nerves of Thigh	8529	15	201
Paralysis, Nerve: Peripheral Nerves- Ilio-Inguinal	8530	15	201
Paramyoclonus Multiplex (convulsive state, myoclonic type)	8104	15	191
Parasitic Disease otherwise not specified	6320	6	92
Pellagra	6315	6	91
Penis: Deformity, with Loss of Erectile Power	7522	10	141
Penis: Removal of Glans	7521	10	141
Penis: Removal of Half or More	7520	10	141

Ailment, Disease, or Disability	VA Code	Chapter	Page #
Pericardial Adhesions	7003	8	112
Pericarditis	7002	8	111
Periostitis	5022	1	38
Peripheral Vestibular Disorders	6204	4	85
Peritoneum, Adhesions of	7301	9	127
Peritonitis, Tuberculous, Active or Inactive	7331	9	131
Pernicious anemia and Vitamin B_{12} deficiency anemia	7722	12	156-7
Pes Cavus (Claw Foot) Acquired	5278	1	61
Pheochromocytoma (Benign or Malignant)	7918	14	175
Pinguecula	6037	3	79
Plague	6307	6	90
Pleural Effusion or Fibrosis	6845	7	106
Pneumoconiosis (Silicosis, Anthracosis)	6832	7	104
Pneumonitis and Fibrosis: Drug-Induced	6829	7	104
Pneumonitis and Fibrosis: Radiation-Induced	6830	7	104
Pneumonitis, Hypersensitivity (extrinsic allergic alveolitis)	6831	7	104
Poliomyelitis, Anterior	8011	15	181
Polycythemia Vera	7704	12	152
Polyglandular syndrome (multiple endocrine neoplasia, autoimmune polyglandular syndrome)	7912	14	174
Postgastrectomy Syndromes	7308	9	126
Post-chiasmal disorders	6046	3	79
Post-Phlebitic Syndrome, Any Etiology	7121	8	122
Post-Surgical Residual	6844	7	106
Post-Traumatic Stress Disorder (PTSD)	9411	16	206
Progressive Muscular Atrophy	8023	15	182
Prostate Gland injuries, infections, hypertrophy, post-op residuals	7527	10	141
Prosthetic Implants: Ankle Replacement	5056	1	40-41
Prosthetic Implants: Elbow Replacement	5052	1	39
Prosthetic Implants: Hip Replacement	5054	1	40
Prosthetic Implants: Knee Replacement	5055	1	40
Prosthetic Implants: Shoulder Replacement	5051	1	39
Prosthetic Implants: Wrist Replacement	5053	1	40
Psoriasis	7816	13	164
Pterygium	6034	3	79
Ptosis, Unilateral or Bilateral	6019	3	78
Pulmonary Alveolar Proteinosis	6827	7	104
Pulmonary Emphysema	6603	7	100
Pulmonary Vascular Disease	6817	7	103
Pruritus Ani	7337	9	131
Pyelonephritis, Chronic	7504	10	139
Raynaud's Syndrome	7117	8	121
Rectum and Anus: Stricture of	7333	9	131
Rectum: Prolapse of	7334	9	131

Ailment, Disease, or Disability	VA Code	Chapter	Page #
Relapsing Fever	6308	6	90
Removal: Cartilage, Semilunar	5259	1	58
Removal: Coccyx	5298	1	63
Removal: Gall Bladder	7318	9	12
Removal: Kidney removal of one	7500	10	139
Removal: Penis Glans	7521	10	141
Removal: Penis, Half or More	7520	10	141
Removal: Ribs	5297	1	63
Removal: Ovary	7619	11	146
Removal: Uterus, including corpus	7618	11	146
Removal: Uterus and Both Ovaries, complete	7617	11	146
Renal Amyloid Disease	7539	10	143
Renal Disease, Chronic, requiring dialysis	7530	10	142
Renal involvement in diabetes mellitus, sickle cell anemia, systemic lupus erythematosus, vasculitis, or other systemic disease processes	7541	10	143
Renal Tubular Disorders	7532	10	142
Retina, Detachment of	6008	3	76
Retinitis	6006	3	76
Rheumatic Fever	6309	6	90
Rhinitus: Allergic or Vasomotor	6522	7	97
Rhinitus: Bacterial	6523	7	98
Rhinitus: Granulomatous	6524	7	98
Resection of the Intestine: Large	7329	9	130
Resection of the Intestine: Small	7328	9	130
Retinal dystrophy (including retinitis pigmentosa, wet or dry macular degeneration, early-onset macular degeneration, rod and/or cone dystrophy)	6042	3	79
Sacroiliac injury and weakness	5236	1	54
Sarcoidosis	6846	7	107
Scapulohumeral articulation	5200	1	45
Scarring Alopecia	7830	13	168
Scars: Burn/scar(s) of the head, face, or neck; scar(s) of the head, face, or neck due to other causes; or other disfigurement of the head, face, or neck	7800	13	160-161
Scars: Burn Scar(s) or Scar(s) due to Other Causes, not of the Head, Face or Neck, that are Deep and Non-Linear	7801	13	161
Scars: Burn Scar(s) or Scar(s) due to Other Causes, not of the Head, Face or Neck, that are Superficial and Non-Linear	7802	13	162
Scars: Other	7805	13	162
Scars: Retina. Atrophy or irregularities	6011	3	77
Scars: Unstable and Painful	7804	13	162
Scleritis	6002	3	76
Scotoma, Unilateral	6081	3	83
Septum, Nasal, Deviation of	6502	7	96

Ailment, Disease, or Disability	VA Code	Chapter	Page #
Shoulder replacement (prosthesis)	5051	1	39
Sickle Cell Anemia	7714	12	154
Sinusitis: Ethmoid, Chronic	6511	7	96
Sinusitis: Frontal, Chronic	6512	7	96
Sinusitis: Maxillary, Chronic	6513	7	96
Sinusitis: Pansinusitis, Chronic	6510	7	96
Sinusitis: Sphenoid, Chronic	6514	7	96
Skull, loss of part of, both inner and outer tables	5296	1	63
Sleep Apnea Syndrome	6847	7	107
Soft Tissue Sarcoma: Muscle, Fat or Fibrous Connective tissue	5329	2	74
Soft Tissue Sarcoma: Neurogenic Origin	8540	15	202
Soft Tissue Sarcoma: Vascular Origin	7123	8	123
Solitary plasmacytoma	7724	12	157
Spinal Cord Injury with Respiratory Insufficiency	6841	7	106
Spinal Fusion	5241	1	54
Spinal Stenosis	5238	1	54
Spleen, Injury of, Healed	7707	12	153
Splenectomy	7706	12	153
Spondylolisthesis or Segmental Instability	5239	1	54
Stomach, Stenosis of	7309	9	128
Supraventricular arrhythmias	7010	8	114
Symblepharon	6091	3	83
Syndrome: Chronic Fatigue Syndrome (CFS)	6354	6	94
Syndome: Cushing's	7907	14	173
Syndrome: Meniere's	6205	4	86
Syndrome: Raynaud's	7117	8	121
Syndrome: Sleep Apnea	6847	7	107
Synovitis	5020	1	38
Syphilis and Other Treponemal Infections	6310	6	91
Syphilis: Cerebrospinal	8013	15	181
Syphilis: Meningovascular	8014	15	181
Syphlitic Heart Disease	7004	8	112
Syringomyelia	8024	15	182
Tabes Dorsalis	8015	15	181
Tarsal or Metatarsal Bones, Malunion or Non-Union of	5283	1	61
Temporomandibular disorder (TMD)	9905	17	210
Tenosynovitis	5024	1	38
Testis: Atrophy, Complete	7523	10	141
Testis: Removal	7524	10	141
Thrombo-angiitis obliterans (Buerger's Disease)	7115	8	120
Thrombocytopenia, immune	7705	12	153
Thrombosis, Brain, vessels of	8008	15	181
Thyroid enlargement, toxic	7901	14	171
Thyroid enlargement, nontoxic	7902	14	172

Ailment, Disease, or Disability	VA Code	Chapter	Page #
Thyroiditis	7906	14	173
Tic, Convulsive	8103	15	191
Tinnitus, Recurrent	6260	4	86
Toxic Nephropathy	7535	10	142
Traumatic Brain Injury (TBI), Residuals of	8045	15	182-3
Traumatic Chest Wall Defect	6843	7	106
Tuberculosis: Bones and Joints, active or inactive	5001	1	37
Tuberculosis: Eye	6010	3	77
Tuberculosis: Kidney	7505	10	139
Tuberculosis: Luposa (Lupus Vulgaris), active or inactive	7811	13	164
Tuberculosis: Miliary	6311	6	91
Tuberculosis: Pleurisy, Active or Inactive	6732	7	102
Tuberculosis: Pulminary, Active, Chronic	6730	7	102
Tuberculosis: Pulminary, Inactive, Chronic	6731	7	102
Tuberculous: Adenitis, active or inactive	7710	12	153
Tuberculous: Pulmonary, Active, Far Advanced	6701	7	101
Tuberculous: Pulmonary, Active, Moderately Advanced	6702	7	101
Tuberculous: Pulmonary, Active, Minimal	6703	7	101
Tuberculous: Pulmonary, Active, Advancement Unspecified	6704	7	101
Tuberculous: Pulmonary, Inactive, Far Advanced	6721	7	101
Tuberculous: Pulmonary, Inactive, Moderately Advanced	6722	7	101
Tuberculous: Pulmonary, Inactive, Minimal	6723	7	101
Tuberculous: Pulmonary, Inactive, Advancement Unspecified	6724	7	101
Tympanic Membrane	6211	4	86
Typhus, Scrub	6317	6	92
Ulcer: Duodenal	7305	9	127
Ulcer: Gastric	7304	9	127
Ulcer: Marginal	7306	9	127
Ureter, Stricture of	7511	10	140
Ureterolithiasis	7510	10	140
Urethra: Fistula of	7519	10	141
Urethra: Stricture of	7518	10	141
Urticaria, chronic	7825	13	167
Uterus: And Both Overies, Removal, complete	7617	11	146
Uterus: Disease or Injury	7613	11	146
Uterus: Prolapse, complete or incomplete, due to injury, disease, or surgical complications during pregnancy	7621	11	147
Uterus: Removal of, including corpus	7618	11	146
Uveitis	6000	3	76
Vagina, Disease or Injury	7611	11	146
Vagotomy, with pyloroplasty or gastroenterostomy	7348	9	134
Valvular Heart Disease	7000	8	110
Varicose Veins	7120	8	122

Ailment, Disease, or Disability	VA Code	Chapter	Page #
Vasculitis, Primary Cutaneous	7826	13	167
Ventricular arrhythmias	7011	8	114-5
Vertebral Fracture or Dislocation	5235	1	54
Visceral Leishmaniasis	6301	6	89
Visceroptosis	7342	9	132
Vision: See also Blindness and Loss of: One Eye 5/200 (1.5/60), with visual acuity of the other eye: 5/200 (1.5/60); 10/200 (3/60); 15/200 (4.5/60); 20/200 (6/60); 20/100 (6/30); 20/70 (6/21); 20/50 (6/15); 20/40 (6/12)	6065	3	80
Vision: See also Blindness and Loss of: One Eye 10/200 (3/60), with visual acuity of the other eye: 10/200 (3/60); 15/200 (4.5/60); 20/200 (6/60); 20/100 (6/30); 20/70 (6/21); 20/50 (6/15); 20/40 (6/12)	6066	3	80-81
Vision: See also Blindness and Loss of: One Eye 15/200 (4.5/60), with visual acuity of the other eye: 15/200 (4.5/60); 20/200 (6/60); 20/100 (6/30); 20/70 (6/21); 20/50 (6/15); 20/40 (6/12)	6066	3	80-81
Vision: See also Blindness and Loss of: One Eye 20/200 (6/60), with visual acuity of the other eye: 20/200 (6/60); 20/100 (6/30); 20/70 (6/21); 20/50 (6/15); 20/40 (6/12)	6066	3	80-81
Vision: See also Blindness and Loss of: One Eye 20/100 (6/30), with visual acuity of the other eye: 20/100 (6/30); 20/70 (6/21); 20/50 (6/15); 20/40 (6/12)	6066	3	80-81
Vision: See also Blindness and Loss of: One Eye 20/70 (6/21), with visual acuity of the other eye: 20/70 (6/21); 20/50 (6/15); 20/40 (6/12)	6066	3	80-81
Vision: See also Blindness and Loss of: One Eye 20/50 (6/15), with visual acuity of the other eye: 20/50 (6/15); 20/40 (6/12)	6066	3	80-81
Vision: See also Blindness and Loss of: Each Eye 20/40 (6/12)	6066	3	80-81
Vitiligo	7823	13	166
Vulva or clitorus, Disease or Injury of	7610	11	146
Weak Foot	5277	1	60
Wrist replacement (prosthesis)	5053	1	40

CHAPTER 19

GLOSSARY OF COMMON MEDICAL TERMS

Medical Term	Easy Definition
Abduction	The movement of a limb away from the midline of the body.
Abductor Muscle	Any muscle that pulls a body part away from the midline.
Abscess	An accumulation of pus anywhere in the body.
Acetabulum	The cup-shaped socket of the hip joint.
Achlorhydria	A lack of hydrochloric acid in the digestive juices in the stomach.
Actinomycosis	Chronic disease with hard masses in the mouth and jaws.
Acute	Abrupt onset of a disease; illness of short duration, rapidly progressive and in need of urgent care.
Adduction	The movement of a limb toward the midline of the body.
Adductor Muscle	Any muscle that pulls a body part toward the midline.
Adhesions	Two opposing tissue surfaces coming together.
Amenorrhea	Absence or cessation of menstruation.
Amyloid	Any number of complex proteins that are deposited in tissues.
Amyloidosis	A group of diseases that result from the abnormal deposition of a protein, called amyloid, in various tissues of the body.
Anasarca	Generalized, pronounced swelling of body tissue due to fluid build-up.
Anatomical	Of or pertaining to human beings.
Anemia	Condition of having a lower-than-normal number of red blood cells or quantity of hemoglobin.
Aneurysm	A localized widening of an artery, vein, or the heart.
Aneurysmectomy	Surgery to repair a weak area of the aorta.
Angle-Closure Glaucoma	Increased pressure in the front chamber of the eye due to sudden or slowly progressive fluid blockage within the eye.
Angulation	Abnormal bend or curve in an organ.
Ankylosis	Stiffness or fusion of a joint
Antineoplastic	Acting to prevent, inhibit, or halt the development of a neoplasm.
Aphonia	Inability to speak.
Apraxia	Inability to execute a voluntary movement despite being able to demonstrate normal muscle function.
Arrhythmia	An abnormal heart rhythm.
Articulation	Where two bones are attached for the purpose of body part motion.
Ascites	An abnormal accumulation of fluid in the abdomen.
Astragalectomy	Surgery to remove the talus bone, or astraglus.
Astragalus	One of the proximal bones of the tarsus.
Asymptomatic	Without symptoms.
Atlantoaxial	Pertaining to the 1st and 2nd cervical vertebrae; atlantoaxial joint.

Atrial Fibrillation	Abnormal heart rhythm where electrical signals are generated chaotically throughout the upper chambers, or atria, of the heart.
Atrophic	A wasting away, breaking down due to lack of use, or diminution.
Atrophy	A wasting away, breaking down due to lack of use, or diminution.
Auricle	The principal projecting part of the ear.
Benign	Not malignant; not a cancer.
Bilateral	Affecting both sides.
Cachexia	General physical wasting with weight loss due to disease.
Caisson	Disease with regions of bone and marrow necrosis
Candidiasis	Serious infection caused by a species of yeast Candida
Cardiomegaly	Enlargement of the heart.
Carpometacarpal	Five joints in the wrist that articulate distal row of carpal bones.
Cellulitis	Spreading bacterial infection under the skin surface.
Cervical	Having to do with any kind of neck, including neck of the uterus.
Cholesteatoma	Abnormal tissue growth behind the eardrum in the middle ear.
Choroiditis	Inflammation of the layer of the eye behind the retina, either in its entity (multifocal) or in patches (focal)- symptom of blurry vision.
Choroidopathy	A diseased condition affecting the choroid of the eye.
Chronic	A condition last a long time- typically three months or more.
Claudication	Limping.
Clavical	Collar bone.
Coccyx	Tail bone.
Cognitive	Having to do with thought, judgment or knowledge.
Comorbid	Two or more disease processes.
Cubitus Valgus	Elbow deformity resulting in an increased carrying angle.
Cubitus Varus	Elbow deformity resulting in a decreased carrying angle.
Cutaneous	Related to the skin.
Cyclitis	Inflammation of the ciliary (hairlike projections) body
Cystocele	Bulging of the bladder into the vagina.
Dacryocystitis	Lacrimal sac infection; causes pain, swelling in lower eyelid.
Degenerative	Relating to or tending to cause degeneration.
Deglutition	The act of swallowing, particularly food.
Diastasis	An abnormal separation of parts normally joined together.
Diplopia	Double-vision.
Disarticulation	Separation of two bones at their joint by trauma or injury.
Distal	The more distant of two or more things.
Diverticulum	A small budging sac pushing outward from the colon wall.
Dorsiflexion	Upward movement (extension) of the foot/toes or hand/fingers.
Dysarthria	Speech that is slurred, slow and difficult to understand.
Dyspepsia	Indigestion.

Dysphagia	Difficulty swallowing.
Dyspnea	Difficult of labored breathing; shortness of breath.
Ectropion	A condition in which an eyelid is turned out, away from the eyeball.
Edema	Swelling of soft tissue due to excess fluid accumulation.
Empyema	Condition where pus and infected tissue fluid collects in a body cavity.
Endolymphatic Hydrops	Inner ear disorder with excessive endolymph fluid build up.
Entropion	Condition where the eyelid, usually lower lid, folds inward.
Enucleation	Surgical removal of an eye.
Epigastric	Upper central region of the addomen.
Epiphora	Watering of the eyes due to excess tear secretion.
Erythematosus	Chronic inflammatory variable autoimmune disease of connective tissue.
Erythromelalgia	Excessive dilation of superficial blood vessels of the feet or hands, with increased skin temperature and burning pain.
Ethmoid	Spongy bone serving as front floor of the skull and roof of the nose.
Etiology	The study of causes of diseases.
Eversion	The act of turning inside out or state of being inside out.
Excision	Surgical removal.
Extension	Process of straightening or the state of being strait.
Extrinsic	Not an essential or inherent part of something, such as a structure.
Fauces	Throat.
Fibula	The smaller of two bones in the lower leg.
Fistula	An abnormal passageway in the body.
Flail Joint	A joint with loss of function due to inability to stabilize the joint.
Flexion	Process of bending, or the state of being bent.
Gait	A manner of walking.
Gastroenterostomy	Surgery to form a passage between stomach and small intestine.
Genu Recurvatum	Deformity of the knee joint, whereas the knee bends backwards.
Granuloma	Number of localized nodular inflammation found in tissues.
Hallux Rigidus	Restricted mobility of the big toe due to stiffness from joint arthritis.
Hemiplegia	Paralysis on one side of the body.
Hemolysis	Destruction of red blood cells leading to the release of hemoglobin from within the red blood cells into the blood plasma.
Hemoptysis	Spitting up blood or blood-tinged sputum from the respiratory tract.
Hepatic Encephalopathy	Brain dysfunction due directly to liver dysfunction.
Hepatomegaly	An abnormally enlarged liver.
Hernia	A protrusion of a tissue through the wall of the cavity in which it's normally contained.
Homonymous Hemianopsia	Vision field loss left or right of the vertical midline.
Humerus	Long bone in the upper arm extends from shoulder to the elbow.

Hyperpronation	Related to an abnormal inward rotation of the foot.
Hypersensitivity	Undesirable reactions produced by the normal immune system.
Hypertrophic	Enlarged or overgrown organ or part of the body due to increased size of constituent cells.
Hypoproteinemia	Condition with an abnormally low level of protein in the blood.
Hypothenar	Prominent part of the palm above the base of the little finger.
Ilium	Upper part of the pelvic bone; forms the receptacle of the hip.
Indurated	Soft tissue that has hardened. Firm, but not as hard as bone.
Infarction	As area of tissue death due to a lack of oxygen.
Inguinal	Having to do with the groin.
Insomnia	Perception or complaint of inadequate or poor-quality sleep.
Interactability	Something not easily controlled or managed.
Interphalangeal	Situated between phalanges; relating to an interphalangeal joint.
Intraocular Hemorrhage	Bleeding in the eye.
Intrinsic	An essential or inherent part of something, such as a structure.
Introitus	An entrance that goes into a canal or hollow organ.
Involucrum	A new bone growing around a piece of dead bone; a sheath/cover.
Iritis	Inflammation of the interior eye structures.
Ischemic	Inadequate blood supply of an area due to blood vessel blockage
Keratinization	When cytoplasm of outmost cells in skin is replaced by keratin.
Keratoconus	A cone-shaped cornea, with the cone apex being forward.
Keratopathy	Non-inflammatory disease of the eye.
Kyphosis	Outward curvature of the spine, causing a humped back.
Labyrinthitis	Inflammation of the labyrinth of the ear; possibly with vertigo.
Lacrimal	Pertaining to tears.
Lagophthalmos	Incomplete closure of the eyelids; eyelids can't close fully.
Laparoscopy	A type of surgery to allow instruments to see the abdomen.
Lateral	Side of the body, or part that is farther from the middle or center.
Lateral Excursion	Sideward movement of the jaw.
Lobectomy	An operation to remove an entire lobe of the lung.
Lordosis	Inward curvature of the spine.
Lumbroacral	Relating to the small of the back and back part of the pelvis/hips.
Lymphadenopathy	Abnormally enlarged Lymph Nodes.
Malignant	To become worse; to invade or destroy nearby tissue; a cancer.
Malleolus	The round, bony prominence on either side of the ankle joint.
Malunion	Not aligning or coming together properly.
Mandible	Jawbone.
Mastectomy	A general term for the surgical removal of the breast.
Masticatory	Used for or adapted to chewing.
Mastoiditis	Inflammation of the mastoid; occurs secondary to ear infections.

Maxillary	Upper Jaw in which bony element are closely fused.
Melena	Stool or vomit stained black by blood pigment or blood products.
Metacarpals	Five cylindrical bones extending from the wrist to the fingers.
Metacarpophalangeal	Involving both metacarpus and phalanges.
Metastases	Process of cancer spreading from its tumor origin.
Metatarsals	Five cylindrical bones extending from the heel to the toes.
Metatarsalgia	General term for painful foot condition in the ball of the foot.
Midaxillary	Imaginary line through the long axis of the body.
Mycosis	Disease caused by a fungus; fungal infection in or on the body.
Myoclonic	An abnormal contraction of muscles or parts of muscles.
Necrosis	The death of living cells or tissues.
Neoplasms	Tumors
Nephritis	Inflammation of the kidney caused by impaired kidney function.
Neuralgia	Pain along the course of a nerve.
Neuritis	Inflammation of the nerves.
Neurogenic	Arising from the nerves or nervous system.
Neuropathy	Any disease or malfunction of the nerves.
Nocardiosis	Infection from bacteria in soil. Strikes lungs, brain and skin.
Nonunion	Not aligned; cannot properly come together at all.
Nystagmus	Rapid, rhythmic, repetitious, and involuntary eye movements.
Open-Angle Glaucoma	Eye condition leading to progressive atrophy of the optic nerve with an open angle. With peripheral vision loss and eye pressure.
Os Calcis	More or less rectangular bone at the back of the foot; heel bone.
Osteitis Deforms	Enlarged, deformed bones due to excessive breakdown and formation of bone tissue; causes bones to weaken and fracture.
Osteomyelitis	Inflammation of the bone due to an infection.
Osteoradionecrosis	Complication from radiation therapy to head and neck resulting in bone death.
Otitis	Inflammation of the ear
Otitis Externa	Infection of the skin covering the outer ear canal due to bacteria.
Palmar	Pertaining to the palm (grasping side) of the hand.
Palpation	To touch or feel for something.
Pansinusitis	Inflammation of all the sinuses on one or both sides of the nose.
Parenteral	Not delivered via the intestinal tract.
Paresthesis	Any abnormal body sensation; ie. numbness, tingling, or burning
Pathological	Indicative of or caused by disease.
Perineum	Area between anus and scrotum (male) and anus and vulva (female)
Phalanges	Bones of the fingers and toes. Singular- Phalanx.
Phalanx	Any one of the bones in the fingers or toes. Plural- phalanges.
Pharynx	Tube running from behind the nose to the top of the windpipe.

Pinguecula	A yellow spot on the eye; possibly due to be a UV light exposure.
Plantar	Having to do with the sole of the foot.
Pleurisy	Inflammation of the pleurae, the membranes around the lungs.
Pneumonectomy	Operation to remove an entire lung or part of a lung.
Polyp	Tissue mass that develops on the inside wall of a hollow organ.
Popliteal Fossa	The hollow behind the knee.
Prolapsed	To fall down or slip out of a designated place.
Pronation	Rotating the arm/hand or leg/foot so the palm or sole is down.
Prosthesis	An artificial replacement of a part of the body.
Proximal	Toward the beginning; the near of two items. Opposite of distal.
Pterygium	A wing-like triangular membrane.
Ptosis	Downward displacement or drooping of a part of the body.
Purulent Pleurisy	Inflammation with pus of the membranes around the lungs.
Purulent Sputum	Pus muscous material from the lungs brought up by coughing.
Pyloroplasty	Surgery to cut and resuture the Pylorus valve of the stomach.
Quadrantectomy	Surgery to remove cancer from the breast, but not the breast.
Radicular	Pertaining to a nerve root.
Radius	The smaller of two bones in the forearm.
Rectocele	Bulging of the front wall of the rectum into the vagina.
Refractory	Not yielding, or not yielding readily, to treatment.
Resection	Surgical removal of part of an organ.
Respiration	Breathing.
Sacroilaic	Joints of the hip formed by connecting sacrum to the iliac bones.
Sarcoma	One of a group of tumors usually arising from connective tissue.
Scapula	Shoulder blade.
Scapulohumeral	Pertaining to the Scapula and Humerus
Scleritis	Inflammation of the sclera; local pain and can cause vision loss.
Scotoma	Partial vision loss / blind spot in an otherwise normal visual field.
Segmentectomy	Surgery to remove: part of an organ or gland; tumor and normal tissue around it; a section of a lobe of the lung.
Semilunar	Either of two valves at the opening between the heart and aorta.
Sequelae	Pathological condition resulting from prior disease or injury.
Sequestrum	A piece of dead bone tissue occurring in disease or injured bone.
Sphenoid	Shaped like a wedge; Sphenoid bone is at the base of the skull.
Spondylitis	Inflammation of one or more vertebrae of the spine.
Sputum	Mucous material from the lungs brought up by coughing.
Stachycardia	An abnormally rapid heart rate.
Stasis Dermatitis	Skin irritation of lower legs typically related to circulatory issues.
Steatorrhea	Excreting abnormal quantities of fat reducing absorption of fat by the intestine.

Stenosis	A narrowing.
Sternomastoid	Involving the sternum, clavicle, and mastoid process.
Stomatitis	Inflammation of the mucous membrane of the mouth.
Subacute	Rather recent onset; between Acute and Chronic.
Subastragalar	Situated or occurring beneath the talus (ankle bone).
Subluxation	Partial dislocation of a joint; luxation is a complete dislocation.
Substernal	Situated or perceived behind or below the sternum (chest bone).
Superficial	On the surface or shallow; not deep.
Supination	Rotating an arm/ leg outward. Arm so the palm faces forward.
Suppurative	Process of pus formation.
Symblepharon	Abnormal adhesion between an eyelid and the eyeball.
Syncope	Partial or complete loss of consciousness with loss of awareness.
Tachycardia	Rapid heart rate; typically, greater than 100 beats per minute.
Tarsal	Part of the foot between the metatarsus and the leg.
Temporomandibular	Joint that hinges lower jaw (mandible) to skull (temporal bone)
Tendo Achillis	Achilles tendon; connects the calf muscle to the heal bone.
Sternomastoid	Involving the sternum, clavicle and mastoid process.
Thenar Eminence	Group of muscles on the hand palm at the base of the thumb.
Thoracolumbar	Relating to the thoracic and lumbar regions of the spine.
Thoracoplasty	Surgery to correct deformity of the chest wall; usually involves removing one or more ribs.
Thromboembolism	A clot in a blood vessel that breaks free and plugs another vessel.
Tibia	The larger of two bones in the lower leg.
Trachomatous Conjunctivitis	Chronic conjunctiva infection due to Chlamydia trachomatis.
Treponemal	Genus of spirochetes in humans that cause syphilis and yaws.
Trophic	Stimulating the activity of another endocrine gland.
Turbinates	Nose bone situated along the side wall of the nose.
Tylectomy	Surgery to remove a tumor from the breast.
Tympanic Membrane	Ear drum.
Ulcerated	Eroded away.
Ulceration	The process of being eroded away, as by an ulcer.
Ulna	The larger bone in the forearm.
Ulnar	Pertaining to the Ulna.
Unilateral	Having, or relating to, one side. Opposite of Bilateral.
Uveitis	Inflammation of the Uvea, the inner layer of the eye.
Vagotomy	Surgery to remove one or more branches of the vagus nerve.
Varices	Plural for Varicose, as in varicose veins.
Vestibular	Relating to the inner ear; generally, to the sense of balance.
Visceral	Referring to the inner organs of the body.

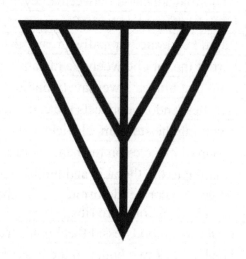

THIS PAGE LEFT INTENTIONALLY BLANK

Veterans Informing Veterans

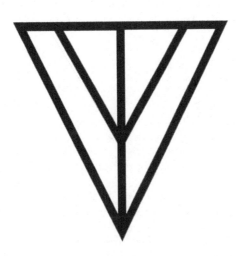

Individual Transition Workbook

My Veterans Service Officer (VSO) or VA rep is:

My VSO or VA rep's phone number is:

My VSO or VA rep's email address is:

My VSO or VA rep's appointment schedule is:

    ☐ Initial Meeting:

    ☐ Update Meeting (if needed):

    ☐ Update Meeting (if needed):

    ☐ Final Meeting:

Checklist of items needed by my VSO:

    ☐

    ☐

    ☐

    ☐

    ☐

    ☐

    ☐

My VSO needs my medical records (circle one):

Single-Sided hard Copy   2-Sided Hard Copy   Electronic (PDF/Disk)

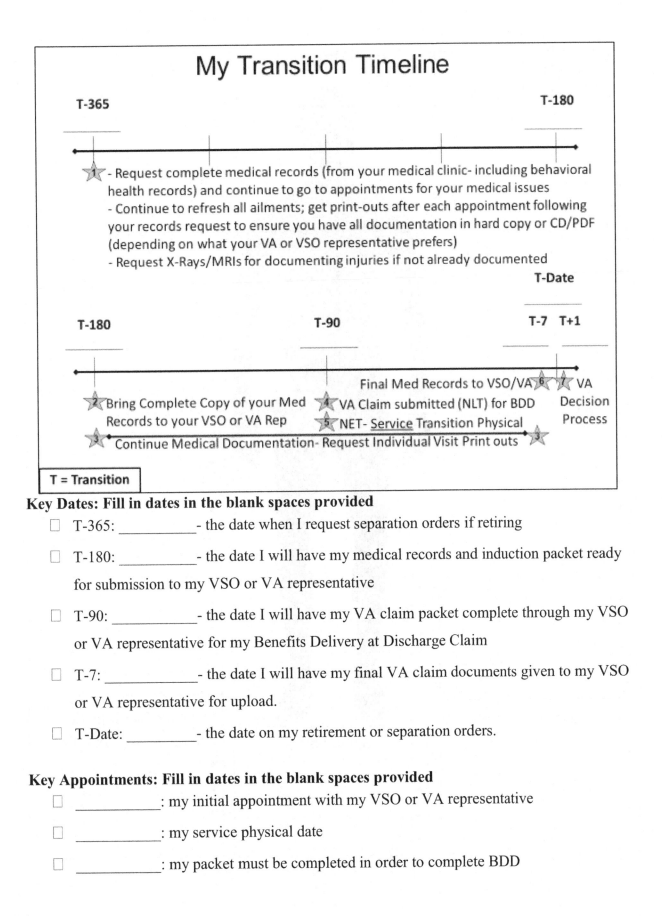

My Transition Timeline

T-365   **T-180**

★1 - Request complete medical records (from your medical clinic- including behavioral health records) and continue to go to appointments for your medical issues
- Continue to refresh all ailments; get print-outs after each appointment following your records request to ensure you have all documentation in hard copy or CD/PDF (depending on what your VA or VSO representative prefers)
- Request X-Rays/MRIs for documenting injuries if not already documented

T-Date

T-180   **T-90**   **T-7 T+1**

Final Med Records to VSO/VA ★6 ★7 VA
★2 Bring Complete Copy of your Med   ★4 VA Claim submitted (NLT) for BDD   Decision
Records to your VSO or VA Rep   ★5 NET- Service Transition Physical   Process
★3 Continue Medical Documentation- Request Individual Visit Print outs ★3

T = Transition

Key Dates: Fill in dates in the blank spaces provided

☐ T-365: _____ - the date when I request separation orders if retiring

☐ T-180: _____ - the date I will have my medical records and induction packet ready for submission to my VSO or VA representative

☐ T-90: _____ - the date I will have my VA claim packet complete through my VSO or VA representative for my Benefits Delivery at Discharge Claim

☐ T-7: _____ - the date I will have my final VA claim documents given to my VSO or VA representative for upload.

☐ T-Date: _____ - the date on my retirement or separation orders.

Key Appointments: Fill in dates in the blank spaces provided

☐ _____ : my initial appointment with my VSO or VA representative

☐ _____ : my service physical date

☐ _____ : my packet must be completed in order to complete BDD

The Silhouette

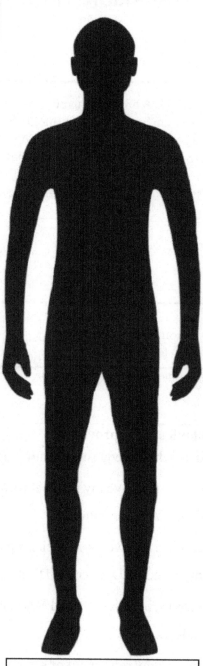

The Head, Brain, and Psych Issues

-
-
-
-

Neck, Throat and Respiratory Issues

-
-
-
-

Left Arm, Elbow, Hand, Shoulder, Finger Issues

-
-
-
-

Left Leg, Hip, Knee, Ankle, Foot, Toe Issues

-
-
-
-

Urology/Gynecology Issues

-
-
-
-

Eyes, Ears, Nose, and Mouth Issues

-
-
-
-

Cardiovascular and Blood Issues

-
-
-
-

Right Arm, Elbow, Hand, Shoulder, Finger Issues

-
-
-
-

Right Leg, Hip, Knee, Ankle, Foot, Toe Issues

-
-
-
-

Spine Issues

-
-
-
-

Digestive, Infectious Diseases, and Skin Issues

-
-
-
-

AILMENTS, DISEASES, AND DISABILITIES TO CLAIM

Claim #	Column A- Claims- Initial	Column B- Claims- Refined
1		
2		
3		
4		
5		
6		
7		
8		
9		
10		
11		
12		
13		
14		
15		
16		
17		
18		
19		
20		
21		
22		
23		
24		
25		
26		
27		
28		
29		
30		

Veterans Informing Veterans

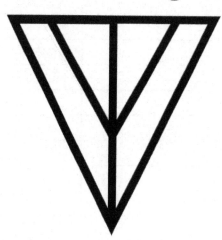

Made in the USA
Columbia, SC
06 January 2020

86414307R00137